Empowerment of Women in Urban Administration

(Experiences and Strategies)

Empowerment of Women in Urban Administration

(Experiences and Strategies)

U.B. SINGH

SERIALS PUBLICATIONS
NEW DELHI

First Published - 2006

ISBN: 81-8387-005-8

Published by

SERIALS PUBLICATIONS
4830/24, Ansari Road, Darya Ganj
New Delhi-110002 (India)
Phone : 91-11-23245225, Fax : 91-11-23272135
E-mail: serials@satyam.net.in,
serialspublications@vsnl.net
website : www.seriealspub.com

CONTENTS

PREFACE

The Indian Constitution provides equal status and opportunities to women in every sphere of life. Despite this, women in general have not been able to attain their due share in the social, economic, political and administrative system of the country. Women are far behind the men folk. The 74th Amendment to the Constitution has taken a lead and provides reservation for women to the tune of one-third in urban local bodies. Such a historical move is a good beginning in right earnest but the experiences of about a decade have not shown the desired result.

The International Community celebrated 1976-1985 as the Decade for Women. 8th March every year is Women's Day. The Government of India declared the year 2001 as the Year for Women Empowerment. A good number of national and international conferences have been devoted to the cause of women, but the impact, a disappointment.

Women in urban areas have a complex characteristic. Their misery is added by complex urban character and socio-economic-cultural-religious situations. They are the victims of role conflict, social disharmony, religious and social traditions, occupational hazards, familial tension, abuses, harassment etc.

In this backdrop, Regional Centre for Urban and Environmental Studies, Lucknow organized a two-day National Seminar on Empowerment of Women in Urban Administration in India at Patna on March 19 and 20, 2002.

The Seminar was inaugurated by Prof. G.P. Lal, Vice-President of the World Federation of Engineers Organization. In his address Prof. Lal said that the mental block about the secondary role of women has to go. He pointed out that the Government of India have focused the role of women in successive Five Year Plans. The first four plans focused attention on various welfare activities with priority to women education. The 5th and 6th Plans shifted the approach from welfare to overall development of women including health, education and employment. The 7th Plan tried to make further dent and in the 8th Plan there was a shift from women development to women empowerment. In regard to urban administration, according to Prof Lal, the role of women is of great consequence. The strategies in urban activity are pre-dominantly health care, education, welfare, cleanliness, aesthetics etc. He felt that in human development and strategy for sustainable development especially through urban administration the role of women is second to none-possibly urban areas will be a better place to live with greater participation of women in administration.

The Editor in his theme paper tracing the history of status of women in Indian continent presents a paradigm shift from women liberation to women welfare, to women development and now to women empowerment. He emphasizes on the need of a change in social mind set up to influence the women with these changing public policies in connection with the women empowerment. In his paper he brings for the some important issues related to women development.

Dr. Kulwant Singh in his paper on "Women in Decision Making" finds women's participation in decision making at all levels as low. He feels that participation of women is an integral part of democratic process and strengthening the quality of civic life. He recognizes that 73rd and 74th Amendments to the Indian Constitution are revolutionary steps. Many countries thereafter have followed and made provisions for reserving the seats of women in local administration. He feels that entry of a large number of women into decision making at local level can radically change the existing situation. Dr. Singh presents the scenario of women's representation at national as well as state level.

Dr. Sanjay Srivastava in his paper entitled "A Study of the Political Aspects of Women Empowerment in India" highlights the prevalent political process in the country and women empowerment. He expresses that even the universal adult suffrage as introduced by the Constitution failed to provide women their due share in political structure. Dr. Srivastava identifies problems in granting political empowerment to women. The first problem, according to him, lies in the fact that political empowerment of women can alter the power arrangement at all levels of political system. It may dislodge the traditional political elite from their dominant position. Another basic hindrance is that they have failed to carry the political mobilization at the grassroots level.

Dr. Supriya Singh in her paper entitled "Empowerment of Women–Need for Larger Participatory Role" expresses that economic independence of women can follow only if they are allowed a larger participatory role in the overall social scenario. She feels that success of development programmes hinges strongly on involvement of the participants and not the beneficiaries in the planning.

Dr. Kumkum Narain and Dr. Mira Mridubhashini in a joint paper entitled "Dynamics of Empowering Women in Urban Development" attempt to highlight the potentials of women in reshaping the urban development. They discussed status of women, urban election scenario, role of women in local governance etc. The authors emphasize on greater involvement of women in urban governance in order to drive the social chariot more efficiently.

Sri Pravin Bhardwaj and Dr. K.K. Upadhyay in their joint paper titled, "The Gender Paradigm in Local Government: Indian Experience" recognize the right of every citizen to participate in public decision as a basic element of democracy. The views and opinions of women are however, largely, represented by others. Such a situation, according to him, is not conducive for social development. In the post-74th CAA scenario, the major task of women in general is to help the new set-up to function properly. The 74th Amendment has sown the seeds for women to emerge as the carriers of power and as equal partners in the politicial process and incoming to power and exercising it. They present case study of many urban local bodies as well.

Dr. S.M. Haider Rizvi in his paper on "Empowering Women through Reservation in Urban Local Bodies – Differences between Theory and Practice" refers to the 74th Amendment Act which provided one-third reservation of seats for women in urban local bodies. He gives an example of Ghazipur Municipality of U.P. and finds that only a few women are active politically in urban local bodies though there is a significant change over the period. Dr. Rizvi presents a package of recommendations for women empowerment in urban local bodies. The suggestions include capacity building, engagement of women in municipal services and functioning, encouragement and promotion of caste and religion based professions and economic activities, regularization of bazaars and melas, access to market, formation and stabilization of self help groups etc.

Dr. M.K. Agrawal in his paper on "Urbanisation and Demographic Bottlenecks in U.P. : Role for Urban Local Bodies" laments upon the emerging demographic scenario in U.P. He maintained that urbanization has not shown its impact on improving the demographic scenario in urban Uttar Pradesh. He says that adverse situation has emerged in urban areas in terms of sex ratio, and urbanization has not been helpful in bringing down the total fertility rate, infant mortality rate and child mortality rate. Dr. Agrawal emphasizes that the urban governments have to do better in terms of their traditional responsibilities and also through new measures.

Ms. Rashmi Sinha in her paper on "Women Empowerment in Urban Governance" says that policy interventions, programmes and strategies have been initiated for women empowerment however, chronic blockages have been responsible for slow progress in this regard. She refers to a case of Andhra Pradesh where community based organizations are performing well. She emphasizes on good governance through its participatory approach which ensures transparency, effectiveness, efficiency, responsiveness, accountability and equality. She calls for the programmes encompassing local people's groups particularly women's groups for poverty alleviation.

Dr. P.K. Banta in his paper on "Women in Local Government" maintains that women have performed well wherever they have been given opportunities. Their faculties have more than matched those of the opposite sex. He further states that 74th Amendment Act has ushered in a new era in democratic process and direct participation of women in local self government. He analyses the constraints and hindrances responsible for women participation in local institutions. He emphasizes on building of technical capabilities in women. He also states that new capacity development plan for elected women in cities towards good governance and effective service delivery is required.

Prof. B.N. Singh laments upon lower status of women and their position in several parts of the globe. He feels that women are facing difficulties, suppression, oppression and are being discriminated on several grounds. Their labour should be recognized in the national accounts. Gender equality has to be ensured to save the survival of the civilization.

Dr. K. Sreeram in his paper on "Role of Women in Urban Governance" focuses on providing employment opportunities to women through community based programmes and role of NGOs in exploring employment opportunities for them.

Sri I.C. Thakur in his paper titled "Women Empowerment: Retrospect and Prospect" explains the various models of women empowerment.

Prof. M.P. Dube in his paper on "Need to Empower Women to End Discrimination" highlights the subordinate status of women in the male dominated Indian society. He points out that women's work is not being counted in the national income–though housework is production not consumption and it should be included in the income accounts. He focuses on the exploitation form of production since women's labour at domestic front being unpaid. Dr. Dube emphasized on the need of identifying and eliminating the obstacles for developing micro-enterprises to enhance the income of female entrepreneurs. Health, education, entrepreneurship development are needed to provide conducive environment, legal reforms in human rights perspective, developing women in groups, cultural pluralism and increased productivity of women's domestic work and also women micro-enterprises are some of the crucial issues to be addressed by local governments. Prof. Dube also maintains that there is need of shifting in strategy and planning to make women economically empowered.

Sri M.K. Dixit in his paper on "Empowerment of Women in Urban Administration in M.P.–Beyond the Constitutional Mandate" focuses on women empowerment in regard to strategies and programmes in the field of urban administration and the ways and means of making them successful and fruitful. Shri Dixit analyses the emerging trends in decentralization and maintains that representation of women in urban local bodies in Madhya Pradesh has increased to more than 33 per cent. He notes that NGO's can play an important role in organizing women and creating awareness about problems being faced by women in urban areas. He also feels that women reservation may not be taken as the end of women empowerment.

Dr. N. Ashok Kumar in his paper "Do Women have Efficiency to run the Urban Administration?" discusses the status of women in Indian society. He examines the role of women in urban administration in the context of 74th Amendment to the Constitution. Dr. Kumar concisely describes the situation of women in Andhra Pradesh.

Prof. S.N. Singh in his paper titled "Participation and Empowerment of Women (The Gaps and the Biases)" focuses on three types of biases of gaps. These are i) bias against gender, ii) bias against equality, and iii) bias against education. He says China was the first country to write women's participation in their development programmes. He reiterates the importance of involvement of women in decision making, which starts from the family and goes up to the Parliament. Therefore 1/3rd participation of women is the need of the hour. By empowering women, we are not favouring the women, but we are favouring the society. The second and third biases relate to regional and social imbalance. Womenfolk can be moderated by education, literacy, training, group discussions and seminars etc.

Dr. A.K. Singh in his presentation on "Empowerment of Female Scavengers: Liberation from Social and Occupational Bondage" emphasizes the role of scavengers in the society. He says that scavengers remain marginalized in Indian society today despite the constitutional provisions which direct the state to promote their educational and economic interests. He highlights scavenging conditions of women in urban area secondly at the national perspective and thirdly in our policies. There is a need to introduce gender sensitivity at the project formulation stage as well as project implementation, both at the governmental and non governmental levels.

Dr. Sanjay Gupta in his paper on "Political Empowerment of Women in Municipal Corporations and the 74th Constitutional Amendment: A Critical Review" feels that unless women are granted space at the political and decision making levels, the question of bringing about social equality is to remain un-filled.

He identifies hindrances on the way and presented future strategies for capacity building for women in urban local bodies.

Dr. Tanuja Singh in her paper on "Empowerment of Women: Myth or Reality" highlights the declining sex ratio in the country. She finds that surprisingly educated women are generally subjected to foeticide.

Dr. K.S. Saxena in his presentation on "Status of Women and Struggle for Political Identity in India" expresses that women in India have played a very significant role in every walk of life. He feels that though delicate and soft, she has a heart far stronger and bolder than of man. But the structure of the family in our country, according to him, creates a lot of problems for women. In fact a systematic violation of the rights of women is institutionalized in the prevailing family system. Dr. Saxena expresses that though by virtue of 73rd and 74th Amendments 33 per cent reservation for women in Panchayats and Municipalities has been granted even then women have to struggle for their political identity as it is the men who are still ruling the roost.

Ms.Renu Shankar and Ms. Suman Lal in their paper "Women Empowerment in Urban Administration: Role of NGOs" feel that the best and the surest method to empower women with knowledge of their rights, duties and responsibilities in education. The second important factor, according to them, is empowerment by granting economic independence. They also highlight the attempts made by NGOs in these fields.

Sri S.K. Sinha in his paper titled "Role of Women in Natural Disaster Management" discusses the reasons, types and impacts of natural disasters in the country. According to him women can play important roles in creating public awareness, capacity building, training and education, incorporating community based approach etc.

Prof. K. S. Padhy presents an empirical study entitled "Women Empowerment: A Case Study of an Urban Council of Orissa. He discusses at length the manipulative tactics of not only male corporators but also the female ones in urban administration.

Aizawl,
January 2005

U. B. SINGH

CONTRIBUTORS

Dr. Kulwant Singh – Formerly Executive Director, HSMI, New Delhi

Dr. M. P. Dube – Professor & Head, Department of Political Science, University of Allahabad, Allahabad.

Dr. S.N. Singh – Professor of Public Administration, University of Lucknow, Luknow.

Dr. S.K. Singh – Professor of Public Administration, University of Lucknow, Lucknow.

Dr. Sanjay Gupta – Reader in the Department of Political Science, University of Lucknow, Lucknow.

Dr. Pawan Kumar Banta – Department of Public Administration, Shimla.

Dr. K. Sreeram – Consultant, IIPA, New Delhi.

Dr. N. Ashok Kumar – Associate Professor, Regional Centre for Urban and Environmental Studies, Osmania University, Hyderabad.

Dr. Sanjay Srivastava – Lecturer in Political Science, Dr. H.S. Gour University, Sagar.

Dr. K.K. Upadhyay – PRIYA, New Delhi.

Mr. Pravin Bhardwaj – PRIA, New Delhi.

Dr. Supriya Singh – Lecturer in Political Science, Government Women's College, Patna.

Smt. Rashmi Sinha – Consultant (Urban), New Delhi.

Sri I.C. Thakur – WALMI, Patna.

Dr. S.M. Haider Rizvi – Coordinator (Urban), Sahbhagi Shikshan Kendra, Lucknow.

Sri M.K. Dixit, IAS (Retd.) – Member Secretary, M.P. State Finance Commission, Bhopal.

Dr. Awadhesh Kumar Singh – Faculty member, Institute of Development Studies, University of Lucknow and Director, Ananya Institute for Development Research and Action, Lucknow.

Dr. M.K. Agarwal – Reader in the Department of Economics, University of Lucknow, Lucknow.

Mrs. Renu Shankar – Social Activist, Patna.

Mrs. Suman Lal _ President, PRAYAS BHARTI, Patna.

Dr. K.S. Padhy – Professor and Head of the Department of Political Science, Berhampur University, Berhampur, Orissa.

Dr. Tanuja Singh – Sr. Lecturer in Political Science, J.D. Women's College, Patna.

Dr. Kumkum Narain – Lecturer in Economics, B.S. College, Patna.

Dr. Mira Mridubhashini – Lecturer in Economics, A.N. College, Patna.

Sri S. K. Sinha – Chef Town Planner (Retd.), Government of Bihar, Patna.

Dr. U.B. Singh – Reader and Head, Department of Public Administration, Mizoram University, Aizawl formerly Faculty Member, Regional Centre for Urban and Environmental Studies, University of Lucknow, Lucknow.

ACKNOWLEDGEMENTS

At the outset I express my sincere gratitude to the Union Ministry of Urban Development for sponsoring the national seminar. We are thankful to the Sustainable Development Forum of the Institution of Engineers (India), Bihar Chapter and its officials especially Professor G.P. Lal, Chairman and Sri Sushil C. Srivastava, Member Secretary and Sri S.K. Sinha for collaborating in this venture.

I am grateful to all the learned scholars, administrators, academics, professionals and practitioners from various corners of the country who made it convenient to come down to Patna, presented a scholarly paper and enriched the deliberations. Their scholarly contributions are unmatched and invaluable.

The family and staff of the RCUES, Lucknow University deserve my thanks for making the seminar a success.

Last but not the least, I am thankful to Shri S.K. Jha, Director of Serials Publications, New Delhi for publishing the volume in a record time.

Aizawl
January, 2005 **U.B. Singh**

Inaugural Address

WOMEN'S EMPOWERMENT IN URBAN ADMINISTRATION

G.P. Lal

I am glad that the Regional Centre for Urban and Environmental Studies, Lucknow University along with the Sustainable Development Forum of the Institution of Engineers (India) have organised a National Seminar on "Empowerment of Women in Urban Administration".

Women constitute half the human population and have to be equal partners in every activity – development, employment, administration, politics etc. The mental block about the secondary role of women has to go. Even now there is a preference to have a male child than a female child which is distressing as would be clear that the female/male ratio of population has declined. The sex ratio in 0-6 age-group was 945 female compared to 1000 males in 1991 which has declined to 927 females against 1000 males in 2001.

The Government of India have focused the role of women in successive Five Year Plans. The fist four Plans focused attention on various welfare activities with priority to women education. The 5th and 6th Plans shifted the approach from welfare to overall development of women including health, education and employment. The 7th Plan tried to make further dent and in the 8th Plan there was a shift from women development to women empowerment. The issue of reservation for women in all levels of government came up in sharp attention. During the period since Independence there has been women development in matter of increased female literacy, life expectancy, lowering of fertility rate, women's presence in Parliament and other elected bodies, employment etc. While the legislative, reformative, educational, health and employment strategies have given Indian women a significant boost in their struggle for equal rights in the society, a lot is yet to be done in terms of giving them enough confidence to carry this struggle further. Not only do they have to fight against the age-old bias, they also have to develop their own personality and capabilities against all odds as they have to maintain the social equilibrium and are the nerve centre of not only the Indian value system but also the guiding factor to our future generations.

We are aware that women comprise over 90 per cent of the work-force in the un-organised sector, like working in the agricultural fields, construction household services and other such sectors in the country. But they not prominently are seen in the organised sector whether in the industries or government. Their presence in positions of decision making levels is still poorer. Though the girls have been doing very well in the university, the number employed in senior positions is still not comparable with the boys. This may be due to individual aspiration, family obligation and social taboos.

Empowerment means acquiring the power to think and act freely, exercise choice and to fulfill position as equal member of the society. The United Nations Development Fund for Women (UNIFEM) include the following factors in its definition of women's empowerment :

- Acquiring knowledge and understanding of gender relation and the ways in which these relations may be changed
- Developing a sense of self-worth, a belief in one's ability to secure desired changes and the right to control one's life

- Gaining the ability to generate choices and exercise bargaining power
- Developing the ability to organise and influence the direction of social change to create a more just social and economic order, nationally and internationally.

Women's empowerment draws an important distinction between equality of opportunity on the one hand and equity of outcomes on the other.

The notion of women's empowerment has been reaching consequences – "Extending the idea of human development to encompass women's empowerment and gender justice puts social transformation at the centre of the agenda for human development and progress of women. Choices for women especially poor women cannot be enlarged without a change in relations between women and men as well as in the ideologies and institutions that preserve and reproduce gender inequality. This does not mean reversing positions, so that men become subordinate and women dominant. Rather, it means negotiating new kinds of relationships that are based not on power over others but on a mutual development of creative human energy. It also means negotiating new kinds of institutions, incorporating new norms and rules that support egalitarian and just relations between women and men".

In regard to Urban Administration the role of women is of great consequences. The strategies in Urban Activity are predominantly health care, education, welfare, cleanness, aesthetics etc. Women can handle these activities with greater care with their interest virtue.

In the human development and strategy for Sustainable Development specially through Urban Administration the role of women is second to none – possibly urban areas will be a better place to live with greater participation of women in the administration.

EMPOWERMENT OF WOMEN IN URBAN INDIA: IN SEARCH OF RIGHT PERSPECTIVE

U.B. Singh

All human beings are entitled to a healthy and productive life in harmony with nature. They have the right to adequate standard of living for themselves and their families, including adequate food, clothing, housing, water and sanitation. The State should ensure that all individuals are given the right to opportunity to make the most of their potential.

The future of development and society lies in the future of women, equally with men because they constitute nearly half of the country's population. Never has it been more apparent that women's issues can not be compartmentalised and isolated as secondary issues in development. One more stark reality is that women not only form a major section of the society but also hold greater responsibilities than men towards many facets of life. Moreover they are directly related with those factors of population change which affect the quality of life.

In the relationship between man and woman, it is the individual with a powerful personality who acquires a position of dominance. Generally, it is a man who commands power over a woman, though in a few cases, a woman also might exercise control over a man.

Besides the physical weakness imputed to women, they were made to believe that nature has made them to bear children and look after the household affairs. They have been designated as 'grihini' which psychologically prepares them to think that the would outside the house is not their concern. This resulted in exclusion of women from main economic activities also and reduced them to status of complete dependence upon males socially, politically and economically. The concept of equality and justice became meaningless in their relation to males. Thus their talent was suppressed and the nation was deprived of their contribution in various fields of social, cultural, economic and political activities. The male dominance was pushed to the extent of complete subjugation of women, torture against them and denial of justice and equality.

Gender Discrimination

In Indian society discrimination on the basis of sex is found since ages. It often starts at the earliest stages of life. In pre-Vedic period the society in India was matriarchal and women occupied the superior place as compared to men. They were rather considered indispensable for certain rites as the man could not be a spiritual whole without her participation.

This much is certain that there was male domination in the society. The Vedic era, however, was the golden era as far as equality of status and freedom are concerned. In "Gurukulas" women studied with men and many women were well versed in the Vedas. They were actively associated with men in every social and religious ritual and ceremony. In this era woman was considered an equal partner and enjoyed equal status and prestige. These were however sporadic instances and not the general custom. In number of places in Vedas there are prayers even for animals but not for daughters. They were not considered fit for politics, as they were considered to be physically weak, of fickle mind and unreliable.

A very important influence on the status of Hindu woman has been the "Manusmriti". In the beginning Manu writes "Brahma separated his body into two parts: from half he created man and from the other part woman. She is therefore, born equal. *'Gods reside where women are respected and where they are insulted all endeavour is useless."* Manu was however partial to men in some other respects by putting women on a pedestal as a source of a daily 'sukh' or comforts for the life. Thus, in the 'Smritik' era the honourable status of woman gradually started declining. Manu stated that there is a vital structure difference between man and woman. A woman could not possess an independent status. It was laid down that she had to depend on man from cradle to grave. They were denied right to property, divorce, freedom and independence.

In Kautilyan 'Arthashastra' it has been said that for a woman there is no greater God than her husband. She was considered to be source of all evils.

Thus women's role was almost insignificant during ancient India. It may however be mentioned that in ancient India many women belonging to aristocracy held power and position and were richly endowed with wealth. It is also clear that two categories of women were empowered, whether they belonged to the Hindu or the Muslim religion or whether rich or poor. The first category were women who devoted themselves to 'Bhakti' or devotion to God and the second were courtesans.

The 19th century was a watershed for women's history. Several Muslim invasions, too, added to the misery of women. There were both political and social movements which impacted on their situation. The condition of women in India, however, came to be worst during the Muslim rule. It was only in the British regime that the attitude, behaviour and living patterns of Indian society changed due to education and the western impact on socio-cultural life. The women organizations took up issues like women's education, abolition of social evils, Hindu law reforms, moral and material progress of women, equality of rights and opportunities and women's suffrage. Thus Indian women's movement worked for two goals: upliftment of women and equal rights for men and women. The former concentrated on reforming social practices so as to enable women to play a more important and constructive role in society, while the latter worked for extension of civil rights engaged by men in the political, economic and familial spheres to women also.

The historical and cultural survey of pre-Independent India shows that the inheritance of the Indian women has depended on the religion, region, caste and class in which she was born. None of these divisions were strictly stratified. The Indian women subjected to patriarchal rule received a position of respect through marriage and mother hood, both of which valued a high level of chastity. In times of uncertainty they regressed and during stability they progressed. One thing however never changed for them, that is the lack of possession of political and economic power as men always remained at the commanding heights of the economy as well as the polity.

In post-Independent period also in terms of every set of indices of development and socio-economic status, women have fared worse than men, in all regions, and in all strata of the population. In work, employment, earnings, education, health status and decision making powers, there is a clear difference between male and female entitlements.

Even when national indices of development show a rise, the benefits of these developments do not percolate in equal measure to men and women, and women end up receiving less than their commensurate share. In fact, women are sometimes victimized by 'development', which leaves them worse off in the wake of technological progress by making them redundant or bypassing their areas of interest.

International scenario is not quite dis similar. Women constitute 70 per cent of the world's poor population. They produce 50 per cent of the food worldwide but receive only 10 per cent of the incomes. Women's access to and ownership of resources is less than that engaged by men, and even among those who own property, the control of its use and dispensation vests more often than not with some male member of the family.

Women and Law

In pre-Independence era, the British Government passed some enactments for the protection and upliftment of Hindu women. These enactments were :

1. Sati Pratha Abolition Act, 1850
2. Caste Disability Removal Act, 1850

3. Hindu widow's Remarriage Act, 1856
4. Female Infanticide Prevention Act, 1870
5. Child Marriage Restraint Act, 1929
6. Hindu Women's Right to Property Act, 1937

Thus, efforts were made in British India also to create awareness among the society and the women themselves about the need to remove social disabilities of women, particularly of Hindu women.

After independence, the framers of the Indian Constitution realized the unequal status of women and assured that women get equal rights. The Preamble itself secures to all Indian citizens "*Justice*, social, economic and political; *Liberty* of thought, expression; *Equality* of status and of opportunity". It further resolves to promote among all citizens "*Fraternity* assuring the dignity of the individual".

The Constitution in Articles 14, 15 and 16 guarantees the principle of equality as fundamental rights.

"**Art. 14.** *Equality before law*–The State shall not deny to any person equality before the law or the equal protection of the laws within the territory of India.

"**Art. 15.** *Prohibition of discrimination on grounds of religion, race, caste, sex or place of birth*–(1) The State shall not discriminate against any citizen on grounds of religion, race, caste, sex, place of birth or any of them.

(2) ....

(3) Nothing in this article shall prevent the State from making any special provision for women and children.

(4) ....

"**Art. 16.** *Equality of opportunity in matters of public employment*–(1) There shall be equality of opportunity for all citizens in matters relating to employment or appointment to any office under the State.

(2) No citizen shall, on grounds only of religion, race, caste, sex, descent, place of birth, residence or any of them be ineligible

for, or discriminated against in respect of any employment or office under the State.

(3) ....

(4) ....

(5) ...."

The Directive Principles of State Policy embody the major policy goals of the welfare state as under :

"**Art. 39.** *Certain principles of policy to be followed by the State*– The State shall, in particular, direct its policy towards securing–

(a) that the citizen, men and women, equally, have the right to an adequate means of livelihood;

(b) ....

(c) ....

(d) that there is equal pay for equal work for both men and women;

(e) that the health and strength of workers, men and women and the tender age of children are not abused and that citizens are not forced by..................

(f) ....

"**Art. 42.** *Provision for just and humane conditions of work and maternity relief*–The State shall make provision for securing just and humane conditions of work and for maternity relief."

Article 51 – A relating to the fundament duties provides that "It shall be the duty of every citizen of India (e) to promote harmony and the spirit of common brotherhood amongst all the people of India transcending religious, linguistic and regional or sectional diversities to renounce practices derogatory to the dignity of women" among others.

The other major social enactments of free India are :

1. Hindu marriage Act, 1955
2. Hindu Succession Act, 1956
3. Hindu Adoption and Maintenance Act, 1956

4. Hindu Minority and Guardianship Act, 1956
5. Suppression of Immoral Traffic in Women and Girls Act, 1956
6. Women's and Children's Institution (Licensing) Act, 1956
7. Orphanages and other Charitable Homes (Supervision and Control) Act, 1960
8. Dowry Prohibition Act, 1961
9. Medical Termination of Pregnancy Act, 1971
10. Family Courts Act, 1984
11. Indecent Presentation of Women's Act, 1986
12. National Commission on Women
13. National Commission on Human Rights
14. 73rd and 74th Constitution Amendment Act, 1992
15. Women Empowerment Policy, 2001

Thus of plethora of laws relating to women exists in the country.

Political Participation

In a democracy, the right to franchise is the first basic right. In India, women along with men got the right to vote as citizens of free India in 1950. Although women exercise their franchise, the percentage of women voters remains comparatively low, because political space has always been monopolized by men. Representation of women among members of parliament and state legislatures has never exceeded 8 per cent, and has typically remained about 5 per cent over the years, despite the increasing visibility of women. Their entry into electoral politics is severely curtailed by the present political climate in the country. Those who do so, enter politics only by the virtue of their familial links with politics. Thus, women's representation at the higher rungs of decision making positions has also been consistently low.

The 73rd and 74th Amendments to the Constitution provide "not less than one third (including the number of seats reserved for women belonging to the Scheduled Castes and the Schedules Tribes), of the total number of seats to be filled by direct election in every Panchayat" (Art. 243 Z (3)) and "in every Municipality" (Art. 243 T (3)) "shall be reserved for women". The offices of chairpersons in the Municipalities and also in the Panchayats are also reserved for women.

Thus, in consonance to the constitutional provisions women have been mandatorily associated with decision making at the grassroots level institutions. This has ultimately broken the ice in the male dominated political scene in the country. For healthy political system and welfare of the people it is necessary that women must come forward and play an active role in political affairs of the country. Without their awareness and active participation nation can not progress. If they remain dormant the country will be deprived of their contribution in nation building process. Their inaction will rather drag the country backward.

Social and Economic Status

Women in India generally dominate the informal sector of the economy. While in informal economic sector, they are mostly disproportionately represented in low–wage positions. The visible and genuine decline in work participation roles, too, is related to a number of trends which adversely affect women : decline in the female proportion of the population, declining representation in decision making bodies, and increasing gap in male and female literacy rates, and unequal access to health and medical services. Even when women are employed outside the home they have to combine the load of double work occupation, house work and child rearing without enjoying a corresponding increase of power in decision making within the family.

Women's earnings are consistently lower than those of men but in the unorganized sector which accounts for 94 per cent of economically active women, earnings are even lower.

Feminisation of poverty has been noticed as a phenomenon in our developing economy. The men move up faster during such development, grabbing grater opportunities that women are unable to access, because of gender handicaps. Even the Official Country Report for India presented at the Fourth World Conference on Women in Beijing in 1995 observed that 'the percentage of women among the extremely poor is disproportionately large' adding that 'intra–house hold inequalities can be significant', necessitating special attention for poor women.

There is a gender asymmetry in the utilization of health services–during illness, fewer women than men seek and receive treatment. Women have neither the time, mobility, childcare assistance, nor leisure to travel to health centers for medicines or treatment. In addition, an ideology that glorifies self effacement and suffering for women make them more inclined to put up with pain and ill health, rather than demand attention and rest.

In terms of food intake, women suffer greater deprivation intra-familialy. A very systematic sex bias is also reflected in higher nutritional deficiency among girls vis-à-vis boys. And because of gender bias in the allocation of food, malnutrition is a significant factor in many of the female deaths.

Education is a key instrument responsible for national development. Education liberates women from ignorance and enhances their self esteem. It enables them to choose their own way and look after their families in a better way. Empowerment of women is directly linked with education. It is unfortunate that even after five decades of independence, the country has not been able to combat illiteracy, and women are far behind their counterpart. The literacy rate is increasing but at a slow pace. The girl child in low strata of society is treated as a helping hand to mother rather than being sent to school. Lack of education, training and low level of literacy not only merely excluded women from social, economic and political power but knowledge power as well. Therefore, while comprising half of the humanity "contributing 2/3rd of the world's work hours she earns only 1/3rd of the total income and owns less than 1/10th of the world resources."

The technological development is proving a curse. In higher level of society female foeticide is prevalent. Dowry is still reigning the roost in all strata of our society. Dowry deaths are a related abominating unique in India. Violence against women has its roots in the subordination of women at the social level and their vulnerability has not decreased but increased as a consequence of social disruptions, backlash and a general degeneration of values. Further more, the cultural construct of son preferences adds to the psychological diffidence of the female child. The growing market mechanism is treating women as a commodity.

Government Interventions

Government programmes for women development began as early as 1954 in India. Although the beginning was made in 1954, the actual participation began only in 1974 with the report of the Committee on the Status of Women in India. In the 1970's, the government dealt with women's issues as part of the wider category of poverty alleviation. In the 1980's the realization came that women are not just a segment but the core of India's poor. This brought to the forefront the need for especial programmes for women as a top priority. Such initiatives included :

(i) National Commission on Self-Employed Women and Women in Informal Sector

(ii) Formulation of National Perspective Plan for Women

(iii) Support to Training and Employment Programmes for Women

(iv) Mahila Samakhya Programme

(v) Women Development Corporations

(vi) Women's Credit Fund

(vii) Development of Women and Children in Rural Areas

(viii) Training–cum-Production Centers for Women

(ix) Awareness Generation Camps for Rural and Poor Women

(x) Centers for Rehabilitation of Women in Distress

(xi) Voluntary Action Bureau and Family Counseling Centers

(xii) Stay Homes for Women and Girls

(xiii) Free Legal and Para-legal training

(xiv) Working Women's Hostels

(xv) CBOs for Urban Poor Women

(xvi) 20-Point Programmes

(xvii) Family Welfare Programmes

(xviii) Maternal and Child Health Care

(xix) Development of Women and Children in Urban Areas

(xx) Balika Samridhi Yojana

(xxi) Self Help Groups for Urban Poor Women

(xxii) Integrated Child Development Scheme

(xxiii) National Adolescent Girls Scheme

(xxiv) National Motherhood Facility Plan

(xxv) Mahila Samridhi Yojana

(xxvi) Vatsalya Yojana

(xxvii) Urban Nutritional Diet Programme

(xxviii) Mid-day Meal Scheme for School Children

(xxix) Urban RCH Scheme

(xxx) Swarna Jayanti Shahri Rojgar Yojana.

Policy Initiatives

The instrument of planning has been the most positive indicator of policy formulation for women. The First Five Year Plan (1951-56) did not say anything specific about the share of women in development policy. The chapter on social welfare said that "social conditions should give women opportunities for creative self expression so that they can make their full contribution towards the economic and social life of the community". The planners laid stress on promoting education of women through enrolling larger number of girls in schools. There was a mention of improving the employability of women through technical training and education of special employment opportunities for them. The planners failed to prescribe administrative structures for women's development as this work had to be done largely through voluntary organizations. The Second Five year Plan (1956-61) did not enunciate any new goals of development for women, either in philosophic or conceptual terms. The need for promoting girls' education, making education more relevant to girls' needs and the need to employ woman teachers was mentioned. The Third Five Year Plan (1961-66) continued to lay emphasis on the welfare aspect of women. Increased allocations for the Social Welfare Boards, and increased assistance to voluntary organizations working in the field were recommended. The Plan emphasized the need to give women special scholarships at the university level and also grants to women's colleges. The Fourth Five Year Plan (1969-74) did not innovate any schemes meant fully for women. The policy parameters continued to stress on approach of assisting voluntary organizations dealing with the welfare of women. The Fifth Five year Plan (1974-79) did not indicate any initiative in this regard. No policy statement was made either.

The Sixth Five Year Plan (1980-85) was a watershed for women's development as, for the first time, a separate chapter on women and development was included in the Plan document. It reviewed the status on situation of women and came to the conclusion that in spite of legal and constitutional guarantees, women had lagged behind men in almost all sectors. It stressed that the main strategy for women's development was three fold-education, employment and health. For the first time, the Plan clearly spelt out that economic independence would accelerate improvement in the status of women. The Seventh Five Year Plan (1985-90) reviewed the achievements of the Sixth Plan for women. It stressed a greater integration between health and family welfare and strengthening of primary health care which benefited women. It also stated that lacunae in existing legislation should be removed. The Plan stated that confidence building and awareness of their rights among women must be accelerated so that women realize their potential for development and their rights to a share from this process.

The Eight Five Year Plan (1992-97) expressed a squeamishness about having a separate chapter on women, and the subject was included in social welfare. The Plan praised the monitoring of beneficiary oriented schemes from which women were deriving. The task of gender sensitization throughout the educational structure was also a creditable achievement. The Department of Women and Child Development prepared a Plan of Action for women for 1988-2000 and set up the Shram Shakti Commission for evaluating the functioning of women in the informal sector and for suggesting steps for ameliorating their condition. There was a stress on the paramount importance of employment for women, the extension of opportunities to them through skill training, a decentralized approach and rural employment. The Ninth Plan (1997-2002) had important objectives for women development. It stated categorically that for empowering women as the agents of social change and development, a policy was needed. Consequently, a National Policy for Empowerment of Women was formulated in 2001. The Plan discussed the need for reservation of seats for women. The most important resolve of the Plan was to have a special women's component to ensure 30 per cent flow of funds to women development sectors.

The approach of the Tenth Plan is to continue with the major strategy of Empowering Women as Agents of Social Change and Development. With this aim in view, the Plan strategy is to adopt a Sector-specific three fold strategy for empowering women, based on the prescriptions of the National Policy for Empowerment of Women. It includes Social Empowerment to create an enabling environment through various affirmative developmental policies and programmes for development of women besides providing their easy and equal access to all the basic minimum services to enable them to realize their full potentials; Economic Empowerment to ensure provision of training, employment and income generation activities with both forward and backward linkages with the ultimate objective of making all potential women economically independent and self reliant and Gender Justice–to eliminate all forms of gender discrimination and thus allow women to enjoy not only the dejure but also the defacto right and fundamental freedom on par with men is all spheres i.g. political, economic, social, civil, cultural etc.

Gender Equality Strategy

The gender equality doctrine is an outstanding contribution of the twentieth century. The social thought has been used as a practical objective for the welfare of the human race. The UN Declaration of Women's Rights, 1967 postulated the egalitarian doctrine of achieving equal rights for women as that of men and advocated its universal recognition in law as an unavoidable necessity. Maximum participation of women as well as men in all fields of human activity is essential for the full and complete development of a country. Any discrimination against equal rights of women or their subordination amounts to injustice to half of the humanity.

India too faced the development crisis, but there was no such women's movement and not even any realization of the interrelationship between the situation of women and the development trends. The movement which had developed along with the freedom struggle had ended by the mid-1950s, with the acceptance of women's claims for complete equality in the Constitution of India. Most of the groups then believed that the women's movement had achieved its objectives and the overall benefits would trickle down in the society with time.

Underlying the Development Dialogue in the 1970's was a general disillusionment with macro-growth theories and techno-economic models of development. The growing problems of poverty, unemployment, malnutrition, socio-economic inequalities, rural stagnation and population crisis compelled a shift in focus, to the need for a more humane strategy for development and narrowing of disparities in income and levels of living and distributional equity within and between the nations. Mid way through the second Development Decade, one notices a conscious search for alternatives in goals of development, which take note of indigenous values. Amongst the many groups searching for better strategies was a section of the new women's movement. This movement has erupted in many countries in the western world from the mid 1960s and had recorded women's protest against their unequal status in society, their images as commodities and unproductive consumers with only the biological role of reproduction to perform their ineffectiveness in decision making on the socio-political front. Pressure from this movement resulted in a Declaration by the UN General Assembly for the Elimination of Discrimination Against Women (1967).

In pursuance of the UN resolution, the Indian government appointed a committee to review the changes that had taken place in the status of women as a result of the constitutional equality, legal reform and educational and other measures introduced by the government since Independence. In view of the declaration of 1975 as the International Women's Year, the committee submitted its report in 1975. An inter-ministerial empowered committee was appointed in 1975, to consider the recommendations and to take decisions thereon. Simultaneously as a follow up measure to the World Plan of Action for the International Women's Decade (1976-85), the Government of India started the preparation of National Plan of Action for Women. In 1976, the Prime Minister announced the constitution of National Committee on Women under his chairmanship. Being a signatory to Non-Aligned Summit, India pursued the related issues and some programmes were specially framed for women.

Despite these rigorous efforts to take the short-cut from the Women Emancipation to Gender Equity, Indian women are still facing seveve development problem. The tration has begqueathed to Indian Women an ambivalent legacy; secondary status in patriarchy, plus the reverence accorded to motherhood. The women are deprived of their fundamental rights of life, health, education, thinking and action. There is today clearly documented evidence to substantiate this claim that women are discriminated against and denied their fundamental right to survival, access to resources and control over their produce. The process of gender socialisation itself is a violation of basic human rights as it attempts to control women's autonomy and their independence of thought and action. It makes them weak, pliant and subservient.

Factors Affecting Status of Women

E.J. Matson has identified five specific factors responsible for the low status of women in India, both in the family and society, and also for female seclusion in our culture. These are –Hindu religion, caste system, joint family system, Islamic rule and British colonialism. The 'purdah' system and dowry are the other social practices, which discriminate against women in a degrading way. Yet another important factor which affects women's self perception and maintains traditional images in spite of social and economic change, is religion.

Justice J.S. Verma feels that "gender equality is more a way of life achieved by a proper perspective rather than one of formal guarantee under the laws. Gender inequality is a fact of continuing substantive inequality in the society". Another factor that affects the status of woman is the institution of marriage. There has been a tradition of early marriages particularly for females which proves disastrous for their mental, physical, social and economic status.

Upliftement Mode

Having studied the women problems over decades the social scientists have realized that there can be five different modes for the upliftement of women :

(a) welfare mode,
(b) equity mode,
(c) anti-poverty mode,
(d) efficiency mode and,
(e) empowerment mode.

Neeta Tapan describes that the welfare mode is one that benefits the most vulnerable group as passive recipients and is suitable at the initial stage of development where there are wide disparities. The equity mode takes special care of gender needs and emphasizes redistributing power. The anti-poverty mode recognizes that a majority of women fall in the category of deprivation. It focuses on the productive role of women. It reflects on the necessity of providing women with better access to resources. The efficiency mode take care of practical gender needs and helps in improving the capability and capacity of women by imparting education, skill training etc. The empowerment mode helps women in making their own choices with regard to their lives and makes them more active players in the society.

Modern Perspective

Several legal and policy efforts over the year have definitely improved the status of women in India. However the process of women's emancipation is yet not complete. The status of women varies from region to region and further on accounts of caste. Social hierarchy, class system, economic inequality, cultural variations and even distribution of power and privileges have made it more complicated. As the Committee on the Status of Women in India admits : "The status of women in India can not be defined simply. General conceptions like equality, role differentiation, legal, social and political rights, dependence or independence are not applicable to all sections of our population. Since a very large section of our society still continues to be under the influence of traditional standards, we had to juxtapose the role conceptions, norms and values in all their wide variety in traditional society, against the new dimensions in women's status and rules introduced by the Constitution and the process of social change".

The socialization of women in the family and in the school reinforce gender roles. As a subordinate group in society women have developed a false consciousness. Thus women are expected to seek occupational roles which stress the aspect of service and cooperation with men, and not competition. Here lies the need of empowering the half of the population.

Urban Complexities

As a result of 74th Amendment to the Constitution women have been associated mandatorily with the decision making process at the grassroot level administration in urban areas. One third of urban local bodies (about 1200) in the country are headed by women representatives. The local administration in about two dozen of larger urban areas having municipal corporations are being led by women mayors. In addition more than 40,000 women members are actively involved in urban governance all over the country.

There may be some cases of 'pati–Adhyaksh', but a new era has dawned and the women have to stay on equal pedestal if not dominating, as far as political empowerment is concerned. A good beginning has been made and the day is not far off when sufficient women may climb to the higher ladder of legislature i.e. state assemblies and parliament.

Economically as well, a large number of women are employed in urban scavenging. They also require a proper deal. In addition good number of girls and adult women are earning their livelihood as rag pickers, as maid servants, in house building activities etc. They all deserve an honourable socio-economic status in the modern society. The women living in unserviced or underserviced areas are the real victim of development and social and health hazards. Thus the urban administration has to counter a complex situation so far as empowerment of women is concerned.

Necessitating Empowerment

The foregone discussion clearly indicates the status of Indian women and the imperative needs for their empowerment. The word 'empowerment' is defined by Chambers Dictionary as 'to authorise'. The Oxford English Dictionary gives two meanings as 'to invest legally or formally with power or authority, to authorize or licence' and "to improve or bestow power to an end or for a purpose, to enable, permit". While there has been much talk of the need to empower women, this has not resulted in specific workable or sustainable measures that would help create a social order based on gender justice.

Women are the agents of change. Therefore it is the woman who matters because if one woman is empowered through education, health and information then a whole family benefits and those benefits are spread over the whole society automatically. In this way, the over all process of development is eased out and accelerated. Thus, empowerment of women is a part of Human Resources Development and cannot be treated independently and the two must necessarily go in tandem for the achievement of sustainable development.

The empowerment and autonomy of women and the empowerment of their political, social, economic and health status is a highly important end in itself. Instead, the issue of women has to be given priority to bring them at par with men as they have been exploited and ignored for long. Human progress is not about income expansion and accelerating commodity production, but about expanding human capabilities. Development is a process of enlarging people's choices. Such choices tend to be very wide ranging starting with some very basic ones to greater social, economic and political freedom, including the opportunities to be creative and productive and enjoy personal self respect and be assured of human rights.

Empowerment in such a context calls for modalities other than mere economic betterment, because much of women's powerlessness stems from non-quantifiable rather than monetary impositions or handicaps. Conventional strategies for development address only poverty, not powerlessness or subordinate status, which are the crucial issues. Thus strategies for empowering women must focus beyond economic restructuring, to include restructuring of social relations which constrain and restrain women. Empowerment of women is not an option today but an infinitive.

In the Indian context, family is a basic social security unit and it has to be strengthened through mutual cooperation in spirit of a fair give and take within its constituents. The society, thus has to change its mind set. While the legislative and other measures may trigger the process, a persuasive approach through mass communication techniques together with involvement of social and family groups will have to be worked out through collective efforts of all concerned. This of course 'has to be aimed at adopting a harmonious path striking a delicate balance between the individual aspirations and family obligations'. Justice J.S. Verma corroborates that the "remedy of in-equality between man and woman lies in the correction of societal aberrations which commence with the birth of a girl child. The infanticide has degenerated to female foeticide". Such a situation poses a big question to the modern Indian society.

A Big Question

Why despite all the concerted efforts there is persistent inequality between men and women and the goal of gender equality, development and peace through women empowerment is still a far off destination?

REFERENCES

Pande, G.S., Political participation of Women in India, New Royal Book, Lucknow, 2001.

Tapan, N., Need for Women Empowerment in India, Rawat, New Delhi, 2000.

Asthana, P., Women's Movement in India, Vikas, New Delhi, 1974.

Boserap, E., Women's Role in Economic Development, George Allen and Unwin, London, 1970.

D' Souza, A. (ed), Women in Contemporary India and South Asia, Manohar, New Delhi, 1980.

Desai, N. and Krishnaraj, M., Women and Society in India, Ajanta, New Delhi, 1987.

Jacobson, D. and Wdley, S., Women in India : Two Perspectives, Manohar, New Delhi, 1977.

Jain, D., (ed) Indian Women, Govt. of India, 1975.

Kapur, P., The Changing Role and Status of Women, Sterling New Delhi, 1972.

Shams, S., (ed) Women, Law and Social Change, Ashish, New Delhi, 1991.

Shastri, H.G., The Manusmiriti (Hindi), 5th edition, Chaukhamba Sanskrit Sansthan, Varanasi, 1997.

Misra, R., Women in Mughal India, M Manoharlal, New Delhi, 1967.

Sarkar, J.N. Studies in Mughal History, Vidya Bhawan, Bombay, 1974.

Forbes, G., Women in Modern India, The New Cambridge History of India, Cambridge Press, 1996.

Annual Report, National Commission for Women, 1992-93 to 1996.

Seth, Mira, Women & Development, Sage, 2001.

Agrawal, S.P., Women's Education in India (1995-98), Vol. III, Concept, 2001.

Ahuja, Ram, Rights of Women (A Feminist Perspective), Rawat, 1992.

Bhasin, K. (ed), The Position of Women in India, Sri Nagar, 1962.

Everett, J.M., Women and Social Change in India, Heritage, New Delhi, 1969.

Hate, Changing status of Women in post–Independent India, Bombay, 1969.

B.B. Ghali, former Secretary General of the UN, welcome speech at the Fourth World Conference on Women in Beijing, 1995.

Agrawal, B., Gender and Command over Property : A Critical Gap in Economic Analysis and Policy in South Asia, in World Development, Vol. 22 (10), 1994.

India : The Road to Human Development, UNDP, 1994.

Norasimhan, S., Empowering Women, Sage, 1999.

National Perspective Plan for Women (1988-2000), Govt. of India, 1988.

S. Singh & S.P. Srivastava (eds), Gender Equality through Women's Empowerment, Bharat Book, Lucknow, 2001.

Purushothaman, S., The Empowerment of Women in India, Sage, 1998.

Seminar, Sept. 2001.

Mainstream, Dec. 14, 1996.

Hans, March, 2001.

Yojana, August, 2001.

Yojana, Dec. 2001.

Employment News, XXVI (48), March 2-8, 2002.

The Gender Advantage on the Basis of General Elections in India

Year	No. of seats Available	Total no. of contestants	Male			Female		
			Total	Elected	Percentage of winning	Total	Elected	Percentage of winning
1952	489	1,874	–	–	–	–	–	–
1957	494	1,518	1,474	467	31.70	45	27	60.00
1962	494	1,985	1,915	459	23.97	70	35	50.00
1967	520	2,369	2,302	490	21.29	67	30	44.78
1971	520	2,784	2,698	499	18.50	86	21	24.42
1977	542	2,439	2,369	523	22.08	70	19	27.14
1980	542	4,620	4,478	514	11.48	142	28	19.72
1984	542	5,574	5,406	500	9.25	164	42	25.61
1989	529	6,160	5,962	502	8.42	198	27	13.64
1991	521	8,699	8,374	492	5.88	325	39	12.00
1996	543	13,952	13,353	504	3.77	599	39	6.51
1998	543	4,750	4,483	502	11.20	267	41	15.36
1999	543	4,649	4,364	494	11.30	284	49	17.0
2004	539	3,545						

Source : Vote, 1998, KBK Pollgraphics. Source for 1999 is the Lok Sabha Secretariat, New Delhi, 1999 Unpublished.

Note : Data for 1952 not available.

Source : Mira Seth, Women & Development, Sage, 2001.

WOMEN IN DECISION MAKING

Kulwant Singh

Democratic and secular India endeavours to provide the necessary conditions for greater participation of women in all spheres of life. Equality of opportunity is guaranteed, and discrimination on grounds of sex, language, religion, class or creed is prohibited. Yet, in reality, women's participation in decision-making at all levels–national to local–is low.

The challenges in seeking to redress this inequality in a diverse and complex country like India are enormous. They are related to overcoming attitudinal, institutional, cultural and social restrictions that have grown over centuries.

There is now, however, an acceptance that women's participation in decision-making in large enough numbers at every level is needed. Women's unique experiences and perspectives would enhance and alter definitions of problems and solutions and would also empower them.

Participation of women is an integral part of democratic process and strengthening the quality of civic life. As they are half the population, women must be in decision-making in all socio-economic and political organizations.

Obstacles which do not let women participate fully need to be identified and removed. Often structures and social norms are barriers, and stem from social conditioning which inhibits women from aspiring to decision-making positions. Governmental and non-Governmental interventions should facilitate and promote women's participation in decision-making.

In the privacy of a home, men and women seem to be keeping decision-making gender based. Micro level studies show that when women determine issues, it is generally in the traditional spheres and at a later stage in their lives. For example, relatively few women decide where and when to invest money or what crops to grow, on their own. Women voicing their feelings, dissent or preferences are the exception, rather than the rule. Women will assume leadership positions and be successful if they are enabled to develop that capability within the domestic sphere and the public sphere.

Is it the opportunity for decision-making for women which must come first or is it many more women in decision-making positions who will make a difference? Both are needed. Entry of a large number of women into decision-making processes can radically change the existing situation. If more and more women are associated at different levels, it is bound to affect public policy. Women issues will be transformed into societal issues. The most critical role for women will be to resist inequality and injustice, not merely for women, but for all.

So far, very few women have risen to high levels without personal sacrifice, suffering or discrimination. This can change when women get into existing patriarchal structures, stay on and exercise women's visions and leadership. Creating a suitable environment for free and fearless participation of women is a necessary pre-condition towards establishment of a just and equitable order.

This is not to cloud gender into an all pervasive homogeneous category. The commonality of sub-ordination and nurturing quality of women which is often advanced in favour of this theory tend to over simplify the complex social factors that influence and govern the construction of gender roles in society. Women's empowerment and participation is however, a political question, linked to changes in power relations. It is through a mutually supportive process of empowerment that women can redirect and influence a political process which has largely failed to tap the energy, knowledge, and ability of women.

During India's freedom movement from British colonial rule, women had a tremendous opportunity to be part of a mass and popular, protest movement. Mostly a non-violent movement, it enabled women from all walks of life to join voluntarily and in large numbers. In the post-Independence period, women have continued to speak out on all issues. The women's movement and women's organizations have advocated policy changes and Constitutional amendments, reflecting and articulating the experiences and aspirations of the nations' women.

While women have often been in the forefront in mass movements, their presence has not been felt strongly in structured decision-making and institutions. Nor are they in positions of power. Even when they have been a Prime Minister or Chief Minister, they have not been able to change the lives of the mass of women. Working in a predominantly patriarchal structure with no gender sensitivity has made it difficult to bring about real and sustained changes for women.

Participation in public life has many facets. It includes activities which have strong bearing on groups and the community, the power to effectively influence elected representatives, decision-making processes as well as policies and actually alter existing situations wherever they are found to be clearly disadvantageous. While women should be positioned in large numbers at crucial levels for significant and effective exercise of power, they need to be equipped with suitable means to shoulder these responsibilities. Otherwise their representation would end up as mere tokenism.

In India, limited adult franchise was granted to women in 1937. After Independence, the Constitution granted equal voting rights. Women have participated in the political process– as voters, as candidates contesting elections, in deliberations in the State Assemblies and the National Parliament. They have held public office at different levels.

Women's participation in elections depends on the mobilization of the political parties, general awareness among the community of the importance of voting, and the overall political culture. No serious effort has as yet been made to mobilize women as a political constituency by any political party. Women are often projected as not being interested in and un-informed about political matters. Women are also not perceived as an organised interest or pressure group, so their needs are not taken into consideration. However, these stereotypes are not borne out by facts.

It is difficult, nonetheless, to generalise about the links between any single factor and political behaviour. They vary and are influenced by factors such as the social status of women, their economic position, cultural norms and above all, the regional outlook towards women's participation in public affairs.

The number of women contestants in Parliamentary elections has not increased significantly over the years. Political parties are still reluctant to field women candidates. The high cost of election campaigning is a deterrent to women candidates (Table 1).

Table 1 : Women's Representation in the Lok Sabha (Lower House)

Term of Lok Sabha	*Total Seats*	*No. of Women Nmembers*	*Percentage*
1952-57	489	14	2.8
1957-62	494	18	3.6
1962-67	494	30	6.0
1967-71	520	31	6.0
1971-77	520	20	3.8
1977-80	542	19	3.5
1980-84*	529	28	5.3
1984-89	542	42	7.7
1989-91**	523	23	4.4
1991-**	536	39	7.2
1996	543	40	7.3
1998	543	43	7.9
1999	543	49	9.02

Source : Election Commission of India.

* Elections were not held in 12 constituencies in Assam and in Meghalaya.

** Elections were not held in J&K and Punjab. Figures include women elected from Punjab during the by elections in 1992.

Even in the Rajya Sabha, where there is indirect election and nomination there has been a low representation of women (Table 2).

Table 2 : Women's Representation in the Rajya Sabha (Upper House)

Year	*Total Seats*	*No. of Women Members*	*Percentage*
1952	219	16	7.3
1957	237	18	7.6
1962	238	18	7.6
1967	240	20	8.3
1971	243	17	7.0
1977	244	25	10.2
1980	244	24	9.8
1985	244	28	11.4
1990	245	24	9.7
1991	245	38	15.5
1992	245	17	6.9
1994	245	20	8.1
1996	245	18	7.3
1997	245	18	7.3
1998	245	18	7.3

Source : Statistical Abstracts, 1998.

Some studies of Parliamentary participation indicate that women members participate more actively in 'women's issues'– health, welfare, atrocities against women, crimes like dowry and violations of human rights. This participation is confined to the more articulate women. In issues of defence, finance, politics etc. their participation is relatively limited.

The data given in Table 3 show women's representation in selected State Legislatures. The situation it appears has not improved much since the 1950s.

Analyses of trends of nominations of women to contest elections to the State Legislatures indicate that there is a gender discrimination which is responsible for poor representation of women (Table 4).

Table 3 : Representation of Women and Men in State Legislatures

States	*Year*	*Total*	*Women*
Assam	1996	122	6
Haryana	1999	90	4
Jammu & Kashmir	1996	87	2
Himachal Pradesh	1998	68	6
Gujarat	1998	182	4
Kerala	1996	140	13
Meghalaya	1998	60	3
Punjab	1997	117	7
Pondicherry	1996	30	1
NCT Delhi	1998	70	9
Nagaland	1998	60	0
Madhya Pradesh	1998	320	26
Tamil Nadu	1996	234	9
Tripura	1998	60	2
Uttar pradesh	1996	424	20
West Bengal	1996	294	20
Bihar	1999	324	19
Maharashtra	1995	288	11
Arunachal Pradesh	1995	60	1
Manipur	1999	60	1
Orissa	1999	147	13
Rajasthan	1998	200	14

Source : Election Commission of India.

At the national level, there is only one woman Cabinet Minister and 6 Ministers of State, in a Cabinet of 70. There is only one woman Governor and two woman Chief Ministers.

Woman Ministers are often given welfare oriented portfolios–women and child development, culture and youth. Science and technology, finance, defence, foreign relations are rarely allotted to women, though women have demonstrated their ability to handle such portfolios.

The maximum number of women at decision making levels have been in the welfare and development oriented sectors or human resource development which includes education, culture, and women and child development.

Table 4 : Candidates Nominated and Contested in the Recent Legislative Assemblies

States/Uts	Year	Total seats	Nominated			Contested		
			M	F	T	M	F	T
Assam	1996	122	1235	45	1280	1183	45	1228
Haryana	1996	90	4609	212	4821	2515	93	2603
Jammu & Kashmir	1996	87	658	21	679	532	15	547
Himachal Pradesh	1998	68	491	44	535	344	25	369
Gujarat	1998	182	1951	89	2040	1076	49	1125
Kerala	1996	140	2001	75	2076	1146	45	1201
Meghalaya	1998	60	313	15	328	293	15	308
Punjab	1997	117	1099	109	1208	641	52	693
Pondicherry	1996	30	470	24	494	252	18	270
NCT Delhi	1998	70	977	75	1052	758	57	815
Nagaland	1998	60	142	0	142	80	0	80
Madhya Pradesh	1998	320	3814	316	4130	2329	181	2510
Tamil Nadu	1996	234	8011	264	8275	4861	156	5017
Tripura	1998	60	304	27	331	249	21	270
Uttar pradesh	1996	424	5842	296	6138	4239	190	4429
West Bengal	1996	294	2583	143	2726	1921	114	2035
Bihar	1995	324	14806	502	15308	8146	264	8410
Maharashtra	1995	288	10672	559	11231	4480	247	4727
Arunachal Pradesh	1995	60	218	7	225	169	4	173
Manipur	1995	60	386	11	397	336	11	347
Orissa	1995	147	1760	96	1856	1338	75	1413
Rajasthan	1998	200	2425	153	2578	1367	69	1436

Source : Statistical Repots, Election Commission of India.

In other wings of Government too, there has been limited representation. For example, there are only few women Judges in the Supreme Court and the High Courts.

A few eminent women have no doubt, occupied important administrative positions such as Secretaries to Departments in the national Government as well as Chief Secretaries to State Governments.

According to available figures only around 5.71 percent of the total number of persons in administrative services are women.

One of the variables that go into the Gender Empowerment measure, as depicted in the Human Development Report, is the proportion of men and women senior levels of government.

It is noteworthy that within the premier civil services of the country, the representation of women is poor (Table 5).

Since relatively few women enter the civil services, several efforts have been made to improve the situation. The Department of Personnel and Administrative Reforms of the Government of India has also provided, whenever possible, women officers on the selection boards for posts and services.

Monitoring the increase in the participation of women at all levels of decision making is essential. Updating of data and preparation of reports on women in administration and management is vital. Facilities provided for posting a working couple to the same place and support services of housing, crèches, and schools need to be better implemented for these initiatives to have the desired impact.

Women also need to be better represented in the public sector undertakings, especially at decision making levels. It is estimated that only about 1.2 per cent of the executive cadre in the private sector are women. They belong mainly to a few selected segments like advertising and hotels.

It is clear that increased participation of women in decision making at the national and regional level will not happen,

Table 5 : Women in Selected Civil Services

Services	Year	No. of Personnel in Position			
		Total	Males	Females	% of Female
Indian Administrative Service	1985	4284	3973	311	7.3
	1992	4928	4498	430	8.7
	1996	5047	4546	501	9.9
	1997	4991	4479	512	10.3
Indian Police Service	1985	2343	2325	18	0.8
	1992	2825	2773	52	1.8
	1996	2947	2883	64	2.2
	1997[1]	2964	2868	96	3.3
	1998[2]	2985	2885	100	3.4
	1999[3]	3115	3007	108	3.5
Indian Foreign Service	1985	535	485	50	9.3
	1992	721	658	83	8.7
	1995	547	481	66	12.1
	1996	567	501	66	11.6
	1997	586	519	67	11.4
	1998	587	520	67	11.4

1. As on 1.11.98 (includes 1998 Batch)
2. As on 1.1.97 (includes 1996 Batch)
3. As on 31.10.97 (includes 1997 Batch)

Sources : Platform for Action : Five years after–An Assessment Department of Women and Child Development Ministry of HRD, Govt. of India, June, 2000.

unless a large number of women are enabled to participate effectively at the local level. The issues and processes here are easily comprehended, and directed to benefit those who need them most. Local Governments are the best training grounds for leadership, participatory planning, administrative skills and expertise.

Since 1959, the representation of women at grass-root level institutions of governance has been through several ups and downs and strategies such as nominations and limited quotas have been tried by States.

After the 73rd Constitution Amendment Act of 1993 all State Legislatures have amended their respective legislations to conform to the Constitutional Amendment and introduced a three-tier system of local governance from the village to the district level. Each Panchayat now has a uniform five year term and elections are expected to be held regularly to constitute new bodies before the term expires. In the event of dissolution, elections are to be held within six months. In all Panchayats, seats are to be reserved for Scheduled Castes and Scheduled Tribes in proportion to their numbers in the population. One-third of the total number of seats are reserved for women. One-third of the Chairpersons of Panchayats at all levels are to be women.

Devolution of financial powers has been contemplated to effectively administer the subjects the local bodies have been allocated. There are as many as 18 functions which are included in the 12th Schedule of the Constitution which defines the functional domain of the local bodies.

Women are governing after being elected through a democratic process of universal adult franchise, multiparty system and mandatory elections at regular intervals. They are a part of the Local Government in their area, at the village, town, city or a larger district level (Table 6).

In States where elections have been held the results have been extremely encouraging. In the States of West Bengal and Karnataka women have gained more than the number of seats reserved for them. In other States, the reserved quota has been

Table 6 : Women in Panchayati Raj Institutions

Sl. No.	State	Year	Gram Panchayats (Village)			Panchayat Samitis (Block)			Zilla parishad (District)			Remarks
	Gram		No. of	Total	No. of	No. of	Total	No. of	No. of	Total	No. of	Rema-rks
		No. of Pan-Chayat (GP)	Women Members	Pan-Members	No. of chayat Smitis (PS)	Women Mem-bers	Zilla Mem-bers	No. of Pari-shad (ZP)	Women Mem-bers	Mem-bers		
1.	Gujarat	1995	13,256	64,052	19,936* (31.1)	182	3,765	1,275 (33.84)	19	761	254 (33.38)	* 1415 more women members are to be elected.
2.	Haryana	1994	5,958	54,159	17,928 (33.10)	110	2,418	807 (33.37)	16	303	101 (33.33)	
3.	Karnataka	1993	5,641	80,627	37,689 (46.74)	175	3,340	1,343 (40.2)	20	919	335 (36.4)	
4.	Kerala**	1995	990	10,700	3,878 (36.2)	152	1,543	565 (36.6)	14	300	104 (34.6)	** Election will be held on 23625 Sept., 1995.

(Contd....)

Table 6 : (Contd...)

Sl. No.	State / Gram	Year / No. of Pan-Chayat (GP)	Gram Panchayats (Village) No. of Women Members	Total Pan-Members	No. of / No. of chayat Smitis (PS)	Panchayat Samitis (Block) No. of Women Mem-bers	Total Zilla Mem-bers	No. of / No. of Pari-shad (ZP)	Zilla parishad (District) No. of Women Mem-bers	Total Mem-bers	No. of	Rema-rks
5.	Madhya Pradesh	1994	30,922	4,43,429	1,47,809 (33.33)	459	9,097	2,991 (32.88)	45	942	315 (33.44)	
6.	Punjab	1993	11,596	60,584	8,776 (14.49)	136	24,024	8,222 (34.22)	14	273	89 (32.60)	
7.	Rajasthan	1995	9,189	1,03,712	36,722 (35.4)	237	5,231	1,738 (33.23)	31	997	331 (33.20)	
8.	Tripura	1994	525	5,427	1,809 (33.33)	16	196	67 (34.18),	3	70	24 (34.29)	
9.	West Bengal	1993	3223	61,011	21,489 (35.22)	328	9,453	3,182 (33.66)	16	656	224 (34.15)	

Figures in brackets are percentages. **Source :** Institute of Social Sciences, PRIs Data Centre, New Delhi.

The Constitutional Amendment (73rd & 74th) is applicable only for 21 states. Four states are exempted. There are about 1 million elected women members in Panchayats and Municipalities in India.

filled. The overwhelming response has been unprecedented in the history of the country.

The 73rd and 74th Amendment Acts have the potential of enabling women to transform State structures from within and are the first best steps of an emerging new grass-roots level leadership. This is crucial in order to change the quality, content and nature of leadership for development. The participation of women indicates that they were ready to avail of the landmark opportunity provided to them.

Surveys indicate that the most significant impact of elections on women has been in the area of social and gender relations and increased self confidence.

These developments have implications for the future which need careful study. Amongst them is awareness of the impediments to the transference of power to women, which could limit the chances of fundamental transformation of politics and socio-economic realities.

Patriarchal control in all aspects of life severely limits the potential and scope of women's actual and defacto participation in public life. Multiple burdens make it difficult for women to avail completely of such politically significant changes. The climate of present-day politics, dominated by elements of criminalisation, corruption, muscle power and violence inhibits women's full participation in the political process. Lack of awareness of the possibilities of political participation, means inadequate contribution to public affairs. Lack of orientation, training and preparation to fulfill the roles and responsibilities, as well as abrupt change in their lives further underscore the nature of challenges to be confronted.

Recognising these obstacles the Government, Non-Governmental Organisations, women's groups and activists have been strategizing to provide appropriate inputs to women. Women have been mobilized to participate in elections as candidates and voters, and to be vigilant citizens where elections have been held. Communities have received gender sensitization to facilitate acceptance of the new roles assigned to women. Leadership and organizational training of women has been conducted to enable them to be dynamic change agents. Networks have been interacting, to influence mass based political structures to provide more space to women.

The 74th Constition Amendment Act extends similar provisions as the 73rd Amendment to the Urban Local Bodies, which are now categorized as Municipal Corporations, Municipal Councils and Nagar Panchayats. It is equally significant in the political empowerment process of women of the country as one third of the seats of elected representatives are reserved in these local bodies. Table 7 gives the total number of urban local bodies as well as elected representatives in India.

Table 8 gives an interesting picture of women candidates contesting in the reserved constituencies of some of the municipalities in India. It only shows growing interest of women in participation of local government affairs and managing their wards affairs.

Decentralisation is essential for effective mainstreaming of women's concerns in development. Identifying women's needs at the micro-level and the constant feedback-data and information of the positive and negative effects of policies and programmes–is an integral part of planning. As individuals and representatives of interest groups, women need to be encouraged to participate in political institutions and processes. The status quo will change when women's concerns gain political prominence and when women are in positions to convert them into a political will.

Women in decision making and leadership roles at the grassroots, regional and national levels is a major change factor. Change no doubt has a different pace in different parts of the country, but its direction surely is towards greater participatory democracy, social equity and gender justice.

(This article is largely based on India's Country Report for the Fourth World Conference on Women.)

Table 7 : Number of Urban Local Bodies and Elected Representatives in India

State/U.T.	*Municipal Corporations*	*Municipal Councils*	*Nagar Panchayats*	*Total*
Andhra Pradesh	07(395)	94(2853)	15(314)	116(3542)
Assam	01	25(353)	42(204)	68(557)
Bihar	06	70	93	169
Goa	–	13(155)	–	13(155)
Gujarat	06(468)	86(2745)	60(1260)	152(4473)
Haryana	01	20	32	53(1359)
Himachal Pradesh	01(25)	19(183)	29(221)	49(429)
Karnataka	06(410)	122(3196)	89(1355)	214(4961)
Kerala	05(298)	53(1597)	–	58(1895)
Madhya Pradesh	02(1067)	106(2527)	283(4537)	409(8131)
Maharashtra	15(1417)	228(4901)	–	243(6318)
Manipur	–	07	20	27
Orissa	02(70)	29(560)	72(1056)	103(1686)
Punjab	03	97	34	134(1699)
Rajasthan	03	11	169	183(4412)
Tamil Nadu	06(480)	102(3494)	611(9794)	719(13768)
Tripura	–	01	12	13
Uttar Pradesh	11(841)	226(5970)	444(5518)	681(12329)
West Bengal	06	112	4	122(2706)
A&N Islands	–	01	–	01
Chandigarh	01	01	–	01
Delhi	01	01	–	02(134)
Pondicherry	–	05	–	05
Daman & Diu	–	02	–	02
Total	101	1430	2009	540(68554)

Note : Figures in brackets indicate number of elected representatives.

Table 8 : Women Candidates Contesting Reserved Constituencies : A Case of Six Municipalities in Orissa

Municipality	*Total Wards*	*Wards Reserved For Women*	*No. of Nominations filed by Woman Candidates*	*No. of Woman Contestants*
Balimela	12	4	18	15
Belpahar	16	6	24	21
Burla	15	5	32	24
Paradeep	15	4	25	16
Rairakhol	11	4	24	21
Sonabeda	24	8	27	25

NEED TO EMPOWER WOMEN TO END DISCRIMINATION

M.P. Dube

The last two-three decades have witnessed rapid urbanization in Indian cities which offer exciting opportunities and high paying jobs, but they are also the site of enormous problems: congestion, crowding, pollution, poverty, dirt, and shortage of civic amenities. No doubt urban migration increases real income. Urban dwellers are more productive than rural people, which leads to increase in their wages. This causes people to migrate to cities.

Despite the fact that migration to urban areas leads to increases in income, there is tremendous poverty in cities. A combination of rapid population growth, dramatic urban migration and inadequate facilities to provide housing, sanitation, safe drinking water, electricity, health care, education, and training leads to a lack of human capital, which in turn leads to low labour productivity and as a result massive urban poverty.

Poor air quality and lack of access to safe drinking water exact a high human health toll in Indian cities, although the dominant source of contamination of drinking water is untreated human waste, both industry and agriculture have polluted rivers and seas with toxic chemicals and carcinogenic heavy metals. Poor urban and indoor air quality also exacts a large human health toll. Urban inhabitants in India also suffer from high concentration of chemicals such as sulfur dioxide and lead in the air. Most of those who are continuously exposed to pollutants are women and children. The subordination of women and household division of labour has made their position much more bad.

The subordination that women experience at daily level, regardless of the class, they might belong to, takes various forms – discrimination, disregard, insult, control exploitation, oppression, violence – within the family, at the place of work, in society. Indian society in general witnesses son preference, discrimination against girls in food distribution, burden of household work on women and young girls, lack of educational opportunities for girls, lack of freedom and mobility for girls, wife-battering, male control over women and girls, sexual harassment at work, lack of inheritance and property rights for women, male control over women's bodies and sexuality, and no control over fertility or reproductive rights are common in India irrespective of class, caste and region.

There is worldwide, gender based division of household labour. The work assigned to a gender is arbitrary, that is any given task can be considered women's work in some cultures and men's work in others. But one thing is usually in practice everywhere is that the task assigned to women are much more time consuming than those assigned to men.

This has been called by some as a patriarchal economy, where household women provide many more of the goods and services needed by household men than vice versa. Men's time is freed up from household tasks to go out and earn income in the economy beyond the household, to formally or informally govern the public sphere of the larger community, to engage in leisure activities or to do all three. Because men have more authority in the larger community, and because most of the income available to the household comes to the men, who thus control the financial resources, the gender division of labour is an unequal one. It establishes and perpetuates the subordination of women to men in the society.

Esther Boserup, in the classic work Women's Role in Economic Development, maintained that in some cases, development results in even 'greater disempowerment of women, expanding men's control over resources and shrinking even those spheres of domestic life where women's influence was traditionally more important. Men leave their subsistence work in the farm fields of the modernizing economy. They leave more of their former household work to women, and their new paid employment displaces traditional informal sector work that used to provide some income to women. This process is summed up by Maria Mies under the concept of "housewifization". However, sometimes development empowers women and increases gender equity.

The gender equity goal is described by the concept of women's empowerment. This is generally defined as a women's increased voice in the everyday decisions that shape her life, especially decisions regarding family formation and family planning; a woman's right to participate equally in the economic, civil and political life of the community and the nation; and a woman's increased experience of the social, psychological dimensions of empowerment, increased economy, and self esteem, along with decreased dependence, fatalism and passivity.

Women's subordination is rooted in patriarchy. It does not originate in the workplace, where sexism is only one of many forms of division and discrimination, but in the patriarchal household, where gender roles are the essence of the division of labour. The idea of patriarchy as a vital developmental stage can be seen in the social theory of Marx, Engels and Weber, and in the psychoanalytic theory constructed by Freud Engel's writing focused on the connection between private property, the patriarchal family and the origins of female oppression. Patriarchal household heads controlled women as the reproducers of children.

Whereas the Marxist approach argues that material structures determine relations between men and women, radical feminists reverse the equation (Daly, 1978; Dworkin, 1981; Millet, 1971; Rich, 1979). For them patriarchal values structure relations between the sexes and these inequalities of gender become paradigmatic of all other social inequalities and are not reducible to any other causes.

Patriarchy is both a state of affairs (i.e. men control social institutions) and an ideology (embedded in languages). Kate Millett's Sexual Politics (1969) was a landmark in the study of patriarchy. Questions of gender, the nature of the family and the process of socialization were highlighted in understanding the nature of male supremacy. For Millett, the political relationship between the sexes was central to patriarchy, and male power was expressed and contained in the sexual act itself.

We see that production and consumption are parts of a continuous process beginning with the extraction of the raw materials of nature and ending with their final human use and return to nature. We decide where on the continuum production ends and consumption begins only by social convention. The convention among economists is to draw the line in the market place, where the product is transferred to the final consumer. Convention assumes that any further processing outside of the market is not significant. Economic activity outside the household is seen as production, work, service, social contribution; all domestic activity is seen as consumption or leisure. Though much processing and value adding activities are done in the domestic sphere, they are not treated as production, e.g. processing of eggs in home makes distinction between production and consumption very difficult. This shows that division between production and consumption is a matter of arbitrary convention. The drawing of the line between the market and the domestic economy serves the ideological purposes of the male members rather than that of the household workers. It is proper that as long as an activity adds rather subtracts utility or use value, we should call that activity production. Thus housework is production, not consumption and it should be included in country's systems of national income accounts, the gross domestic product (GDP).

The household is divided into two classes. One is the working class of domestic production, the term commonly used for them is *dependents* and the other is leisure class called *heads of households*. However, reality is that the leisure classes are always more dependent for their survival on producing classes rather than vice versa. Domestic or patriarchal household production is an exploitative form of production, because the labour is almost wholly produced by the female dependents within the household and because the male head of the household consumes the use values produced by his dependents.

The question is what compels female dependents to do this? It is fact that in foregoing their own self-interest for the benefit of their household heads, women are driven by the power of economic, legal and ideological sanctions backed by the threat of force. Women's denial of access to ownership of capital for domestic production has compelled them to work as household dependents. At the same time legal and ideological norms prevent them from establishing themselves as independent heads of their own households. In many developing countries domestic property laws still make it difficult or impossible for women to legally possess their own residences independent of their fathers or husbands. Gender role norms, once embodies in law but now largely legitimized only by ideology, lead women to believe that the performance of their labour is a natural and inevitable aspect of their gender roles as women, as their family roles as wives and mothers, or of their roles as partners in heterosexual love relationships. These ideologies constitute the norm of what Nazzari called the support service marriage.

In order to extract the household labour from women, role of violence and threat of violence cannot be neglected. Historically wife-beating permeated most societies. In some countries (including U.S.A.), it was permitted by law. Generally, fear of violence is part of the bond tying women to their household heads. Generalized male violence against women, where women are victimized by men outside of their own households, lends ideological and material support to domestic production by making women unsafe unless they are protected by their ownhousehold heads. Under these conditions men can exchange ideologically justified protection for exploitation.

Gerda Lerner makes a Telling Point: "men and women live on a stage, on which they act out their assigned roles, equal in importance. The play cannot go on without both kinds of performers. Neither of them "contributes" more or less to the whole; neither is marginal or dispensable. But the stage set is conceived, painted defined by men. Men have written the play, have directed the show, interpreted the meanings of action. They have assigned themselves the most interesting, most heroic parts, giving women the supporting roles."

In other words, the problem is not with what women do or are, it is with how they are valued and who has the right to assign value to people. It is not that women are absolutely excluded from power or prestige in patriarchy – the problem is with the framework itself, and the framework is determined by men.

Here the pertinent question is what should be done to end subordination and exploitation? For development to lessen discrimination, there is needed shifts in consciousness and shifts in strategy. No doubt development harms women when it domesticates them, forces them back into the household from economic roles they play outside. Development helps women when it draws them partway out of the domestic economy, providing them with incomes and economic lives independent of their household patriarchs.

On the one hand, solution in urban areas is to make all dependents to participate in the paid labour force and they should sell services in the market that the domestic economy has traditionally provided (child care, elder care, household maintenance). On the other hand, approach should be to go to the sector where women predominate and where poor women obtain most of whatever cash income they do earn, micro enterprise production. The idea here is to identify and eliminate the obstacle to micro enterprise expansion to increase the income of female micro entrepreneurs. In it the potential exists to help many women from barely productive and poorly compensated work in this sector to more substantial and economically independent roles. Access to utilities such as electricity, running water, fuel, access to vaccination, preventive health care, most simple drugs, literacy, numeracy and access to home economics information lead to increased labour productivity as they build self-esteem and broaden access to extra household income opportunities. Four other variables have an impact on women's empowerment, but their impact is greatly increased when combined with increased income, education or both. These are (1) legal reform resulting in human rights equality for women under the laws of the country; (2) women's self-organization, or the formation of women-oriented membership and self-help groups in civil society, (3) cultural pluralization; and (4) increased productivity of women's domestic work.

Urban governments tend to be technically weak. Institution building is needed on a vast scale to help local governments perform necessary functions. Part of this should involve granting the private sector a much larger role in providing urban services. Many cities are now experimenting with private provision of urban services such as, transportation, education, and garbage collection. Urban governments need help with their enormous environmental problems. Several studies demonstrate that the latest technologies in Japan and Germany, which have tough environmental regulations, pollute less and are more efficient. Thus one no longer has to choose between preserving the environment and increasing productivity. If these technologies are appropriate for use in India, which typically has more labour and less capital than developed countries, they should be adopted.

Women are much more likely to participate in the organizational life of civil society and democratic politics if they have enough education to achieve literacy and enough income security to escape the day-to-day desperation of the lowest levels of poverty. Women are more likely than men to engage in political activity with modest and pragmatic goals and less likely to accept totalistic goals of revolutionary or fundamentalist societal transformation. The greater the participation of women in political life, the more democratic pluralisms furthered in its political culture.

PARTICIPATION AND EMPOWERMENT OF WOMEN

(The Gap and The Biases)

S.N. Singh

Women constitute almost half of the population in India and their active involvement at various levels of formal and non-formal interaction should be considered a sine qua non for the socio-economic and political development of the country at large. It is noted that India and China are the two most populous country in the contemporary world. There are many things uncommon between the two neighbors but economists have tried to draw lessons from the development that China could achieve while India could not. The lesson is that because of the participation of the women folk in the developmental process China reached this stage. It has lessons not only for India but for the entire underdeveloped world. The fact that China was able to put a burgeoning workforce to productive work explains the rapid economic growth of China.[1] The realization came here too but late with the 73rd and 74th Constitution Amendment Acts, 1992. These are the historic steps which have provided for 33 per cent reservation for women in various urban and rural local bodies across the country. It is worth noting here the comments of the International Conference on Population. It says that the empowerment and autonomy

1. Development Paradigms: China and India 1949. Arun Chosh in Society and Development in China and India. Ed. Kuttar Mahedevan and Others, B.R. Publishing Corporation, Delhi, 1994.

of women and the improvement of their political, social, economic and health status is a highly important end in itself. In addition, it is essential for the achievement of sustainable development. The full participation and partnership of both men and women is required in production and reproductive life. Including shared responsibility for the care and nurturing of children and maintenance of household. The power relation that impede women's attainment of healthy and fulfilling lives operates at many levels of society, from the most personal to highly public.[2] These are the concern voiced at the international conference on population and development.

The present paper makes an attempt to look into the gaps and biases in the participation and empowerment of women in formal and non-formal structures as well as at the various levels of these operative structure. Our focus is on the urban India though parallels have been drawn from the rural India too. There may be several gaps and biases in the participation and empowerment of women. However, we have confined here to only three of them:

1. Gender
2. Region/Places
3. Cultural/Traditional

Gender Bias

We would analyse the question of participation and empowerment with above these components. We have taken up the question of participation prior to that of empowerment in view of the fact that participation leads to somewhat empowerment, and both could be considered complementary too. A brief survey of the socio-political process shows that menfolk have generally dominated and women were relegated to a subjugated position. Gender biases can be seen in various

---

2. Para 4.1, Chapter IV on Gender Equality, Equality and Empowerment of Women, Programme of Action (POA), International Conference on Population and Development (ICPD) 1994.

forms and various levels. In order to give women a fair representation in governance the 73rd and 74th Constitution Amendment Acts, 1992 provided for 33 per cent reservation in urban and rural local bodies as referred earlier. How far this has made the participation and empowerment is a matter of debate at best.

During the early 90's when these reforms were introduced, even after getting elected to various positions in the urban local bodies, it was their male counterpart which eventually was the decision maker even in public offices. The enactment did provide for participation, the empowerment has still to come. Last ten years or so had shown some change and readjustment in the power structure and power sharing in the urban local bodies. It could, therefore, be considered a matter of time before the effective empowerment of women takes place. It should be a matter of satisfaction as the change could be seen settling in.

Regional Imbalances

The gaps and biases could also be seen in the different regions and places across the country. Regional imbalances in terms of growth and empowerment could well be seen in the country. Different states account for different levels of development which is reflected in different levels of empowerment. The difference in the level of participation and empowerment is also because of regional biases. For example, the states having high literacy rates account for more participation and empowerment than the ones where the literacy level is low. Though literacy may be taken as a variable it is the region which is of concern here. The regional biases have to be taken into account while considering the question of participation and empowerment.

Cultural/Traditional

The third factor to be considered crucial for the participation and empowerment of women is concerned with culture and tradition. As another matter of fact this is the most important component which influences and has been influencing the empowerment of women. As referred earlier, India is a traditional society with modern state system. The traditional social order in a modern political system often creates paradoxes which becomes difficult to resolve. At times the traditional value system alongwith traditional social attitudes are not in consonance with modern political system. The reforms initiated in the form of 74th Constitution Amendment in the year 1992 often failed to respond to the traditional ways and attitudes towards life and matters of states. The problem being faced by the women folk in this regard generally has it's roots in our traditional social (family) system.

It can therefore, be observed that the participation and empowerment of women is conditioned by the aforesaid three factors apart from several others. In order to have an effective and realistic participation and empowerment changes and moderation are needed at different levels of the formal as well as the non-formal social and political system. Efforts have no doubt been introduced at the formal levels but the new focus is required for the non-formal socio-political structures which should try to ensure attitudinal changes in the behaviour patterns. It's a process which is going to take time, the beginning has already been made, let us hope that the desired objectives are achieved sooner than later.

WOMEN EMPOWERMENT IN INDIA : EMERGING LEADERSHIP IN URBAN U.P.

S. K. Singh

The basic quest of all human endeavors is always to seek a better life. The quality of life of the people of a nation can be effectively improved by raising the standard of living of the common man. Empowerment in general and women empowerment in particular is very fundamental towards achieving this goal. Within the democratic framework, great opportunities exist for synergying women and economic growth programmes to deliver better quality of life in the shortest time. Against this backdrop, the present paper tries to review women participation in political institutions in India at the urban local level and also presents a critique of emerging trends in their leadership.

Gender equality and women empowerment have been differently interpreted to suit varied sociopolitical perspectives. Its rhetoric has acquired an important place in government policy, non-governmental advocacy, the media and also in the academic research. These two terms (women empowerment and gender equality) determine the direction of diverse discourses on women both nationally and internationally. The Beijing Conference (1995) was the first milestone towards ensuring gender equality and women empowerment. The goals of this conference were: (i) sharing power equally; (ii) obtaining full access to the means of development; (iii) overcoming poverty; (iv) inspiring a new generation of women to work together for equality and equity. Even earlier the action plan, recommended by International Conference on Population and Development held at Cairo (1992) included (i) establishing mechanisms for women's equal participation and equitable representation at all levels of the political process; (ii) promoting the fulfilment of women's potentials through education, skill-development and employment, giving paramount importance to the elimination of poverty, illiteracy and ill health, (iii) eliminating all practices of discrimination; (iv) adopting measures to improve women's ability to earn income beyond traditional occupations, achieve economic self-reliance and ensure their equal access to labour market and social security systems; (v) eliminating violence against women; (vi) eliminating discriminatory practices by employers against women; (vii) making it possible through laws, regulations and other appropriate measures for women to combine the roles of childbearing, breast feeding; and child rearing with participation in the workforce, and (viii) strengthening policies and programmes that improve, ensure and broaden the participation of women in all spheres of life as equal partners, and improve their access to all resources needed for the full exercise of their fundamental rights.

Political power has become the cornerstone of development planning and many matters pertaining to human rights of women are integrally linked to political empowerment. Equal participation of women in the political sphere plays a pivotal role in the process of their advancement and enjoyment of human rights. It is a necessary condition instrumental in increasing their ability to demand and secure their rights and entitlements. Their active role in political decision-making processes is necessary for redefining the political agenda and gender justice that may address the women's rights, and entitlements.

Indian women are at the crossroads. There is a great upsurge in consciousness of their rights among all sections and classes of society. A tremendous increase in developmental activities for women has been witnessed since 1980's with a great leap forward in the 1990's. The country has entered the new millennium with the hope of achieving greater equity. The principle of gender equality is enshrined in the Indian Constitution in its Preamble, Fundamental Rights, Fundamental Duties and also Directive Principles. The Constitution guarantees equality and also empowers the state to adopt measures of welfare, development and empowerment. Accordingly laws have been enacted and the policies, plans and programmes have been launched for women's advancement in different spheres from time to time. The National Women Policy (2001) also aims to bring about the advancement, development, and empowerment of women. Its objectives include: (i) creating an environment through positive economic and social policies for development of women to enable them to realize their full potential; (ii) the de-jure and de-facto enjoyment of all human rights and fundamental freedom by women on equal basis with men in all spheres: political, economic, social, culture and civil; (iii) equal access to participation and decision-making in social, political and economic life of the nation; (iv) equal access to health care, equality, education at all levels, career and vocational guidance, employment, equal remuneration, occupational health and safety, social security and public life etc.; (v) strengthening legal systems aimed at elimination of all forms of discrimination; (vi) changing social attitudes and community practices by active participation; (vii) mainstreaming a gender perspective in the development process; (viii) elimination of all forms of violence against women and the girl child; and (ix) building and strengthening partnerships with civil society, particularly women's organizations.

In India, the plight of women is no better than that of women in other developing countries. Despite the honour and reverence accorded as deities, the ground realities speak otherwise. In a patriarchal society like India, the unfounded belief that only man is the bread winner, the male child gets the best of the limited facilities and resources within the family and the girl child runs the risk of being aborted. She is deprived of equality in school education because she has to take care of siblings at home and since she is to be married off soon, investing in her education is considered wasteful and a liability. Despite the fact that women are massively involved in almost all sectors of economy, their activities as producers are not reflected in National Income Statistics, thus making their contribution unrecognized and invisible. In an effort to uphold cultural heritage, the past is glamorized and with it, the trend of equality of women and enhancement of their role in development gets inhibited. This unfortunate state of affairs emanates from the fact that the role of women in overall development has not been fully understood, nor has it been given weightage in the struggle to fight poverty, inequality and injustice. The Human Development Report, 1995 published by the UNDP, presents a gloomy picture on the status of women in the world. The most striking point the Report has made is that there is not a single country where women enjoy equality with men. Women perform $11 trillion worth of unpaid or invisible economic activity world wide and, in fact, contribute more than half of the wealth of nations. Yet they are denied economic, social and even political and legal rights and privileges, that such a contribution entitles.

As the largest democracy, India has been experimenting with a number of forms, structures and modes to achieve women's equality. The replacement of institutional structures and formations from time to time and their modifications, renewal as well as organic growth have come as a response to emerging concepts on women's issues. The institutional structures have undergone changes in response to these evolving concepts which have changed from welfare to empowerment and beyond, in response to experiences of social reality at the field level as well as factors governing external environment. The state has accepted women as active agents, participating in development programmes and schemes and thereby achieving their own development.

The UNDP in its Report on Human Development (1995) observed; "there is unwitting conspiracy on a global scale to under value women's work and contribution to society." It also suggested a plan of action in this regard. Promotion and protection of human rights has been a major preoccupation of the United Nations since its inception when it resolved that the horrors of the Second World War should never be allowed to occur. Respect of human rights and dignity is the foundation of freedom, justice and peace in the world. Over the years, a network of human rights instruments and mechanism has been developed to ensure their primary and to confront their violations. The Commission on the Status of Women recommends to the Economic and Social Council on the promotion of women's rights in political, economic, social and educational fields.

No strategy of entitlements to women can be successful unless it is coupled with appropriate policies, programmes and projects of empowerment from cradle to grave. They should be articulated and coordinated in such a fashion to yield the desired results. A strategy should encompass the problem areas of constitutional and legal provisions, discrimination, exploitation, participation in political and administrative institutions and development programmes which should be tackled on a priority basis while taking a holistic view in an integrated manner.

Political Rights

Sweden was the first country to accord its women the right to vote as early as in 1861. Since then majority of nations have given this right to their females in the early part of 20th century. Australia (1902), Soviet Union (1917), Canada (1918), Germany (1918), U.K. (1918), United States (1920) and Sri Lanka (1931) extended this right to women in the first half of the century. In 1917, in the USA the first woman got elected to the legislature followed by Netherlands (1918), Austria (1919), Sweden, Canada and Belgium (1921). But the right to franchise to women was not extended in all the developed countries in the first half of the 20th Century. Switzerland, the premier country of the First World gave its women this right as late as in 1971. In India, universal adult suffrage was extended simultaneously in 1950 when the new Constitution was adopted and women got elected to legislature in the first general elections itself (1952). The imperative for women's equality is rooted in part-III of this document. Articles 14 and 15 proclaim the right of women to equality before the law and prescribe a bar on discrimination on the basis of sex by the State. Article 15 also forbids any disability, liability, restriction or condition, on the basis of sex, in the access, or use of, any public place or service. Article 16 guarantees equality of opportunity in matters of employment under the state. Political rights of women are rights to vote, to context election, to hold political office and to vote in legislature. Equal participation of women in political life plays a pivotal role in the process of their advancement, development and empowerment and also in strengthening their role in governance and decision-making at all levels. However, their equal participation in political institutions is largely under represented at most levels. This is so because politics is still being viewed as men's privilege and therefore male centred functioning of political parties discourages women.

Political Participation

Historically women have played a very significant role in the growth and development of parliamentary democracy in India. They have held important positions both in the legislature and government. Their contribution to the development of parliamentary procedures and practices is in no sense less significant than those of their male counterparts. Their areas of interest in the debates of parliament and state legislatures cover not only the issues concerning women upliftment but also the issues of national and international importance. Time and again, they have, in various capacities mooted important bills many of which have become laws. Even outside the legislature, they have been socially and politically active. Social reforms, concerning women, intended to impart political consciousness among them seem to be one of the important vocations of the women parliamentarians, legislators and panchayat members.

Political participation of women can be classified into following categories: (1) aspirant; (2) hesitant; (3) reluctant; and (4) resistant. In the first category are those women who are active and aspire for higher political posts. They generally belong to a family having political background and experience and are being inducted in politics by their near ones. The second category consists of women who want to enter into politics but its criminalisation inhibits their participation. They also lack money and other support. Third category consists of women who are neither opposed to idea of participation, nor are they willing to come in politics. Politically they are indifferent and remain content in their traditional role. The fourth category consists of women, who are opposed to the idea of coming in politics and express their unwillingness. Majority of women in general, are reluctant to join politics because of socio-cultural barriers. The role conflict among working women and particularly those who are in political bodies at grass root discourages them to participate effectively.

Women constitute half of the country's population but they do not even have a 10 per cent representation of the total members of National Parliament and state legislatures. The analysis of women's participation in general elections over the past five decades bring out the significant facts that (1) the extent, nature and level of their participation is much greater than in most other countries – developed or developing; (ii) the participation has been steadily increasing over the years; (iii) the gap in the voter's turnout between men and women is getting narrowed; and (iv) the percentage of women getting elected has been increasing.

Indian women's involvement in politics in the modern era started in the early 19th century. Although British imperialism profoundly influenced the political engagement of both elite and non-elite women, its impact on the character and purposes of their engagement was very different. A number of social organisations were founded by women both Indian and British for women rights and welfare. Muthulakashmi Reddy, a Tamilian doctor became one of the first female legislators in the country. During the freedom movement also many women leaders actively participated and strongly advocated the protection of women's interest and their rights.

In Independent India, the Constitution, after guaranteeing equality to women in all spheres, left the political representation to their own willingness, opportunity and support while providing for reservations for Scheduled Castes and Scheduled

Tribes in Parliament and state legislatures. Several committees on local self government advocated reservation for women representation at the grass-roots. Balwantrai Mehta (1957) also suggested a token co-option of two members in the rural local bodies. The Committee on States of Women in India was set up in 1971 to look into all aspects of women's status in India, specially their political participation. It recommended separate women's statutory panchayats at the village level. To give them more opportunities to participate in the formal political process, the Committee recommended that political parties fix a quota for women in the municipal councils. It also recommended the setting up of a permanent independent Commission on Women at both state and national levels.

The National Perspective Plan for Women was drawn as a long term action blueprint for 1988-2000 but women's groups pointed out several shortcomings in its approach, coverage and methodology. The National Commission for Women, set up in 1992, has initiated planning process involving women and protecting their interests. It has intervened even in the judicial process resolving problems related to women's welfare, upliftment and development. However, the 73rd and 74th Amendment Acts became the watershed for women's political empowerment at the grassroots political institutions providing for 1/3rd reservation of seats for women in rural and urban local bodies, in the country.

In Governance

The proportion of women at the ministerial level in 2000 as per Human Development Report 2002 was recorded as high as 55.00 per cent in Sweden followed by Finland (44.4%), New Zealand (44%), Norway (42 per cent), UK (33.3 per cent) and USA (33 per cent). It was recorded lowest Sri Lanka (4.4 per cent) in Kenya (1.4 per cent), Jordan (1.3%). During 2000, proportion of women parliamentarians in the lower house was recorded highest in Sweden (42.7 per cent) followed by Denmark (38 per cent), Norway (36.4 per cent) and Sweden (42.7 per cent) followed by Denmark (38 per cent), Norway (36.4 per cent) and Netherlands (36 per cent). Similarly in the upper house their percentage depicted highest ratio in Barbodas (33.3%) followed by Canada (32.4%), Trinidad and Tobago (32.3%) and South Africa (31.5 per cent).

In India, during 1952 to 1999 representation of women in Lok Sabha as per their seat candidature was as low as 0.31 per cent. The ratio of women candidates has been computed 3.5 per cent while their winning ratio has been reported as high as 87.5 per cent (Table 1). The main political parties who fielded woman candidates in 1999 Lok Sabha elections were Congress (10.99%), BJP (7.74%), and Communist Parties. In 11th Lok Sabha (1996) election woman candidates comprised just 3.4 per cent while 7.9 per cent of them were elected recording as high as 66.67 per cent for the Congress (I), and 56.52 per cent for the BJP.

Table 1 : Woman Contestants in Lok Sabha Elections (1952-1999)

Year	*Contestants per seat*	*Share Among Contestants(%)*	*Success Rate(%)*
1952	0.10	2.7	43.1
1957	0.14	4.4	38.6
1962	0.14	3.4	50.0
1967	0.13	2.8	47.0
1971	0.17	3.1	25.6
1977	0.13	2.9	27.1
1980	0.26	3.1	19.7
1984	0.29	2.9	27.7
1989	0.37	3.1	14.3
1991	0.60	3.7	12.0
1998	0.90	3.4	7.9
1999	0.51	7.0	17.5
Average	0.31	3.5	27.5

Source : Compiled from the CSDA Data Unit, New Delhi, 1997 and the Rashtriya Sahara, New Delhi.

During 1952-1999 in Lok Sabha on an average there were 31 woman members in the House constituting 5.95 per cent. Uttar Pradesh sent 6 members accounting for 19.35 per cent. Interestingly, their representation in Lok Sabha was reported highest in 1999 (49%) followed by 1984 (44%) and 1998 (43%).

Out of total contestants (4000) in 1999 women numbered 280 accounting for 7 per cent winning ratio being 11.12 per cent. In the 1998 poll, total woman contestants were 271 accounting for 5.44 per cent only and their winning percentage was 7.9 per cent. Women representation from UP was reported highest (9 members) in 1996, 1998 and 1999 and the lowest (3 members) in 1957 and 1991. The share of U.P. in total number of woman parliamentarians was reported highest in 1952 (27.27%).

Women's representation in Rajya Sabha during 1952 to 1996 demonstrates that woman members comprised 9.51 per cent only. It was recorded highest in 1991 (115.5%) followed by 1985 (11.4%), 1978 (10.m2%) and 1977 (10.m2%). It was reported lowest in 1952(7.3%) and 1971 (7.0%).

During 1952 general elections 97 women contested and their per seat average was 0.19. Average per seat was the highest in Haryana followed by Delhi, U.P., Sikkim while it was the lowest in Nagaland followed by Arunachal Pradesh, Manipur, Mizoram and Jammu and Kashmir. Interestingly, percentage of woman contestants was recorded highest in Sikkim. The success rate was reported to be the highest in Arunachal Pradesh and lowest in Manipur (Table 2).

During 1952 to 1997, average representation of women in the state legislatures in India was recorded 4.0 per cent only. It was the highest in Haryana (6.2%). In Uttar Pradesh, the average number of woman legislators from 1946-47 to 1996 has been computed to 15 members only constituting 3.8 per cent of the legislature (lower house). It was reported the highest in 1957-62 (6.03%) and the lowest in 1974-77 (94.46%). Interestingly, highest number of woman members in the state legislature (26) was reported in 1957-62. Major political parties have been advocating reservation for women in the legislature both at the centre and state levels but their attitude towards the fair sex is not reflected in the allotment of tickets for the general elections. In U.P. State Assembly elections 2002, only 341 women contested, out of which 171 were supported by various political parties. Congress (32), BJP (31), SP (26), RKP (25), IND (15) and NCP (9) were the main political parties which fielded them. Besides, 170 women contested as independents. Out of the total contestants so fielded and the independents supported by the political parties only 26 could make it to the legislature. The success rate accordingly has dipped to as low as 7.62 per cent only while numerically they have increased their representation to the last election (22 women). Out of the elected women legislators now twelve belong to SP, six to BSP and another six to BJP. No other party could get its woman candidates elected to the Assembly.

From 1952 to 1995 the Upper House of the State legislature was represented by 41 women. A few of them graced the House for a quite long time being re-elected or nominated again and again. Smt. Indra Mohini, Smt. Indira Hridesh, Smt. Premwati Tewari, Smt. Kudasia begam, Smt. Beena Duggal, Smt. Shakuntala Devi, and Sanya Sood are few names which made a distinct mark in the proceedings of the Upper House of the state.

In Local Bodies

The Indian nation has already entered the new millennium and has celebrated the tenth anniversary of the 73rd and 74th Constitution Amendment Acts. It is quite heartening to observe that women are playing pivotal role in the decision-making process at various levels in the local self government institutions. These Amendment Acts have stipulated one third reservation of seats and posts for women. Significantly, the participation of women in these institutions is considered essential not only for ensuring political participation in the governance but also for realizing the developmental goals of urban and rural development which involves them as : (1) voters; (2) member of political parties; (3) candidate; (4) planners, implementers and monitors and evaluators of programmes; (5) member of various committees, core groups, associations, task force etc.

In the 1995 election to urban local bodies, in the state of Uttar Pradesh 193 women were elected as Mayors/presidents whereas 4243 women were elected as ward members. Women secured more than one-third share in Nagar Palika Parishads and Nagar Panchayats because they also got elected on the general seats defeating their male counterparts. Their representation, in case of chairmen/presidents was reported least in Nagar Nigam and slightly higher in Nagar Palika Parishads and Nagar Panchayats. Similarly, women members have much higher share in Nagar Panchayats (37.60) and Nagar Palika Parishads (35.81) while it was just one-third (33.49) in case of Nagar Nigams. Importantly, no women belonging to Scheduled Tribe elected as president of a municipal body in 1995, although they got elected as members to Nagar Palika Parishads and Nagar Panchayats (Table 3). Perhaps it was due to non reservation of posts and seats in the local institutions by the government.

After 2000 elections (excluding Uttranchal state), 227 women were elected as mayor/presidents of the municipal institutions in the state. In the Nagar Nigams, one OBC Woman was Elected While in nagar Palika Parishads, 9 Scheduled Castes and 20 OBC women were elected and in Nagar Panchayats 40 OBC women were elected. Thus, women's representation was recorded higher in Nagar Panchayats, and Nagar Palika Parishads while it was recorded lower in Nagar Nigams (Table 4).

Emerging Leadership Trends

Empirical studies have revealed quite a few interesting as well as starting facets of women leadership in urban areas in the state. Prominent among them have been given speial attention as following:

1. In majority of cases, women leadership emerges from the old and traditional caste leaders who have all along been in the forefront of the political, social and cultural life of the areas. It is quite natural that the spouses of these leaders either come forward by themselves or are driven by inlaws and relatives to take up the mantle of caste leadership. It is quite heartening that the young, energetic and broadminded women accept this role willingly to contribute their bit to the empowerment of their brethren. Nevertheless it has its own pitfalls. Many a time, caste leaders put forward their spouses just to

Table 4 : Reservation of Seats in Urban Local Bodies

(2000-2001 Election)

Particulars	*Nagar Nigam*	*Nagar Palika Parishad*	*Nagar Panchayat*
Chairman/President	11	225	446
Scheduled Castes women		8	21
Scheduled Castes	1	17	42
Scheduled Tribes women	–	–	–
Scheduled Tribes	–	–	–
OBC women	1	20	40
OBC	2	40	80
Women	2	46	88
General	5	93	175
Total Women	3(27.27)	75(33.33)	149(33.41)

Source : U.P. State Election Commission, Lucknow.

Note : Uttranchal state is excluded in the data.

grab political power by proxy as many of their protigees simply do not understand their roles and responsibilities of the urban government under the new Constitutional dispensation.

2. The second category of leadership easily discernable is that of women whose spouses hold influential positions in the government and politics. Perhaps they are baptized by their menfolk to take over the positions in urban local bodies, or may be just to reate a new hold on population specially the women of the area, which might help them only in securing political mileage and fortunes. This leadership is welcome only if the womenfolk take up the responsibility to lead the masses by themselves, last their powers and privileges, in most of the cases, are arrogated by their male counterparts. This is really a very dangerous trend and needs to be nipped in the bud itself.
3. The third category of leadership which attracts attention is that of women dependents of the political leaders.

These leaders want to cash on their performance, charisma and clout to give their dependents a break in the political life which by no means, is unjust or inappropriate. It is, in fact a welcome step to keep going the political hegemony, but harmful only when the elders themselves try to exercise the power which is statutorily bestowed in their women.

4. A survey of the election data in the state of U.P. reveals that the majority of women elected to the urban local bodies belonged to the middle age group i.e. above 40 years. This naturally gives them an advantage over the younger lot specially those who are uneducated or less educated. Their experience of life and the time spent on struggling with the real life situations, could put them far ahead of the young girls, who have very little first hand experience of social and political life. In fact, in the meetings of the local institutions it has been well observed that these elderly women only participate actively and are sometimes vociferously vocal to put up their poit of view.
5. It has been observed that very few educated women get elected and therefore their participation in the political process and sharing of power is naturally very nominal. Even then, they register their presence quite distinctly in the meetings at all levels. In fact, these educated women are quite sensitive and positive thinking persons who want to contribute to the well-being of the urban loal bodies as the units of self governance.
6. One major factor inhibiting the natural growth of women leadership in urban areas is the availability of monetary resources. The women who really want to contribute are also equipped qualification wise and feel concerned about the urban administration and its problems, get discouraged to contest elections as it involves a huge amount of money to contest and win. As a result, quite a few women educated or uneducated, who have an ardent desire to serve the people, do not

venture in the elections and are forced to take a resigned view of the whole issue.

Though women have been enthusiastically participating in politics and its process, at the some time they have been facing difficulties, challenges and problems related to the initiation of development programmes. Their low level of active participation in the political process is the predominant problem for the administrators and the policy makers to address. The proxy in election process, meetings, participation in development programmes, and decision making has caused a serious damage to women empowerment. Husbands, in-laws and close relatives have become the main decision makers relegating the real women representatives to the background. Moreover, role conflict has also increased while managing house hold responsibilities and political activities simultaneously. Since male dominating society is reluctant in accepting the women as decision makers, they are being abused and harassed by officials, caste leaders, elected representatives and also musclemen. They are also facing revengeful attitudinal behaviour in the society, since they have defeated influential persons of the other sex. Moreover, desire for political power, status and sustainable source of black money has caused social tensions affecting immensely the women representatives. Importantly, low level of education, poor communication skills and awareness and inadequate leadership quality have not allowed them to actively participate in the municipal governance and contribution their bit earnestly.

Conclusion

A close look at the present trends unmistakably points out the stark reality that the new millennium is unlikely to bring about qualitative improvement in the economic and social postures of women in the country. Unfortunately, Indian women still continue to be crowded in a limited number of low paid, low productivity and uncertain jobs which hold out little prospects for advancement and career building. The reason for this sad state of affairs is that so far none of the potential change agents have seriously challenged the household patriarchal controls over women's labour. Women administrators, executives and managerial workers are increasing significantly, however, their share in decision making process is very low and their effective participation could not be ensured. Women are making sincere and concerted efforts around the world to see that their rights are respected, their voices heard, their opportunities widened and their multiple contribution in various fields evaluated as to ensure gender equity and social justice. Indian women though not at par with their sisters in developing countries are leaving no stone unturned to give their efforts a fillip in this direction. The emerging leadership in the urban local bodies is a positive sign in this regard. Yet they have a long way to go. With the determination and commitment which some of them have shown and thus have become the torchbearers in the area of women empowerment at the grassroot level will certainly guide their comrades to make a concerted efforts in this direction which will bring them at par with their brethren of the developed countries.

REFERENCES

Agrawal, S.P., Women's Education in India: Present Status, Perspective Plan and Statistical Indicators, Volume 3, Concept Publishing Company, New Delhi, 2001.

Ahuja, Ram, Rights of Women: A Feminist Perspective, Rawat Publications, New Delhi, 1992.

Butch, Nirmala, Panchayats and Women, Kurukshetra, Vol. 49(7), April, 2001.

Government of India, New Women Policy (2001), Ministry of Social Justice and Empowerment, Delhi, 2001.

Joshi, I and Kang, B., The Female Principle, Outlook, January 19, 1998.

Krishnaraj, M., Towards Alternative Development Strategies; Problems and Possibilities for Women, Mainstream, December 14, 1996.

Narasimhan, S., Empwering Women, Sage Publication, Delhi, 1999.

Pandey, G.S., Political participation of Women in India, New Royal Book Company, Lucknow, 2001.

Pandey, J.S., Mahilayon Ki Rajnitik Sahabhagita: Uttar Pradesh Se Chuni Gayi Mehiloyon Ka Samaj Shashtriya Adhyyan, Ph.D.

Thesis, Department of Scoiology, Lucknow University, Lucknow, 2000.

Purushothaman, S., Empowerment of Women in India, Sage Publications, Delhi, 1998.

Sengupta, A.K., & Singh, A.K., Empowerment of Women: An Operational Strategy, MMEM Business Review, Vol. II, Jan., 1998, Institute of Development Studies, Lucknow University, Lucknow.

Seth, Mira, Gender and Development, Sage Publications, Delhi, 2001.

Sharma, Shamsuddin, Women, Law and Social Change, Ashish Publishing House, Delhi, 1991.

Singh, S.K., Dalit Women: Status and Issues, New Royal Book Company, Lucknow, 1999.

Singh, S.K. and A.K. Singh, Women Empowerment: Emerging Leadership in U.P. in Democratic Decentralisation and Panchayati Raj in India (ed.) M.P. Dube and M.Podalia, Anamika Publishers and Distributors, New Delhi, 2002,

Singh, Surendra & Srivastava, S.P., Gender Equality Through Women's Empowerment: Strategies and Approaches, Bharat Book Centre, Lucknow 2001.

Singh, U.B., Revitalised Urban Administration in India, Kalpaz Pub., Delhi, 2002.

Tripathi, Rajmani, Panchayati Raj Vyavastha Aur Mahila Sashasktikaran, Kurukshetra (Hindi), Vol. 46(5), March 2001.

Yojana (Women Empowerment), August, 2001.

POLITICAL EMPOWERMENT OF WOMEN IN URBAN LOCAL BODIES AND THE 74th CONSTITUTION AMENDMENT : DISPELLING DOUBTS AND DEVISING FUTURE STRATEGIES

Sanjay Gupta

Good governance, decentralized administration and transparency in government functioning are considered to be the hallmarks of an enlightened democracy and a responsible civil society. During the last two decades there has been a marked increase in the rise of public consciousness around the world which has exerted considerable pressure on their respective governments in order to bring about the required changes for creating an environment which could directly enhance the living standards of the people. This leads to the question of good governance and its role towards the civil society, particularly, its contribution to the most vulnerable section of the society, i.e., women. Good governance is understood to be as implying participatory and representative governance where all constituencies are included in the political, economic and legal planning and decision-making processes involving collection, distribution and use of urban resources for the development of the city.[1] Thus, participatory democracy, decentralized government, human rights, type of

1. Nora Fernandes, Coordinator, Asian Women and Shelter Network (AWAS), Phnom Penh, Cambodia.

political regime, and social justice are the various components that involve the concept of good governance without which the goal of empowerment of the needy sections would remain unfulfilled.

The need for giving reservation to women at the political and decision-making levels was long-felt. Women's organization had for long advocated the need for providing representation to women through constitutional amendment for bringing about social transformation and social justice to the deprived sections, including women. These women organisations asserted that greater the number of women involved in the decision-making process, greater would be the improvement in their social, economic, legal and cultural conditions. This would enhance the women's status and would lead them to more opportunities to influence the outcome of political deliberations. Thus, in the backdrop of this realization coupled with the long-felt need for women's reservation in urban governance where they were long found to be under-represented, the 74th Amendment to the Constitution was enacted. This enactment provides for 33 per cent reservation of seats to women in the urban local bodies with the ultimate objective of securing them political participation and enabling them to take decisions concerning their development at urban grass-root level. The increase in political participation requires improvement in their educational level and the acquisition of economic means since failing which, the development of women in other spheres would be incomplete and weak.

Outstanding Doubts

Notwithstanding government's efforts and intention towards women's cause, many doubts have been raised over the government's policy of legislative intervention and 'selective discrimination' for bringing women into the seat of authority. Observers and analysts have been skeptical of the 74th Amendment (also 73rd Amendment) which they say that without strengthening their social and economic status, their political and administrative roles would be reduced to a mere show of puppetry. They have held the view and rightly too, that the increase in political participation requires improvement in their educational level and the acquisition of economic earns since failing which, the development of women in other spheres would be incomplete and weak and that without giving them sufficient exposure to handle political and administrative affairs, reservation is meaningless.

The incorporation of women into the political and administrative seats of authority through constitutional amendments may although appear to some, a back-door entry in the name of social justice and gender-balance, a look at Bangladesh, one of our neighbours, who share almost the same social, economic and cultural backgrounds, would lead us to a understanding that women's empowerment through their political and administrative coronation is being ushered in by legislative intervention. In Bangladesh, Article-9 of the Constitution promoters special representation of women in local government. A few years back, there was a vociferous demand from the academic citizens and women's groups, for the Union Parishad Amendment Act 1997. This amendment accepted the demand of women's organizations for reserved seats in local governments through direct election. As a result, women's representation over the last few years has increased in local governments.

In stark contrast to this, women in Sri Lanka, Nepal, Pakistan, and Afghanistan are grossly under-represented. In Sri Lanka, women constitute a mere 1.2 per cent in all Municipal Councils and Provincial Councils. The population of the city of Colombo is 1.2 million and there is only one woman Municipal Councilor in the Colombo Municipal Council which means only one woman is representing the problems of women in a population of 1.2 million!

In Nepal, 90 per cent of the population lives in rural areas. Though the percentage of urban population is increasing which at the same time is also becoming quite influential, women are yet a neglected lot. NGOs have taken a lead in espousing the cause of women's representation but little has been achieved.

Not much different is the case of women of Pakistan. In Pakistan, local government structures exist, but as in the case of Karachi, it has been dissolved by the central government and replaced by a local administrative system headed by the Commissioner of Karachi. However, women are a discriminated lot and they have hardly made any impact on politics. There is no provision of representation for women of the local levels although it did exist in the Parliament in very miniscule numbers. In Maldives, there is local administration but no local government.

Thus, India and Bangladesh are the only two countries in South Asia where constitutional provisions have been enacted to grant political and administrative representation to women through popular election. As a result of legislative interventions, more women are coming into the political systems of these two countries and now there is a perception that women are bringing change in the process of governance. Thus, the issue of legislative intervention or even 'selective discrimination' has been a useful tool in uplifting the position of women and bringing them into the mainstream of national life.

But what is really of concern is the fact that the provision of one-third reservation granted to women in local governments was not the outcome of their consciences demand or efforts, rather it was handed over to them and women were caught unprepared. As such, their involvement in the public space created for them by the system is still in its infancy and needs time to mature.[2] Thus, most unintentionally, it has also been referred to as a 'quiet revolution', which brought in nearly a million women now occupying positions as members and chairpersons of local bodies.[3]

---

2. Madhushree Sekhar, World Bank Mc Namara Fellow, Institute for Social and Economic Change, Bangalore, India.

3. Statement made by Mrs. Asha Das, Secretary, Department of Women & Child Development on March 6, 1998 at the Commission on the Status of Women during a General debate at the United Nations.

Unlike women's representation in India or in any other South Asian country, women's representation in a developed country like Canada is characterized by the fact that the emergence of women in seats of authority has come about not as a result of any state concession granted to them but by virtue of their won initiative and struggle at the grassroots. Women work as volunteers in their neighbourhood or involve themselves in community development programmes which sufficiently gives them exposure to social, economic and political problems of their communities. This prior socialization of women has facilitated their self-initiation into the governance process as people's representatives. Lessons should be drawn from the Canadian experience, and it could be suggested that in India too such self-help community associations can be encouraged to involve the locals, including women, in their own development activities. This would prepare them to understand the problems faced by them and would also ensure that in the longer run women and other socially marginalised groups are better empowered to occupy formal representational positions created for them in the governance process. It is pertinent to note that like India, women in Thailand too have been able to bring about legislative change to mainstream issues of women and have generated a great deal of debate on women's participation in local government.

Another debatable issue has been whether the reservation provided to women through the 74th constitutional amendment resulted in the genuine political empowerment of women alongside their male counterparts? It has been held that while the strategy of reserving seats for women in the local bodies has resulted in quantitative changes in women's representation in local politics, qualitative changes in their representational role has not yet taken place as per expectation. A prime reason for this has been that a majority of women entering into local councils have come from families where male members were exercising or had experience of exercising political power or families which enjoyed a pre-eminent status in the society in terms of social or economic standing. Besides, the bureaucracy, who is traditionally attuned to dealing with men in power, has found it difficult to adjust itself with the rising number of women entering into the local councils or in other institutions of urban governance. The problem in question here is not the making of women but the bureaucracy itself who still treats the male member of elected woman representative's family as the real elected member. Besides, lack of gender sensitivity amongst officials and growth of fundamentalism had reinforced tendencies that gave women minimum participation in the decision-making process. This is true for almost the whole of South Asia where local governments continue to be dominated by rich, powerful and upper caste males. Women in Pakistan who enter politics are the ones who have received politics as a legacy from some male relatives, a brother, father or husband. As feudalism dominates the politics, women politicians with family connections enjoy the advantage of inheriting a political life.[4]

Critical Hindrances

Although the 74th Amendment provides a vast opportunity to women to participate in their urban local areas, they have not been able to effectively utilize the opportunity due to many factors such as, the "domestic responsibilities, lack of financial clout, rising criminalisation of politics and the threat of character assassination" which have made it increasingly difficult for women to contest elections.[5]

1. Patriarchal social system
2. Socio-cultural prejudices
3. Financial dependence of women
4. A high degree of politicization in development processes
5. The criminalisation of politics
6. Lack of media support and lack of exposure to political processes and training opportunities for women
7. Fund crunch in the municipality

---

4. Mohammed Yakoob, Trainer, Political Education of Women Project, Aurat Foundation, Karachi.
5. Times of India, February 5, 1998.

8. Casteism
9. Security of self
10. Household responsibilities

A major factor behind the low performance of women in municipal council has been their low educational status. A study conducted by MARG on women members of Delhi and Karnal Municipal Councils revealed that due to the difference in the educational status of woman members of these two councils, woman members of Municipal Corporation of Delhi (MCD) were better informed about the important provisions of Delhi Municipal Corporation Act, while the case with regard to woman members of Karnal municipal Corporation (KMC) was vice-versa. The study further revealed that unlike their counter parts from Delhi, elected woman representatives (EWRs) of Karnal were largely dependent upon their spouse and other male members of family. The woman members of MCD being more educationally sound, have learnt a lot from their personal exposure and day to day work. Their interactions with male colleagues and bureaucracy have been to their benefit in the professional discharge of their duties. Besides, their contact with their political parties and area MLAs have enabled them to perform their duties without much hindrance from vested interests and thus has increased their efficiencies. However, things have not been so in the case of KMC woman councilors.[6]

Doubts have been expressed over the issue of women remaining largely untouched by corruption. While some hold the view that even if some of the obstacles militating against woman councilors were lessened, far to talk about removing them, women can prove to be better administrators as they are more sensitive to problems, more caring and less prone to corrupt deeds. However, skeptics doubt the merits of the argument and contend that as women are yet new to the functioning of urban governance they appear to be more honest

6. For details, see "Daughters of 74th Amendment", a book based on the study conducted by MARG (a research group), 1999.

and efficient. But once women learn the art of administration and as they get used to power, they would gradually get corrupt like men and would employ various tactics to fulfill their vested interests by aligning with corrupt and criminals.[7]

Besides, accusing fingers have been raised by the Report of the Ministry of Urban Development and Poverty Alleviation to the Eleventh Finance Commission for 2000-2005 which says that the status of Municipalities in the country continues to be low and characterized by neglect as compared to Panchayati Raj Institution in India. Major constraints have been put on the Urban Local Bodies (ULBs) by increasing their responsibility without giving them proper financial supports. The financial position of the ULBs is far too inadequate vis-à-vis the requirements.......There exists a wide gap between the powers granted to the ULBs on paper and the actual situation they face at the time of their implementation. Besides, the report has cast adverse remarks on the District Planning Committee, Ward Committees, the obstructing role of bureaucracy, and the lack of accountability and cooperation within the elected representatives, councilors and the municipal staff.

However, the apprehensions on women becoming corrupt is by and large not shared by many, particularly by the academia who say this is a bogey raised by the vested interests including the conservative and fundamentalist forces to malign the newly acquired roles by women under the 73rd and the 74th Amendment Acts and thus, stall the genuine devolution of powers to women by these two amendments.[8] Notwithstanding various hindrances, women are gradually

7. This was the view of some government officials of Directorate of Women's Welfare, Lucknow Municipal Corporation, State Urban Development Agency (SUDA), Directorate of Panchayati Raj whom the author of this paper visited and interviewed. Interestingly, these departments or corporations are related to the implementation of the 74th Amendment Act.

8. The issue of corruption among womenwas discussed at the seminar on where the views expressed by various government officials was decried and was termed as a 'hypothetical' issue.

proving their efficiency. While functioning under the 74th Amendment, women have belied the doubts expressed against their cooption into urban governance through reservation at least to some extent by bringing about qualitative changes. There is a marked awareness on such developmental issues as education, primary health care, drinking water and sanitation, and livelihood systems, including environmental concerns. In Karnataka State, women far excess of the 33.3 per cent quota have been elected, implying a spread-affect process within the system. Perhaps keeping this in mind, former President K.R Narayanan remarked that women had made an impact on democracy (India) at the grass roots and that it would be only logical to carry forward this process of empowerment of women to state legislatures and Parliament. He further added that "women's empowerment in politics might well be a decisive factor that will purify and save the democratic politics of India from the deterioration of standards and values it is experiencing today".[9] But as women's representational role is shaped by the feudal and patriarchal elements still dominant in the Indian society, it will take some more time for women to come out and effectively occupy the public space alongwith their male counterparts.[10]

Future Strategies for Capacity Building for Women in ULBs

Women's reservation in urban councils has come to stay in India by virtue of the 74th Constitution Amendment Act. The democratic decentralization of power aimed at providing the governing space to women in urban governance is an affirmative action which could be utilised to the optimum only by pursuing a well-defined and comprehensive strategy as reservation by itself cannot solve the problem for women. The following measures can be initiated to make women more effective and visible in urban local governance.

9. Republic Day Speech, 2001.

10. Madhushree Sheker, Ibid.

Imparting Legal and Political Literacy to Women

In the process of empowerment of women, the principal focus should be on increasing women's participation in formal politics and this is possible only when they are imparted training in legal, political and constitutional systems of the country and their operation. This will lead to the development of political literacy among women, which is so important for the political empowerment of women and the obligation for this rest on the government. Women organizations' leaders have advocated changes in education syllabuses so as to involve and strengthen civic engagement of women and adopting counseling in social action programmes to encourage and support women advocators. Besides, it has also been recommended that women experts in the field of city planning, waste management, water supplies, pollution control and other related areas should establish an organisation to help the representatives in case of technical problems.[11]

Organizing Training Programmes for Selected Women Councilors

Training is a critical component in preparing women for the effective exercise of powers granted to them. Training is necessary not only in the period proceeding women's entry into local governments but even in the post-entry period for developing leadership and communication skills to enable them to function effectively. Therefore, women leaders have been particularly emphasising on the necessity of training. Women who are elected for the first time, they are educated but they do not know how to work with corporations, but the issues that they deal with are very much related to women.[12] It has been found that women representatives were more sensitive

---

[11] Kalyani Pandey, mayor, Municipal Corporation, Jabalpur at the Regional Workshop on "Women in Urban Local Government in South Asia" organised by the Economic and Social Commission for Asia and the Pacific (ESCAP), 1998.

[12] Bhavna Joshipura, former Mayor, Rajkot City, at the ESCAP Conference on Women, 1998.

to urban management issues and problems. They were more accessible and approachable for other women and vulnerable urban groups such as, the disabled, poor, ethnic groups and minorities. They were better managers of the scarce resources and if trained, could develop a better organisational capacity. Hence, it has been felt that women should be trained in such critical areas of urban governance as environment, health, water, conservation, education, sanitation. Womer should be given sufficient financial resources to solve the pressing problems facing the people of their area.

Providing Means of Economic Activities and Self-employment

A number of economic schemes have been initiated by the government to help the urban and rural poor. But due to illiteracy and ignorance, women have not been able to take advantage of the schemes. They did not have the required skills to compete in the national and international market. There were minimal marketing outlets for their products. They faced security problems while at work, which gives them fewer opportunities to succeed in the economic filed. NGOs were playing a significant role in mobilizing women through programmes such as, literacy, savings and credit schemes and through providing training and basic services. Although there is no dearth of promising women who have potential to enter the politico-administrative system, the lack of economic support have kept them away from entering into public offices through elections. Besides, women were not sufficiently aware of the various economic schemes launched by government for their economic well-being. For example, in Maharashtra women had the rights to land and property. There was a reservation of 40 per cent for women in all the government-introduced economic schemes. While the government has taken a big initiative for the economic empowerment of women, it is the government itself which is to be blamed for the poor communication of such schemes for the target group, i.e, the women.

Building a Positive Image of Women as Efficient Administrators

The contribution being rendered by women in urban local councils should be thoroughly studied, recorded and given a wide publicity to make their work and performance visible in local governance. Efforts should be made to build a positive image of women in the society which could serve as an inspiration to other women who want to enter into local councils.

Sensitizing the State

The role and function of women councilors in urban local bodies has suffered due to the lack of gender-sensitivity and apathy of the state government. There is a pressing need to sensitize the state and its various agencies–the legislature, executive, bureaucracy and the election commission through organizing training programmes and special sessions to make them aware of the problems of women councilors. Hence, in the process of strengthening the capacity of women in local governments, local authorities need continuous sensitization and awareness raising on gender issues.

Restructuring the Planning Process to Create Space for Women Members

The District Planning Committees (DPCs) that have been set-up for a joint rural and urban effort in planning for economic and social development of the district urgently needs to incorporate elected women representatives. Women's interest and issues in urban governance can get priority only through the DPCs. Similarly, Ward Committees and Standing Committees too need to include women members in its planning process. Recently, Kerala has introduced a bottom-up planning exercise which adopted a process of discussion and debate in popular conventions and ward committee meetings to ensure that planning was done according to the priorities of the communities, including women. The creation of bodies, such as, ward committees was proposed as a medium to ensure accountability to the public. However, a report of the

Ministry of Urban Development passed critical remarks against the functioning of DPC and Ward Committees. Thus, a complete streamlining of these bodies is needed in order to give proper representation to women in these bodies for backling issues which are of vital concern to women of their constituency.

Generating Pressure on Political Parties to Give Greater Representation to Women

Pressure needs to be exerted on political parties by women groups and lobbies to give enhanced representation to women aspiring to contest elections for local councils outside the 33 per cent quota reserved for them. The role of women elected to various elective offices – State Assemblies, Parliament and urban/rural local bodies should be analyzed in the light of having infused new values in the administration, work culture, lessening of corruption and cutting down irrational expenditure in the administration. Based on the assessment of their contribution to the cause of women and society in general, political parties should give representation to women in large numbers to establish gender-balance, social justice and infuse a healthy political environment in urban local councils in the real sense.

Conclusion

Women's political participation in urban local governance is crucial to the upliftment and emancipation of fellow-women. It is difficult, if not impossible, for men to understand and internalize the issues that women regard as central to them and their lives. Neither the continued dependence of women on men would address their problems, nor would the instrument of reservation help to solve their multifarious problems. Reservation is just at road not a destination. The destination can be known and reached only by developing the required strength and the insight. Women's destination to power-sharing in urban local governments could be made possible and ever-lasting only by following a definite strategy of capacity building. Where proper care has been given to train women in ULBs, they have created new avenues on untrodden ground. They have fought against corruption and vested interests, and have taken up issues that are of central importance to their community. However, a lot still needs to be done before one can safely conclude that women are better administrators and more efficient than men. But this conclusion would be difficult to be arrived at unless the society changes its traditional mindset, disapproves and dismantles the hurdles posed by vested interests in the path of women acting as decision-makers, and accepts her newly emerging identity of being the master of her own gender and her fellow-community, it would be difficult for her to prove her administrative skills not only in urban governance but at all levels of political and administrative governance.

WOMEN IN LOCAL GOVERNMENT–INTRODUCTION

Pawan Kumar Banta

Today, the world has six billion people, out of this about fifty per cent are women. About thirty-three per cent of households, worldwide, are estimated to be headed by women and in quite a few developing countries the proportion is even higher. The most striking is the fact that the women's contribution in the world's wealth has been assessed to be the marginal. The need of the hour is to focus on the role of women as decision-makers in our urban society, and the need to address urban issues that are of particular relevance to women. These were highlighted in the message of the Secretary General of the United Nations, Mr. Kofi Annan, on the occasion of the World Habitat Day. Mr. Annan called for a greater involvement of women in the governance of urban neighborhoods. In a rapidly urbanizing world, where over 2.5 billion people live in town and cities, the concerns of half of this population are not represented. The UNCHS indicates that the females representation in the highest circles of government was less than ten per cent in 1990 and only 3.5 per cent of the world's cabinet ministers were women. The proportionate representation of women in the national level legislature in Asian countries has been estimated to be 14.1 per cent on an average. The UNCHS also indicates that the representation of women in local governments is generally better than that at the national level, but in no way equal to men's representation. In Africa the percentage of women in local government is estimated to be five per cent and in European countries, the average percentage of women in municipal councils is indicated as twenty-three per cent.

The discrimination practiced against women has been rooted in false beliefs and attitudes that got entrenched over time in custom and law. With greater wisdom, man of these assumptions about women have been resoundingly discredited. The theory of physical weakness itself appears dubious. Though-out the developed world and much of the developing world, the life expectancy at birth for women exceeds that of men. Intellectually, wherever women have been given the opportunity, their creative faculties have more than matched those of the opposite sex. It is quite evident that assumed disparities in mind and body were fallacious and will not stand scrutiny in an environment of equal opportunity.

The interest in women and local governance has recently developed at global, national and local levels, and providing some statistics on women's representation in politics worldwide to help put our concerns into perspective. At the same time we have seen the development of women's movements at local level, operating through the processes of civil society where women have worked individually and collectively in autonomous women's groups to further their cause and raise awareness of women's continuing disadvantaged position. More recently, these groups have been engaged in debate over involvement with institutionalized, more formal, structures of party politics.

The number of women in politics at the local level prior to 1993 has been very small, and their influence negligible. As stated by Kumari and Kidwai (1996), prior to 1990, the women in local politics were generally either politicians who had lost membership of higher institutions and those who were given such an opportunity to serve the purpose of publicity. In many cases, the motive was partially also to satisfy the aspirations of these few women, since they could be kept under virtual control and denied higher aspirations. The insignificant presence of women at these levels was an important indicator of two basic facts : one that women who are planted at the top often lacked the kind of training required for effective participation, secondly, the society was unable to accept women in politics, particularly at the grass-roots level.

If we examine the reasons for low participation, as stated by Nath, Kamle (1997), "down the ages women have always been treated as subordinate to men in every aspect of life. Their place of work was confined to the domain of the household with household chores and rearing of children. Her identity was attached to that of her father, husband or son, i.e. she was given a status in accordance with that of her male partner. It is not the women in the past have not contributed substantially in politics, but because of their secondary status and low esteem, most of them were denied entry in political decision-making".

The 74th Amendment of the Indian Constitution in 1992 ushered in a new era in the democratic process of the country as it not only provided constitutional status to the municipal bodies but also provided an enabling environment of women to direct part in the local self government and brought women to the forefront and center of local development.

The different political parties in India have shown great reluctance to field women candidates. Reservation of seats at Municipal level have put pressure on political parties to locate and field more women candidates. Sharing power and responsibilities with immense control over resources for city development and social change will be an empowering instrument for women in India.

Women's Participation in Local Government

The 74th Amendment to the Indian Constitution, has served as a major breakthrough towards ensuring women's equal access and increased participation in local government. The Constitution (74th Amendment) Act, 1992 aims at Constitutional guarantees to safeguard the interests of urban local self governments to enable them to function as effective democratic and self governing institutions at the grass root level. This Amendment provides for reservation of $33^{1/3}$ per cent of elected seats for women at level of local government in urban and rural areas. There is also a one-third reservation for women on posts of chairpersons of these local bodies. A very active role for women in local governance is envisaged as compared to governance at the state and national levels in India. These provisions have provided great opportunities and challenges to women in India, particularly in local government field. This is of great significance, since this grass-roots level participation has considerably broaden the base of women's participation in politics at city level.

Involvement of women in the political arena and in decision-making roles are an important tool for empowerment as well as monitoring standards of political performance at local level. However, in the present political process of entry into decision making political institutions, there is growing influence of money and muscle power, backroom dealings, communalization and criminalisation. In many respects women and men elected representatives face similar problems on election to office. Above all there is a need to understand just how to be a good local people's representative. The role of political representatives at local level is demanding needs time to gain experience and to understand the rules, regulations and procedures governing the administrative bureaucracy with which they now have to work-often quite closely in urban service delivery system.

Some of the major constraints that prevent women from effective participation at local level are observed as follows :

1. Lack of orientation / training in urban development issues and municipal administration.
2. No proper knowledge / orientation about municipal acts and rules and regulations.
3. No prior experience about dealing with multidimensional urban development issues / civic issues and its complexities.
4. Lack of knowledge about technical inputs related to urban service delivery system.
5. Lack of support from senior male / female colleagues in the party / municipal body.
6. Less co-operation from municipal officials understan-

ding about various facets of the budget, such as allocation of budget at ward level (at central / ward level).

7. Lack of party support and poor organizational structure.
8. Lack of money and resources to sustain the electoral campaigns (inspite of code of conduct by election commission).
9. Discrimination in decision making at party level.
10. Specific notions towards politics and political atmosphere.
11. Fear and insecurity.
12. Lack of confidence in public speaking.
13. Criminalisation of politics and use of money power.
14. Family responsibilities.

Political system in India works through political parties who contend for power by invoking popular support. Therefore it is necessary that if women want to share power they have to make a place for themselves within the political parties through which Indian democratic system operates. The experience of the last 52 years show that inability to create 'this space' and recent studies show that there has been no significant change in either the nature of women' functioning or in the political parties' approach to women and women's issues. If we examine women's participation (prior to 1993) it is seen that the political parties have given less importance to women's issues in terms of ideology, either in priority in their party manifesto or in terms of the number and importance of the position that women occupied as individuals in political parties. Women are not seen as a vote bank to be approached, and once the men are mobilised, women will merely endorse their choice of party and candidate. Male candidates rarely have access to the female electrorate and there are not enough women involved in political campaigns to be able to reach out to a large section of women even in big cities. As a result, the exposure of women to political debates and issues has always remained indirect. The analysis made by Kumari and Kidwai (1996) stated that political parties have dominated the conservative 'cultural' perspective and no conscious attempt has been made to increase active participation of women. Women in India today are agitating at the doors of Parliament, demanding reservation for $33^{1/3}$ per cent of the seats. The issue at stake here is more complex than it may seem. It is not only a question of a few more or a few less women in the corridors of Parliament and legislatures but also a response to the fact that a large section of society has historically been denied its legitimate share in the exercise of political power, power that ultimately determines its destiny. In this demand for reservation, women are also raising their voice against a system, which has consistently denied them space by harnessing the forces of tradition in order to marginalize their role. Reservation of seats for women in Panchayats / Municipal bodies have shown that it has tremendous implications not merely in terms of the number of women entering the public arena and holding public office, but also in terms of the social, economic and political impact that these reservations have had for the total system.

It is for these reasons that women are increasingly demanding political role for themselves. They recognize that constitutional guarantees do not ensure effective participation and that these can not ensure political equality. Hence the need to gain entry into political institutions and in the functioning of the state, and to share control over the power the state exercises. This alone would lead to a situation where women are able to reverse the existing situation, which has consistently been against their interests, and bring about the necessary changes in policy and the social structure so as to ensure a more equitable and humane order.

The role of women's participation in local bodies should not be undervalued. Elections are after all a forum for self government and democracy, they are significant in drawing the attention of the nation to the problems and needs of disadvantaged section; the manifestos, campaigns, promises made by individual candidates, track record and future course of action of political parties are indicative of national concerns as well as mandates for action.

Strong and dynamic women who would not dream of appropriating privileges are today talking of reservation because they have come to recognize that they will not get "easy entry" in the corridors of power without reservation. This hierarchy is so rigid that the natural processes of democracy and constitutional guarantees have not been able to make a dent in these fortresses of power. The demand for reservation should not therefore be seen as either a gift or a privilege that women are seeking. For most women it is the last straw and measure to ensure their coming into the political mainstream. Their participation becomes vital in the context of the adoption of development strategies that are negative and harmful to women. Today most of the political parties in India have taken some initiatives to activate political participation of women and develop their capacities. However, most of the political parties have not yet developed any special programmes to meet the requirements of women in urban or rural areas, despite the fact that most of the women activists felt that if planned efforts were made, they could be easily mobilised. Different debates concerning struggles of women as well as various actions by women's groups, NGOs and CBOs on local as well as national problems have forced the mainstream political parties to accept women's concerns in their political agenda. The political parties started changing their attitude towards women which is reflected in their election manifestoes, their attitudes towards women candidates, speeches and slogans.

Statistics on women's participation in the electoral process are not very encouraging. It is important not only to pressurize the political parties but also to make the leaders understand the significance of organizing systematic training of women possessing leadership qualities, of carefully selecting women candidates and ensuring financial, technical and human resources or affirmative action (Patel, Vibbuti, 1992).

The need to strengthen women's participation and leadership is constantly emphasized by various institutions, including All India Institute of Local Self-Government which is actively involved in capacity building for women elected members at city level.

As stated earlier, 74th Amendment to the Constitution and its implementation has added another level 'in' political participation in politics at local level. The question arises whether these women are able to function effectively? Are they able to serve as effective elected representatives and meet people's aspirations.

Reservation for women in local government is not just a question of getting a certain number 'in' but develop their capacities to play their rightful roles in the development process and which would make an important difference as the local government deals mostly with the quality of life for citizens. Municipal responsibilities relate both to women's strategic needs and their strategic needs. The better we meet women's strategic needs, the better they are able to contribute to good city governance.

With rapid growth of urban population, there is servere pressure on local governments in cities to cope with the provision of basic services and infrastructure, which pose enormous challenges to the elected representatives, particularly women members, who are quite enthusiastic but many times lack the requisite knowledge and skills for local level decision-making. There is now a perceived need for improved managerial and technical capacities. This would require new capacity development plan for elected women members in cities towards good governance and effective service delivery and to become more efficient, dedicated and effective elected members of the public service.

ROLE OF WOMEN IN URBAN GOVERNANCE

K. Sreeram

In India, urbanization has been increasing steadily for decades. It is expected to raise considerably over the next 25 years. The Ninth Five Year Plan suggested that it will reach 605-618 million during 2021-2025, that is nearly 50% of the total population. Although other sources predict lower figure, all forecasts indicate that the urban population growth rate will be significantly large.

The impact of urbanization is immense. The National Institute of Urban Affairs (1998) estimated that urban India's contribution to be more than 50 per cent and likely to increase by 2001 at 60% of the Gross Domestic Product (GDP). Alongside, there has been a parallel growth in urban poverty. Some of the important statistics are that around 35% of the urban population lives in recognized slums in major cities and 68% of the urban poor are estimated to be women and children. Trends in urban poverty suggest the number will increase considerably in future in the absence of a better articulated strategy. Evaluation of strengths and weaknesses of current urban policy and programmes is also called for in order to ensure that available scarce resource's utilization has a perceptible impact on poverty.

In India, definition of poverty is officially related to the expenditure required by an average household to meet a specific minimum nutritional norm measured in terms of calories. Based on the calorific intake model, different research institutions in India have estimated that the percentage of urban population Below the Poverty Line (BPL) varies between 30 to 70 per cent.

Economic definitions are unidimensional and neglect the importance of neighbourhood and environment. Poverty needs to be looked at a range of perspectives. Poor women and children experience poverty in their daily life. Within the poverty circle itself individuals experience poverty differently according to their gender, age, caste, class etc. Further enabling environment does not necessarily support the needs of the poor. At the same time, access to basic public services is, generally, restricted.

The Constitution (74th Amendment) Act 1992 gave a new orientation to these issues. The statement of objects and reasons for enacting the Act highlights the inadequacies of the then existing system of urban local governments and considered it necessary to incorporate provisions relating to urban local governments particularly for :

- streamlining the relationship between the State Government and the urban local bodies with respect to functions and taxation powers and arrangements for revenue sharing;
- ensuring regular conduct of elections;
- ensuring timely elections in the case of supersession; and
- providing adequate representation for the weaker sections like Scheduled Castes, Scheduled Tribes and women.

Article 242T(2) states that not less than one third of the total number of seats to be filed by direct elections in every municipality shall be reserved for women and such seats may be allotted by rotation to different constituencies in a municipality. Further, Article 243(T) lays down that the office of Chairpersons in the municipalities shall be reserved for Scheduled Castes, Scheduled Tribes and women in such manner as the legislature of the State may by law, provide.

Thus the role of urban poor women which was considered peripheral hitherto assured a central role. It was realized that unless women are involved in the governance of their neighbourhoods, and until women's concerns become the concerns of the entire community and larger body polity, the urban crises will continue to be problematic. Local Government being closest to the citizens, it was considered in best position, both to involve women in the decision making process and also effectively use their knowledge and capabilities in promotion of sustainable development.

Women in India : A Profile

According to provisional Population Tables of Census of India 2001 (Series 1, Part-1 of 2001), India's population as on 1st March 2001 stood at 1027 million out of which 531 million were males and 495 million were females, thus becoming the second country to cross one billion mark (after China). The decadal growth rate (1991-2001) was (+) 24.34 as against a growth rate of (+)23.86 registered during 1981-1991.

The State of Uttar Pradesh is the most populous state with more than 166 million people accounting for 16.17 per cent of the total population. The State of Bihar takes third place with 82 million population accounting for 8.07 per cent of the total population (ranks third). The State of Madhya Pradesh consists of 60 million population accounting for 5.88 per cent of total population (ranks seven) and Orissa with 36 million consisting of 3.57 per cent of the total population (ranks 11).

Sex Composition

One of the basic demographic characteristics of human population is the sex ratio which is essential for any meaningful demographic analysis. Variations in sex ratio indicate the underlying socio-economic and cultural patterns of a society. Sex ratio defined as the number of females per 1000 males in the population, is an important social indicator to measure the extent of prevailing equity between males and females in a society at any given point of time. Sex ratio is the outcome of the interplay of differentials in mortality sex selective migration,

Distribution of Population in the Selected States : 2001

State	*Total*	*Males*	*Females*	*Density*	*% to total Population of India*
India	1027015247	531277078	495738169	324	
Uttaranchal	8479562	4316401	4163161	159	0.83
Uttar Pradesh	166052859	87466301	78586558	689	16.17
Bihar	82878796	43153964	39724832	880	9.42
Jharkhand	26909428	13861277	13048151	338	2.62
Orissa	36706920	18612340	18094580	236	3.57
Chattisgarh	20795956	10452426	1034530	154	2.03
Madhya Pradesh	60385118	31456873	28928245	196	5.88

Source : Census India, 2001, Series 1 Provisional Population Tables (Part 1 of 2001).

sex ratio at birth etc. According to the Census of India 2001 the sex ratio stands at 933 for the country as a whole (1991 Census recorded 927 females per 1000 males) which is a welcome improvement.

The following table indicates sex ratio of total population and child population in the age group of 0-6 in 1991 and 2001 in the selected states in the country.

It is interesting to note that sex ratio in the States of Uttar Pradesh, Bihar and Madhya Pradesh which ranks 1, 2 and 7 by population size and constitute nearly 30.12 per cent of country's population are in the category of below national average.

The sex ratio among the child population in the age group of 0-6 which was 945 during 1991 decreased to 927 during 2001 and among the population aged 7 and above increased for 923 in 1991 to 935 during 2001 at the national level. The sex-ratio in this age group showed a decrease during 1991-2001 in all the states under study. Probably this needs an undepth study.

The sex-ratio in the population aged 7 and above, the national average which was 923 in 1991 increased to 935 in 2001. State-wise analysis indicates that though in Uttar Pradesh, Madhya Pradesh and Bihar, sex ratio in this category increased between 1991and 2001 (in U.P. from 863 to 895, in Bihar 895 to 916 and in MP from 905 to 918 respectively) still the figures in these states is below the national average.

The State-wise analysis of the above data throws up interesting and intriguing factors. In the age group 0-6, sex-ratio in the States of Uttar Pradesh and Madhya Pradesh is below the national average which is a critical factor. Another significant factor is that the sex-ratio in this age group (0-6) showed a decrease in all the states under study between 1991-2001.

The imbalance that has set in this early age group is difficult to be rectified and would continue to affect the population growth for a long time to come.

Social Scientists forwarded several factors to explain the consistently low levels of sex ratio, important ones being :

Sex Ratio of Total Population and Child Population in the Age of 0-6: 1991 and 2001

State	Total Population		Sex ratio (females Per 1000 males)			
			Child Population in the age group 0-6		Population aged 7 and above	
	1991	2001	1991	2001	1991	2001
India	927	933	945	927	923	935
Uttaranchal	936	964	948	906	933	976
Uttar Pradesh	876	898	927	916	863	895
Bihar	907	921	953	938	895	916
Jharkhand	922	941	979	966	908	936
Orissa	971	972	967	950	972	976
Chattisgarh	985	990	984	975	986	992
Madhya Pradesh	912	920	941	929	905	918

Source : Provisional Population Tables, Census of India 2001, Series 1, Paper 1 of 2001, Statement 19, pp. 92-93.

(a) neglect of girl child resulting in higher mortability at younger ages;

(b) high maternal mortality;

(c) sex selective female abortions; and

(d) female infanticide.

Status of Literacy

Literacy is an important indicator of development and forms an important input in the overall development of individuals enabling to understand their social, political and cultural environment better and respond it appropriately. The Census considers a person aged seven and above as literate who can both read and write with understanding in any language.

Number of Literates and Illiterates Among Population Aged 7 Years and Above and Their Change– India; 1991 and 2001

Literates		**(in millions)**	
Year	*Persons*	*Males*	*Females*
1991	358	228	129
2001	562	336	225
(Increase in 2001)			
Over 1991	203	107	0.95
Illiterates			
1991	328	128	200
2001	296	106	189
(Increase in 2001)			
Over 1991	(–)0.31	(–)0.21	(–)0.10

Sources : Ibid, Statement 25.

During 1991-2001, the total number of illiterates has come down from 328 million to 296 million, thus registering a decline in absolute number. On the other hand during this period the contribution to the total decrease of 319 million among illiterates, is dominated by males with 214 million as compared to the females 105 million.

The following table gives a picture of decadal variation in female illiterates between 1991 and 2001.

Number of Female Illiterates, and Decrease in Female Illiterates 1991-2001 (Selected States)

State	*No. of females illiterates*		*Decadal decrease*	*Percentage contribution in decrease (All India)*
1991	*2001*			
Uttaranchal	1636908	1405350	231557	2.20
Uttar Pradesh	36833350	36504260	329091	3.13
Bihar	18857757	21169173	(–)23111416	(–)21.99
Jharkhand	6182038	648777	299739	(–2.8)
Chattisgarh	5111612	4108199	1003413	9.54
Madhya Pradesh	13052783	11840248	1212535	11.53
Orissa	8470782	7634546	(–)836236	7.95

The above figures indicate a gloomy picture especially in Bihar and Jharkhand and dismal picture in U.P.

The following table shows the ranking of the States under study by literacy rate and sex.

The above table reveals that :

(a) except for the States of Uttaranchal and Chattisgarh literacy rate in the rest of States is below national average for the total persons

(b) the States of Bihar, Jharkhand and Uttar Pradesh fall below the national average in the case of male literacy; and

(c) except for Uttaranchal, in the rest of the States the female literacy is below the national average

Situation of Women : A Glance

The number of females per 1000 males declined from 972 in 1971 to 933 in 1981 and to 927 in 1991 registered an increase in 2001 with 933. The child population in the age group of 0-6 which was 945 in 1991 decreased to 927. The decrease in the sex ratio is explained largely by poor health, inadequate nutrition and a higher mortality rate among females.

Ranking of States by Literacy Rate and Sex : 2001

State	*Persons(%)*	*Males(%)*	*Females(%)*	*Rank in all India Ranking*		
				Persons	*Males*	*Females*
Uttaranchal	72.28	84.01	60.26	14	12	18
Chattisgarh	65.18	77.86	52.40	23	18	25
Orissa	63.61	75.95	50.97	26	23	27
Madhya Pradesh	64.11	76.80	50.28	25	20	28
Bihar	47.53	60.32	33.57	35	35	35
Jharkhand	54.13	67.94	39.38	34	31	34
Uttar Pradesh	57.36	70.23	42.98	31	30	32
All India	65.38	75.85	54.16	–	–	–

Out of 30 years of reproductive life, a woman spends 16 years in pregnancy and lactation by typifying the malnourished state of women.

Further, it is estimated that an average Indian woman becomes pregnant eight times and gives birth to 6-7 children of which 4-6 children survive.

Life expectancy at birth is generally lower for women than men.

Literacy rate for the country as a whole in 2001 worked out 65.38 per cent for the population aged seven years and above. The corresponding figures for males and females are 75.85 and 54.16 per cent respectively thus showing male and female literacy gap rate of 21.69%.

Policy Interventions to Empower Women in Urban Areas

The Urban Basic Services Programme initiated during the Seventh Five year Plan for Urban Poverty Alleviation, for the first time highlighted the active role of women in urban areas mostly belonging to economically weaker sections of the society. UBSP is a dynamic process which functions within the broad goal of creating a facilitating environment for a significant improvement in the quality of life of the urban poor. This is envisaged to be achieved through community organization and mobilization, empowerment of communities, especially of women, in order to equip them in the roles of decision making and community management and a process of convergence to enhance the reach and effectiveness of the existing sectoral programme for the urban poor who are found not only in slums but in a wide range of conditions and places. It aims to introduce a pro-poor orientation in the design of new programmes and evolve innovative partnership arrangements to fulfil the community's critical needs. It aims to ensure a sound foundation and evolve new approaches to promote the participation of the urban poor in their development as well as improvement of towns/cities within the context of the 74th CAA.

The UBSP is to contribute positively towards participative strategies and plans encompassing the needs, concerns;

experiences and opportunities among all city/town residents including the poorest to achieve eradication of poverty by poor themselves with focus on women and children in receiving common efforts and support.

More importantly, among others, to establish and support self-relient community based women's and other organization to actively participate in planning, implementation and monitoring of community development programmes.

In order to operationalise the participative framework, the programme promotes :

(i) Community organization and mobilization of women with supportive and facilitating mechanism responsive to the groups' needs of development, but moving towards self-reliant community based organization and liking them with city/town and sectoral processes; and

(ii) The community organizations include Neighbourhood Groups (NHG). Neighbourhood Development Committees (NDC) or Neighbourhood Committees (NHC) and Community Development Societies (CDS).

Neighbourhood Group is an informal association of women living in a mohalla or basti or neighbourhood group of manageable size (preferably 10 to 40 to represent urban poor or slum females); geographic contiguity and homogeneity should be the basis to carve out the boundaries of NHGs, one woman resident among them who is willing to serve as a volunteer should be selected as a Resident Community Volunteer (RCV).

The responsibilities of RCV include: to serve as a channel of communication and information among the females in the cluster; to represent the views of the group in the neighbourhood committees and community development societies and other forums; to support planning, implementation and monitoring of activities at the neighbourhood level; and foster and encourage participation in community improvement.

Neighbourhood Development Committee (NDC/NHC) is a more formal association of women from the Neighbourhood

Groups located in close proximity and as feasible within the same electroral ward. These Committees consist of all the RCVs from the neighburhood groups. It may form special and need based sub-groups i.e. Primary Education, Health etc. as and when required. The NDC/NHC is responsible to :

- identify local problems and priorities;
- provide suggestions for group involvement in meeting community needs and goals (mini-plans)
- support local action with partnership of responsible agencies including community contracts;
- provide feed back to agencies of programme effectiveness and out-reach especially for children and women
- develop community capacity through training in association with community development societies; NGOs and other sectoral departments,
- develop community-based thrift and credit systems.

The NHC/NDC may be registered and may apply directly for grants-in-aid under various schemes.

Communidy Development Society (CDS) is a formal association of the NHCs at the ward or city level based on common goals and objectives. The Society consists of elected or selected representatives of NHCs/NDCs and other interest groups (NGO, sectoral departments etc.). The CDS is responsible to :

- represent the needs of all the communities, etc. especially women and children;
- liaise and link-up with agencies and departments to promote action in the community towards fulfillment of their needs;
- identify specific training and arrange for their organization; and
- prepare community plans and proposals, mobilizing resources from the community; city/town or other sectoral departments.

The CDS may be registered to provide access to grants-in-aid under various schemes and for a wider financial credit and base.

Representation to NHCs in CDSs should be provided in ward level committees in cities/towns under the 74th CAA.

Role in Planning Process : Need based planning and action through community participation and convergence is the basis of UBSP programme. The Community based organisation (CBO) set up has an important role to play. Critical areas in which their intervention is envisaged are :

- *Rapid appraisal* of all low income communities focusing on specific problem areas to understand the reasons, behaviour and willingness of communities to participate in the programme to be undertaken by city/town level UPA cell in which the community needs to actively participate.
- *Needs Assessment* to gain a proper perspective, assessment of community's felt-needs and their provisions should be undertaken by the NHGs and NHCs/NDCs with the support of town level UPA cell. This involves mostly community self-surveys and community spatial mapping exercises.
- *Developing Action Alternatives :* Support the town level UPA cell to review the convergence processes for meeting prioritised and appraised needs and develop action plan alternatives by mobilizing resources from community city/town; state departments etc.
- *Community Action Plans :* The NHC/NDC based on action alternatives and community's own priorities should develop a community action plan for discretionary functioning from the funds allocated to the NHC/NDC.
- *Need Linked Credit Plans :* The CDC and NHC/NDC need to prepare credit plan to meet the specific contextual needs of the NHC/NDC and explore the prospects for loan/finance/grants from financial institutions.

The detailed framework evolved during the operation of the UBSP became the bed-rock for further policy interventions to make women active participants in the governance of urban local bodies. The subsequent programme of Swarna Jayanti Shahari Rozgar Yojana (SJSRY) further strengthens this process.

Swarna Jayanti Shahari Rozgar Yojana (SJSRY)

The SJSRY seeks to provide gainful employment to the urban unemployed or underemployed poor through encouraging the setting up of self-employment ventures or provision of wage employment. This programme relies on creation of suitable community structures on the UBSP pattern and delivery of inputs under this programme is through the medium of urban local bodies and community structures.

The SJSRY consists of :

(a) Urban Self Employment Programme (USEP) and

(b) Urban Wage Employment Programme (UWEP).

The salient feature of SJSRY is that it rests on the foundation of community empowerment. Rather than rely on the traditional method of top down planning and implementation, this programme relies on establishing and promoting community organizations and structures to provide supporting and facilitating mechanism for local development. Towards this end Community Organisations like Neighbourhood Group (NHGs), Neighbourhood Committees (NHC) and Community Development Society (CDS) are to be set up on the UBSP lines.

Role of CDS : The CDS in the focal point for purposes of –

- identification of beneficiaries;
- preparation of applications;
- monitoring of recovery; and
- providing necessary support to the programme.

The CDS will also identify viable projects suitable for that particular area.

The CDS may also set up itself as Thrift and Credit Society to encourage community savings and other group activities. These agencies will endeavor to link local resource generation efforts with wider institutional finance and will have access to funds under various schemes.

The CDS being the federation of different community based organizations will be the nodal agency for this programme. It is expected to lay emphasis on providing the entire gamut of social sector inputs to their areas through convergence of schemes being implemented by sectoral agencies.

The Urban Self Employment Programme (USEP) consists of the component for assisting the groups of urban poor women for setting up gainful self employment ventures. Thus sub-scheme is known as "the Scheme for Development of Women and Children in the Urban Areas (DWCUA)".

One of the target groups of SJSRY is the women belonging to Scheduled Castes/Scheduled Tribes etc. The percentage of women beneficiaries under this programme shall not be less than 30%. Further the scheme lays that at other conditions being equal, women beneficiaries belonging to women-headed households are to be ranked higher in priority.

The scheme of DWCUA is distinguished by the special incentive extended to urban poor women who decide to set up self employment ventures in a group as opposed to individual effort. Groups of urban poor women can take up an economic activity suited to their skill training, aptitude and local conditions. Besides generation of income, the group should strive to empower the urban poor women by making them independent and also providing a facilitating atmosphere to self-employment. Other factors expected for the group consists of getting to know each other well, understand group strategy and recognize the strength and potential of each member of the group. In addition, every effort needs to be made to encourage the group for set itself up as a Thrift and Credit Society.

In the planning and implementation of Urban Wage Employment Scheme the CDS plays a vital role: surveying and drawing up of available basic minimum services in their areas; identification of missing basic minimum services first and listing of other physical infrastructure services subsequently, prioritization of the services as listed etc. These lists alongwith remarks of the CDS with respect to location of service provided to be is forwarded to the Town Poverty Eradication Cell at the beginning of the year.

In order to operationalise this institutional mechanism, it is essential to initiate necessary actions. One is the, after formation of community groups, it is essential to promote a proper understanding and appreciation of their role among the community groups and also dispel their misconceptions. This will enable building a meanginful partnership between local government and the economically weaker sections. Regular discussions and meetings with community groups also facilitate a proper understanding of the objectives and philosophy among women. This will enable for promoting a confidence among women to shoulder the responsibilities enlisted to them from time to time.

Attitudinal change, both among the officials and political executives, is essential for the effective functioning of these institutions. They need to look at these structures as an integral part of administrative approach.

These community based organizations need to be free from political affiliations and do not be seen as alternative political centers to the existing local government institutions. Both need to work in close cooperation and collaboration in the overall interests of urban community, in general and women in particular.

DO WOMEN HAVE EFFICIENCY TO RUN THE URBAN ADMINISTRATION

N. Ashok Kumar

Woman–Her Place

The bygone times saw the male's hegemony over the woman. Women were subjected to subordination to men. But, there has been sea change in gender prejudices and discrimination over the past decades. Abolition of the practice of Sati, and introduction of English/Western education had a runaway impact on the improvement of woman's place in her own family and outside. There is a growing evidence that, not only understanding between men and women has been improved but also a climate of mutual respect of values has been created. All over the world, awareness on the concepts of equity and equality has been increased in men as well as in women. Based on various research studies concerning women, it is revealed that women are in most advanced position in the West. The stark reality is that, in the European region, women constitute forty one per cent of the total workforce as against fourteen per cent of women having full time employment in organized sector in India. The root causes are many for this marked disparity between the European and the developing countries. Prime among them is adoption of equal opportunity laws by the European countries since last twenty years.

It is said that nature has made woman powerful. But in reality it is not true. It is evidently seen that more often woman finds it difficult to reach top position in their work place challenging male's claim irrespective of their qualifications and experiences. This is a universal phenomenon. It is amazing to note that, on one side gender conflict is fast disappearing in education and labour force sectors in European countries but number of women reaching top positions in management is very negligible. On probing, majority of the woman employees reacted that, if they failed to become top boss in their organizations it is necessarily because of male chauvinism and their ego. In its report, (breaking through the glass ceiling: women in management, 1996), the ILO has also made similar observation. Slowly things have been moving in favour of women at least in business sector in developed countries. There has been significant increase in the number of women becoming because the kind of educational system which the countries in the developed region have adopted over the past few years. Situation in the developing region on the other hand is not notably sound. For example, America prior to 1978 nothing was known about female entrepreneurs in the US. But between 1978 and 1990, one out of 10 women of the age group of 35 years and plus was involved in entrepreneurial venture. Experiences in New Zealand and France on the other hand exhibited different scenario. In these European countries, not only women were under-represented in managerial capacities but also they are being paid less salaries in comparison to men both in private and public sectors. Though New Zealand boasts that, it is the first in the world to grant women the power to vote in 1893, women in this country are still fighting for gender equality. Sensitizing the groundswell, the New Zealand government has adopted a strategy called, 'platform for action' with a view to address several issues pertaining to women with development, inter alia, gender perspective in all the developmental activities, remunerated work for women, difference in salary structure, indigenous women, participation of women in developmental activities, building capabilities of women and involvement of women in decision making process.

Similar situation prevails in Australia too. Australian women have been pressing for equality. It was in 1970s this issue has drawn the attention of the government of Australia. Though a few Australian states have introduced anti discrimination legislation, Federal legislation in this regard was not possible to be introduced until the government of Australia has taken up an initiative to reduce sex discrimination in employment sector in 1980s. Now Australia is reviewing affirmative action. Despite, Australian government has taken potential strides during the past decades, women in this country have been failing to get equal opportunities in employment both in private and public sectors. Therefore, vomen's place is still at the crossroads in this country. This again reminds us undoubtedly that, gender discrimination is still persistent in some of the developed countries too.

This Paper

The scope of this paper is very limited. In this paper, woman's place in the contemporary society has been examined against the backdrop of the developments that have taken place across the globe. This apart, impact of the 74th CAA on woman's participation in local government was also examined in the light of Andhra Pradesh experience. To add, advantages and disadvantages of empowering women in urban administrtion have been discussed.

Indian Women–A Case

People often discuss about humanity, morals and law. But the question is to what extent people follow them in practice? Individuals commit mistakes for various reasons. Husbands beating their wives is still prevalent among all classes of society of course with a degree of variance. Is it not a crime? Yet women wish to live with their husbands in accordance with the patriarchal norms tolerating violence against them by their husbands and sometimes blaming themselves for their ashamed and wounded condition. Cases of husbands turning violent when their wives attempt to earn independently or when they become mobile and autonomous are humpty.

In our traditional patriarchal system man always tries to restrict woman from encroaching into his space. Is this not a humiliation to woman? This is what is called male hegemony. It seems our education and knowledge have not made any good impact on our thinking in advancement of our women. This is the major root of all miseries and sorrows with which we have been suffering over the centuries. The rate of crime against women such as domestic violence, sexual abuse, rape, etc. has been increased. Often we see in the daily news papers about indulging sexual abuse on lady civil servants too (Punjab and Kerala cases).

Future of the Woman at Cross Roads

Partly women themselves are responsible for their present place in the society. Determined social activists, woman leaders, feminists, NGOs raised a banner against the male chauvinism voicing their concern for gender equity and equality in all spheres of life particularly equal chances in job opportunities and in administration. Their participation has awakened womanhood.

Factors for Backwardness of Women

Lack of education coupled with poverty, large family size, poor access to information, poor infrastructure, callousness of the policy makers are some of the major factors responsible for the backwardness of women in the society. It is because of these factors women have been failing to become autonomous in their thinking and in playing managerial role in domestic and community development affairs on an equal basis with men. Another major reason is that, hesitation on the part of women to share her expertise, views with their fellow men on aspects concerning their domestic or the society at large. And because, of this most of the women have been loosing right opportunities to claim equal opportunities in sharing of resources on an equal basis with men. On probing, majority of the women however said that, lack of leisure/time on one hand and the prevalence of patriarchal values in the system restrained them from becoming more mobile, autonomous and independent economically, socially and politically. There is a growing evidence that, domestic tension and conflict are very common in such families where women volunteered to involve in activities other than that of domestic. To add all these, man exhibits his reluctance to share of the house work along with his life partner. This is because of his strong feeling that house work is women's primary responsibility. It is man's fear that if given a chance, woman may over ride him in all spheres of life and this fear of man is continued to be a major stumbling block for women's progress over the centuries since Manu's time.

Government's Initiatives

Government of India and the non government organizations including feminist groups, NGOs among others have committed to initiate action for ensuring gender equality in our social system. This resulted in enactment of 73rd and 74th Amendment Acts by the Parliament in the year 1992. This apart, the Union Government has constituted National Commission for Women. Other initiative which the Government of India has taken was establishment of a National Center for Gender Training, Planning and Research at Mussoorie in collaboration with the DFID. These are some of the initiatives which the Government of India has taken during the past few years. Of these, 73rd and 74th CAA have quietly become a force to reckon with. Through these Constitution Amendment Acts, a provision relating to local bodies was incorporated in the Constitution for reservation of seats in local bodies for women to the extent of not less than one-third of the total number of seats. The government is also contemplating to extend this provision to state assemblies and the Parliament too. It is in this regard it has introduced a bill couple of times in the Parliament in the form of 81st and 84th Amendments to the Constitution but it failed to get the bills adopted by the Parliament. However the 73rd and 74th CAAs have empowered women to participate in the local government administration.

Empowerment–The Concept

The concept of empowerment could be defined as a right to know about one's own rights, entitlement to have access to resources and information and the legal right to participate in matters concerning one's own growth and development. It is a tool which enables the individuals to swing into action. The age old Manu Sastra cloaked all possible avenues for women to live with dignity on an equal basis with men. Empowerment is generally linked with gender analysis. Policy makers, social activists and the NGOs both at the national and global levels oft repeatedly have been adopting this concept over the past years in the context of interpersonal relationships, economic and political developmental process, discrimination on the basis of feminity. The basic objective of this concept is to bring people into the decision making process from outside the decision making process both with in the family and outside the family.

International agencies like the UN and the World Bank have made strides with a view to resphape the network of social relations in the society focusing on women development. They argued that, as long as women keep themselves away from involving in the community development process so long they remain lower to men in social, economic and political spheres. It is in this backdrop, they advocated participatory approach which according to them would enable women groups to share knowledge and transform of that learning to other women in the service of 'total women development' and the community.

Participation of Women in Administration

The very idea of participation of women in development process has gained momentum in the post 1970s. Declaration of 1975-85 as an International year for Women by the UN, International Women's Conference held in Nairobi in 1985 and the global women's conference held in Beijing in the year 1995 have drawn the attention of the world on this topical issue of empowerment of women in administration. This resulted in mushrooming of woman's forums echoing their voice for improvement of the conditions of women all over the world, particularly in the third world countries like India, Bangladesh, Pakistan, etc.

Ever Lasting Fight

74th CAA has given room for women to have access to information. By gaining access to information sources, women could aim at their rights of equal status and this will enable them to shift the balance of power at home and outside the home as well. In this direction only, determined law makers, social activities, development planners, journalists, opinion shapers among others determined to continue their fight for the cause of women. Their fight has just began and they will continue their fight till they meet their just demand. As sunshine is the best disinfectant, raging a war against gender is also a right thing. It is a best medicine to clean up our democracy.

Women Administrators–Their Efficiency

Women entering the civil services have been increased over the past few years. At the district level women heading the departments like education, health, commercial tax, revenue, etc has become more common. We are seeing women becoming district collectors, police officers of different cadres, governors, professionals, judges, university vice-chancellors, ministers in the state and the union cabinets, ambassadors, chief ministers, Prime Ministers, Presidents both in India and else where in the world. Late Indira Gandhi, Margaret Thatcher, Chandrika Kumarathunga, Jayalalitha are classic references in this context. The Union External Affairs Ministry, Government of India was lately headed by a woman. For the first time the Government of India has appointed a woman as a Joint director for CBI (Archana Ramasundram). All these references confirm the fact that, women in no way are inferior to men in administering the things either as managers or chairpersons or chief executives of the state or the nation. If given a chance they can even excel men. One could quote Kiran Bedi in this context.

Women in Urban Administration

In urban development department, the number of woman administrators like the municipal commissioners, planning officers, municipal engineers, or for that matter chairpersons of the municipal councils is very small. In Andhra Pradesh for instance the number of woman municipal commissioners in the state is nine. There are 109 municipalities in the state. At the state level, only the commissioner and one of the three joint directors in municipal administration department are females and the remaining senior officers are males only. This is the first time for the government appointing a lady IAS officer as the director and commissioner of the municipal administration. In the case of the Town and Country Planning Department, there is no woman senior officer at the state level. All senior officers including the director of this department are males. So is the case with the state public health department. This shows that female representation in the urban administration is very poor at the state level. Is it because women have no capabilities to run the municipal administration on an equal basis with men they were deprived of the opportunities to involve in the urban administration? If that is the case there were occasions of governments at the state and Central levels appointing women as ministers of urban development/municipal administration.

On probing, women have given their own versions in regard to their liking and/or disliking of the administrative jobs in the municipal/urban development department. Some felt that heading a municipality or a corporation is a Herculean task and more than their capacity. Others said that, though they have that capacity to manage the department they are not interested in entering the municipal administration because neither they can satisfy the citizens nor the political leadership or even their own supporters. On the other hand, woman administrators who are already in service often complain that, they failed to get cooperation from the male dominated administration. Some others feel that they need to build their knowledge and experiences in municipal management. They suggested on the job training. Many of them fear of political pressures and rowdyism. Support from the state government in running the municipal administration in view of bad municipal finances is very much needed. In relation to management of basic civic services like water supply, solid waste management, drainage, provision of dust bins, etc. many of the woman urban managers said that, as women they are aware about the priority sectors in which investments are to be made.

The basic requirement of woman municipal managers is building their capabilities, knowledge and experiences. This could be met by allowing them to get experience through various learning processes. Prime among them is organizing capacity building workshop training programmes on a regular basis. The government of Andhra Pradesh has taken an initiative in this direction. At the instance of the state government the RCUES and the ASCI undertook a series of orientation programmes and training workshops for the newly elected members of the municipal councils and the administrators on various aspects of urban administration. Evaluation reports show that these programmes had runaway impact on the performance of the municipal personnel and the political executives.

Problems

Though woman administrators claim that they can offer resistance to all kinds of stress and strain there is certain void in their claim. Husbands/brothers/or the political party workers escorting woman municipal chairpersons when they are on the official job has become more common. It has also become common women political executives acting as hence – women of their husbands/their supporters in urban development policy making matters. At times they restrain from attending the councils due to fear of attacks and involvement of rowdies in the administration. Therefore, entering the urban administration field especially for females a challenging task. But by entering they have scope to share their mite of comforts for the welfare of their fellow women, urban poor, street children on one hand and for the over all development of the community at large.

Gender Training

NGOs across the globe have been playing an active role in gendering. Many of the NGOs, especially the female headed NGOs have been imparting training for women in different areas including urban management.

Conclusion

Empowerment of women in administration on one hand would reduce gender conflict and on the other hand it will enable for the formulation of gender neutral policies. It is a tool for economic, political and social mobility for women. Similarly, in the case of urban administration, women's involvement could solve many a problem. Implementation of income generating programmes for the urban poor, managing the municipal finances, minimizing corruption in the municipal personnel, involving women in keeping the city clean and green programmes, management of select basic services like sanitation and water supply are some of the tasks which woman urban administrators could undertake successfully.

A STUDY OF THE POLITICAL ASPECTS OF WOMEN EMPOWERMENT IN INDIA

Sanjay Srivastava

Political Process in India and Women Empowerment

The countries of the Europe took four centuries to establish first a strong State, then internal security (law and order), then a sense of nationalism and finally democracy. But in Asia these four political revolutions are telescoped into one and people hope to consummate them in their own life time.[1] In this context, democracy in India, as originally conceived and institutionalised and subsequently operated in the political system, is the most outstanding deviant case from stereotype Parliamentary Democracies of the Western vintage[2].

The Indian experiment of a predominantly parliamentary democracy, superimposed on a highly centralized federal structure, in its effort to realise the goals of social and economic revolution through the apparently irreconcilable mechanism of planning for economic development and Panchayati Raj, has carved out a category of its own, offering a new direction and model for future. The real test for democracy, therefore, lies not merely in its concern for safeguards, but even more in its success in peacefully resolving social conflicts and recurring collective participation in a common national endeavor[3].

This very collective participation and a common national endeavor have been lacking since very inception. According to the Cabinet Missions Plan of May 16,1946, a Constituent Assembly was formed, but critics enumerate that Constituent

Assembly was not a real representative body of the people of India. Not only it was elected by minority (about 20 to 24 per cent) of population eligible to vote on property or educational qualifications, this election too was indirect. In these circumstances, most of the members of the Constituent Assembly belonged to an extremely small westernised professional middle class molded by nineteenth century. English education system sustained in the cities. The members of this class were drawn from higher caste backgrounds and inherited a radical and alien social perspective based largely on the European experience in the twentieth century. Women, who constituted 48% of the population were given negligible representation, exceptionally the All India Women's Conference was given representation but it was not adequate.

The introduction of electoral politics under these conditions tended at the outset only to reinforce the strategic position of the dominant landowning castes by enlarging their role as intermediaries in relationship between the village and outside authorities in the administration and government. They were the "link men", in the constituencies, whose support was courted by the political parties because they controlled the "vote banks" built on the loyalties of local faction members[4]. In this system of "link men" politics women had almost negligible role to play, their interests, priorities and necessities remained veiled due to the domination of traditional political elite. So even the, universal adult suffrage as introduced by the constitution failed to provide women, their due share is political structure. Moreover, when country got independence and First General Elections were held in 1952, only eighteen percent of the population was literate, and level of political socialization, political participation and political mobilisation, was very low, in this typical situation women folk mostly illiterate, having background role in family and society, could only participate as humble and obedient voters of the dominant political elite, they failed to put popular pressure from below to accomplish peaceful implementation of social reforms of their interests.

Following Tables very well reveal this point-

Table 1 : Participation of Women in National Elections

Election Year	*Voting % of men*	*Voting % of Women*	*Total Seats Contested by women*	*Seats won by women*	*% seats won of contested Seats*	*Total Seats*	*% of women embers*
1952	53.00	37.10	51	23	45.09	499	4.40
1957	56.00	38.77	70	27	38.57	500	5.40
1962	62.10	46.63	68	35	51.47	503	6.70
1967	66.70	55.48	66	31	48.43	523	5.90
1971	69.70	49.15	86	22	27.50	521	4.20
1977	65.62	54.96	70	19	25.70	544	3.40
1980	57.69	51.22	142	28	19.70	544	5.14
1984	63.61	68.17	421	159	28.30	544	7.90
1989	70.90	43.90	189	28	14.80	525	5.30
1991	52.56	47.42	307	33	10.75	503	6.60

Source : PIB. Government of India, 1998.

Indian political system may be called a Congress System upto 1967, (Fourth General Election), as it remained single dominant party and ruled at Center and in most of the states. Francine R. Frankel points out that despite their professed aim of carrying out elaborate, development and welfare functions, the elected governments after Independence were able to establish only a token administrative presence at the village level. Instead, like the colonial regimes before them, they relied primarily on the co-operation of established local leaders to organise peasant participation on behalf of national economic and social policies. Similarly, the process of "party building" involved little more than pyramiding alliances among district and state factional alignments that at their base often turned out to be the personal following of local leaders. The Congress party, which had dominated politics since the turn of the century, mastered the art of political accommodation to the highest degree. They succeeded by adapting local power structures, using the natural building blocks closest at hand. Within each region they recruited from among those who were typically members of the dominant land owning castes and were the leading members of the large land owning caste. Such local notables put together the basic units of the Congress party organisation. The units were composed of the leaders kin, caste fellows, and economic dependents, and the position of women in this political setup dominated by the traditional political elite was relegated into the background. They failed to enjoy their due share, proportionate to their number in the political process[5].

The Congress umbrella was so broad that it included, almost all the social groups viz. forward castes, backward castes, landowning class, working class, schedule castes, schedule tribes and women as well. The typical Congress mentality something to everybody. Hence again women failed to achieve success to get just share in the decision making process and their interests remained unfulfilled.

But, the political socialization has helped to build an awareness of self-interest among various groups, and to deepen group conflicts and inequalities of the society. The group based on gender identity has become more self conscious and such along vertical cleavages, hitherto quiescent have been socially mobilized as they have been inducted into political process. Women having discovered that they are different from other groups, they have become conscious of their separated identity and are seeking political expression for their newly discovered identity i.e. to claim their due share in the authoritative allocation of values and decision & law mak·ng process[6].

Table 2 : Women Representation in the Rajya Sabha (Upper House)

Year	*Total*	*No. of Women*	*Percentage*
1952	219	16	7.3
1957	237	18	7.6
1962	238	18	7.6
1967	240	20	8.3
1971	243	17	7.0
1977	244	25	10.2
1980	244	24	9.8
1985	244	28	11.4
1990	245	24	9.7
1991	245	38	15.5
1992	245	17	6.9
1994	245	20	8.1
1996	245	18	7.3
1997	245	18	7.3
1998	245	18	7.3

Source : Statistical Abstracts, 1998.

Thus with increased political socialisation, political education and political mobilisation, women have come to realise that their interests are different from other groups and this self-identification has put them at loggerheads with other groups in the society.

However Table Nos. 1, 2, 3 & 4, also reveal that there is a consistent increase in women participation in elections and political activities. Modern day women in India are accepting the challenges of the life and are able to bear the responsibilities of administration and governance.

Table 3 : Women's Representation in Selected State Legislatures

Assam	1996	122	6
Haryana	1999	90	4
J&K	1996	87	2
Himachal Pradesh	1998	68	6
Gujarat	1998	182	4
Kerala	1996	140	13
Meghalaya	1998	60	3
Punjab	1997	117	7
Pondicherry	1996	30	1
NCT Delhi	1998	70	9
Nagaland	1998	60	0
Madhya Pradesh	1998	320	26
Tamil Nadu	1996	234	9
Tripura	1998	60	2
Uttar Pradesh	1996	424	20
West Bengal	1996	294	20
Bihar	1999	324	19
Maharashtra	1995	288	11
Arunachal Pradesh	1995	60	1
Manipur	1999	60	1
Orissa	1999	147	13
Rajasthan	1998	200	14

Source : Election Commission of India.

Women role in All India Services has also increased, though not considerably, in Indian Administrative Services out of total personnel, 10.3% were women in 1997 as against 7.3% in 1995; the same trend is true about Indian Police Services and Indian Foreign Services. The massage is clear, that educated young women are breaking the traditional shackles to face the challenges of modern day society; table No. 5 substantiate this point.

But actual problem lies in the fact that political empowerment of women shall alter the power arrangement at all levels of political system; it shall dislodge the traditional political elite from their dominant position, the entire structure of dominance shall crumble, for this very reason the traditional elite are challenging the concept of women empowerment, to maintain their own political hegemony.

Table 4 : Number of Urban Local Bodies and Local Elected Representatives

State/Union Territory	*Municipal Corporation*	*Municipal Council*	*Nagar Panchayat*	*Tatal*
Andhra Pradesh	07(395)	94(2853)	15(314)	116(3542)
Assam	01	25(353)	42(204)	68(557)
Bihar	06	70	93	169
Goa	–	13(155)	–	13(155)
Gujarat	06(468)	86(2745)	60(1260)	152(4473)
Haryana	01	20	32	53(1359)
Himachal Pradesh	01(25)	19(183)	29(221)	49(429)
Karnataka	06(410)	122(3196)	89(1355)	214(4961)
Kerala	05(298)	53(1597)	–	58(1895)
Madhya Pradesh	02(1067)	106(2527)	283(4537)	409(8131)
Maharashtra	15(1417)	228(4901)	–	243(6318)
Manipur	–	07	20	27
Orissa	02(70)	29(560)	72(1056)	103(1686)
Punjab	03	97	34	134(1699)
Rajasthan	03	11	169	183(4412)
Tamil Nadu	06(480)	102(3494)	611(9794)	719(13768)
Tripura	–	01	12	13
Uttar Pradesh	11(841)	226(5970)	444(5518)	681(12329)
West Bengal	06	112	4	122(2706)
A&N Islands	–	01	–	01
Chandigarh	01	–	–	01
Delhi	01	01	–	02(134)
Pondicherry	–	05	–	05
Daman & Diu	–	02	–	02
Total	**101**	**1430**	**2009**	**3540(68554)**

Notes : (i) Figures in brackets indicate number of elected representatives.

(ii) 1/3rd are women elected representatives in India.

Another basic hindrance in the way of women empowerment is that they have failed to carry the political mobilisation at the grassroots level; instead of exerting popular pressure from below to accomplish their goals, they are

Table 5 : Women Selected all India Services

Sr. No.	Services	Year	Total	No. of Personnel in Position		
				Males	Females	% of Female
1	Indian Administrative Service	1995	4284	3973	311	7.3
		1992	4928	4498	430	8.7
		1996	5047	4546	501	9.9
		1997	4991	4479	512	10.3
2	Indian Police service	1985	2343	2325	18	0.8
		1992	2825	2773	52	1.8
		1996	2947	2883	64	2.2
		1997	2964	2868	96	3.3
		1998	2985	2885	100	3.4
		1999	3115	3007	108	3.5
3	Indian Foreign Service	1985	535	485	50	9.3
		1992	721	658	83	8.7
		1995	547	481	66	12.1
		1996	567	501	66	11.16
		1997	586	519	67	11.4
		1998	587	520	67	11.4

Notes : 1. As on 1.11.98 (Includes 1998 batch).
2. As no 1.1..97 (Includes 1996 batch).
3. As no. 31.10.97 (Includes 1997 batch).

basically relying on few women or feminist groups and counted women leaders. In the democratic system the decision making process works as input-output system, on the issue of women empowerment. The input i.e. demand is of quite low intensity and it is unable to penetrate the decision making process, as their is no mass mobilisation on part of women on the issue of women empowerment.

Moreover, women groups have failed to influence the electoral politics, through tactical voting to press for their demand. Women voters have been unsuccessful in making "women empowerment" an issue in the elections. As political parties and pressure groups hold the key to decision making process at the highest level, women groups so far have not succeeded in influencing political parties or groups. The political parties and pressure groups only keep lip sympathy with them, women basically vote in the election and are loyal to a political party, without having bargained with them for their political interests. Thus women groups have neither aggregated nor articulated their demand properly. They perhaps lack strong leadership also.

In challenging the decision making process they appear to be quite casual in their approach, they lack a well set organisation determined to fight for the demand of reservation. Their demand get expression only in the political forums of different political parties, and even their in subjected to the mercy of traditional political elite.

Rigid caste system also perpetuate the plight of women, particularly the women of backward castes in UP and Bihar are not allowed to play decisive role in the society, due to social restriction imposed by their caste rules, and opposing the women reservation issue, as for them it will enhance the domination of forward castes, with caste, class also coexist in Indian polity, women of upper class are now more educated and aware of their rights and liberties, this class is supporting the demand of women reservation.

Another important point to be noticed, is the planet and satellite relation between metros and other rural areas, in metros women enjoy gender equality, this supports the demand for women empowerment but for women of rural areas, this demand is of no worth as they are busy in their traditional background role. Thus, the women empowerment movement may be called an urban upper and middle class phenomenon.

Women in Urban Government

The 74th Constitution Amendment Act (CAA) 1992 revitalised the institutions of municipal body by providing them the Constitutional status. This Constitution Amendment Act, basically deals with the municipalties and has inserted Part IX A, in the Constitution, which contains Articles 243 P to 243 ZG. These provisions also provided conducive environment for women to take active part in the local governance by providing 1/3rd reservation for women in urban local bodies.

Now women shall be directly playing an important role in the decision making process and shall be at the forefront of local development, this shall definitely lead to grater women participation in urban management. Details of the provisions of women reservation provided by the 74th CAA 1992 are following.

Article 243 T (I) of Constitution Amendment (1992) states as follows:

"Reservation of Seats

243T1. Seats shall be reserved for the Scheduled Castes and the Scheduled Tribes in every Municipality and the number of seats so reserved shall bear, as nearly as may be, the same proportion to the total number of seats to be filled by direct election in that Municipality as the population of the Scheduled Castes in the Municipal area or of the Scheduled Tribes in the Municipal area bears to the total population of that area and such seats may be allotted by rotation to different constituencies in a Municipality.

2. Not less than one-third of the total number of seats reserved under clause (1) shall be reserved for women belonging to the Scheduled Castes or, as the case may be, the Scheduled Tribes.
3. Not less than one-third (including the number of seats reserved for women belonging to the Scheduled Castes and the Scheduled Tribes) of the total number of seats to be filled by direct election in every Municipality shall be reserved for women and such seats may be allotted by rotation to different constituencies in a Municipality.
4. The office of Chairpersons in the Municipalities shall be reserved for the Scheduled Castes, the Scheduled Tribes and common in such manner as the Legislature of a State may by law, provide.
5. The reservation of seats under clauses (1) and (2) and the reservation of office of Chairpersons (other than the reservation for women) under clause (4) shall cease to

have effect on the expiration of the period specified in article 334.

6. Nothing in this Part shall prevent the Legislature of a State from making any provision for reservation of seats in any Municipality or office of Chairpersons in the Municipalities in favour of backward class of citizens."[7]

But the constitutional guarantee alone con not lead to metamorphosis in the status and role of women in urban governance; following are the difficulties women face, while making active participation at local level management-

1. Lack of orientation / training in urban development issues and municipal administration.
2. No proper knowledge / orientation about municipal acts and rules and regulations.
3. No prior experience about dealing with multi-dimensional urban development issues / civic issues and its complexities.
4. Lack of knowledge about technical in-puts related to urban service delivery system.
5. Lack of support from senior male / female colleagues in the party / municipal body.
6. Less co-operation from municipal officials understanding about various facets of the budget, such as allocation of budget at ward level (at central / ward level).
7. Lack of party support and poor organisational structure.
8. Lack of money and resources to sustain the electoral campaigns (in spite of code of conduct by election commission).
9. Discrimination in decision making at party level.
10. Specific notions towards politics and political atmosphere.
11. Fear and insecurity.

12. Lack of confidence in public speaking.
13. Criminalisation of politics and use of money power.
14. Family responsibilities.[8]

Besides these, role of money power, muscle power, backroom dealings, communalisation and criminalisation of politics also prevents women in making active participation in local governance.

Kumari and Kidwai (1996) have analysed that political parties have dominated the conservative 'cultural' perspective and no conscious attempt has been made to increase active participation of women. Women are not considered as a vote bank in Indian Politics, and once the men are mobilised, the women shall follow suit. In the election compaigns, mostly men are involved, they hardly have access to female voters, this impedes the political socialisation of women.

Nath Kamale (1997) points out that "women's movement has been a powerful agent of empowerment and has provided an alternative perspective for fundamental structural changes". The 74th CAA 1992 is the right step is this direction, through 1/3rd reservation to women it ensures women participation in local urban affairs. It develops their capacities to play their rightful roles in the development process.

Attention is being paid to proper training and skill development of women involved in local government, as elected representative, so that they can over come various personality related and procedural difficulties. Some of the important training institutions imparting training and offering Orientation Programmes to elected women representative are following-

1. State Womens' Commissions in all States in India (to deal with women and development issues).
2. All India Institute of Local Self Government branch offices at Mumbai, Ahmedabad, Vadodara, Bhubaneshwar, Bhopal, New Delhi, Panaji, Bangladesh.
3. Regional Centre for Urban and Environmental Studies (RCUES) of AIILSG, Mumbai.

4. Regional Centre for Urban and Environmental Studies (RCUES), Hyderabad.
5. Regional Centre for Urban and Environmental Studies (RCUES), Lucknow.
6. Indian Institute of Public Administration.
7. National Institute of Urban Affairs (NIUA), New Delhi.
8. Uttar Pradesh Academy of Administration (UPAA), Nainital / Lucknow.
9. Rajasthan State Institute of Public Administration (RIPA), Jaipur.
10. Kerala Institute of Local Administration (KILA), Trichur.
11. Administrative Training Institute (ATI), Guwahati.
12. Institute of Local Government and Urban Studies (ILGUS), Calcutta.
13. Centre for Urban and Environmental Studies, Trivandrum.
14. National Institute for Habitat Management (NIHM), Bhubaneshwar.
15. Tamil Nadu Institute of Urban Studies, Coimbatore.
16. Professional Development Centre (PDC), Maharashtra.
17. Housing and Area Development Authority (MHADA), Pune.
18. National Institute of Human Settlements, Bhopal.
19. Environmental Training Institute (ETI), Madras.
20. Training Institute of Housing Development Finance Corporation (HDFC), Lonavala, Maharashtra.
21. Indian Institute of Education, Pune.
22. Yashvantrao Chavan Pratishthan, Mumbai.
23. Rambhau Mhalaji Pratisthan, Mumbai.
24. P. V. Mandlik Trust, Maharashtra.
25. SNDT University, Mumbai.[9]

The main purpose of urban management training is to develop capacities of officials to deal with the complex urban problems in a holistic manner to achieve efficiently the aim of municipal bodies and of the urban sector as a whole. These institutions cover the main areas for orientation / training or capacity building in urban development and municipal administration field.

1. Urban Development Management.
2. Municipal Administration.
3. 74th Amendment to Constitution (1992) & its implementation.
4. Information Technology and Application of Computers in Municipal Administration.
5. Project Planning and Management.
6. Urban Infrastructure Planning & Development.
7. Municipal Finance and Resource Mobilisation.
8. Urban Environment Management.
9. Housing and Slum Programmes.
10. Urban Poverty, Poverty Alleviation Programmes & Convergence
11. Traffic and Transportation,
12. Solid Waste Management,
13. Water and Waste Water Management,
14. Shelter Upgradation Programmes,
15. Women and Development
16. Municipal Legislative Framework.
17. Laws of Meetings.
18. Motivation Techniques and Communication skills,
19. Disaster Management,
20. Public Health and Management of Healthcare programmes in cities.

21. Management Information System in Municipal Administration.[10]

Despite these efforts, to increase women participation in urban administration, not much resulted has been achieved so far. Domination of men still continues, the elected women representation are often the puppet politician, the real string is held by the male member of their (women's) families; these male members take the decisions on behalf of women representatives. Often right from the beginning, the entire election campaign and election strategy is made and executed by the male members of the family and women contestant is reduced to just a rubber stamp; after elections the major decisions, policies and plans are decided by these male members and often financial matters are also controlled by the male members of the family, the women representative has virtually no say in these matters, despite of people's mandate. The stories of virtual control of *Sarpanch Pati* and *Parshad Pati* over the local governance have become a very common thing.

Thus the legal empowerment of women in urban administration has taken place, by the 74th CAA 1992; but the goal of actual political empowerment of women is yet to be realised.

REFERENCES

Gurnnar Myrdal, Asian Drama, Vol. I.

Saminendra Nath Roy, "Democracy and Development Experience in India, Teaching Politics", Vol. VIII 1 and 2, p. 1.

ibid p. 3.

This idea is very elaborated by A.S. Narang, Indian Government Politics, 1987, New Delhi, pp. 201-2002.

This tactics of congress politics is explained by Narang, Op. Cit.

Narang, Op. Cit.

India Report, State of Women in Urban Local Government, UNESCAP, 2000. Available on website: www.unescaporg\ huset\ women\ reports

India Report, Op.Cit.

India Report, Op.Cit.

India Report,Op.Cit.

THE GENDER PARADIGM IN LOCAL GOVERNANCE : INDIAN EXPERIENCE

K.K. Upadhyay and Pravin Bhardwaj

Introduction

The recognition of the right of every citizen to participate in the public decision is a basic element of democracy. Which, to be effective, requires that the needs and the interest of all members of the society is respected and represented. This cannot happen if any one group is consistently excluded from taking part in decision making. The fact that others might claim to be speaking for them is no guarantee of social justice, as is evident from the situation of women in most part of the world and particularly true in developing countries where male always represented the feelings and views of the women for many centuries.

The 74th constitutional amendment has guaranteed the elections at the local level every five years. All the councilors who have been elected are the new entered into politics either men or women. The reservations of the seats to the women have given a new bend to the political process at the local level because at the national and the state level the representation of the women is still less and it is considered to be the sole domain of the male members. This can be generally attributed to the fact that the 81st reservation bill that talks of the reservation for women at the national level is still pending in the parliament.

As all the elected representatives are new and most of them has fought on the party ticket it was observed that because they want to please the leaders at the state level they give more priority to the party than the work at the local level. This case has been witnessed in most of the states and to have a regular place in the political party more interest is shown towards the political parties agenda then to the problems at the local level.

Women in Parliament

Women presence in Lok Sabha and in the assembly election has been less since independence and they haven't got enough chances at the central and the state level to participate in the elections. Women in these election have shown an overwhelming response as far as voting is concerned. The results of the various elections shows that the winning percentage of the women has been high in all these elections. Though India is having a low representation of women in parliament but due to the 73rd and the 74th constitutional amendments atleast at the local level 33% of the representation has been assured. This is a very welcome step. Few of the developed countries have even not taken the decision to increase the women representation even when the education level is high.

Reservation at Local Level : An Issue

Though the Constitution of India guarantees the right to the Indian women but there exists huge gap between Constitutional guarantees and the realities of the women's lives. It is important to acknowledge these gaps, because the time has never seen more appropriate to make a huge concentrated effort to bridge them–to identify and overthrow the barriers that prevent the realization of freedoms and equality for half of the Indian population.

The inequality is very clearly and visibly built into the structure, as in the case of some religious hierarchy or exclusive clubs, where women are debarred from high office. In both these cases, customs and traditions are quoted as justification for this discrimination. At times the inequality lies not in the structure but in the way it operates. For instance, even there is no law that debars women from contesting elections to the Lok Sabha, very few women become the members of the parliament.

Current Reservation Guarantees to the Indian Women at the Local Level

- 1/3 reservation to women
- Reserved seats for SC/CT and OBCs
- Reservation based on rotations

Factors Affecting Women's Political Representation at the Local Level

Political Party

Inspite of the fact that most of the national political parties have stated in their manifestos that they support reservations for women in Parliament, very few women candidates have been given chance to contest election. Following data indicate that, so far, there are relatively few political parties which have establishes electoral mechanism aimed at increasing the proportion of elected women, in either their internal structures or indeed in parliament or other elective bodies.

Political Party Wise Distribution of Elected Representative

Party support to contest elections at every level is very essential. In a democratic system party provides a platform and an identity to individual. Again contesting elections is much more streneous stake as far as mental, social and financial factors are concerned. Therefore the analysis of the party wise distribution of elected representatives show that winning chance of independent candidate is very low as compared to the party supported candidate. Therefore for women candidates it's more desirable to contest election as a party candidate. The electoral process includes all activities concerning elections. i.e., right from the filing of the nomination papers to the declaration of elections results. In between there are number of activities like canvassing, collection of elections funds, arranging and attending elections meeting, participating in elections rallies and finally exercising the franchise. It is a tedious task and requires party support to get elected.

Getting the Party Nomination and Electoral Support

However, whenever it is enquired from the political parties that why they do not nominate adequate number of women candidates for contesting the elections, they answer that it is difficult to find a woman with both the necessary political status and readiness to accept nomination. This seems to place the burden on women but in fact it poses the question on how women can have access to the governing structures of parties because it is universal fact that parties tend to nominate their elite, who inevitable concentrates at the top. In most political parties, women are still very rare in high decision–making spheres.

Family

Family plays a greater role as far as women participation in sphere of life is concerned. In common Indian families, women have very little say even in the matters affecting their own lives. For most Indian women, marriage itself is not a matter of choice–only a small minority, even among educated women of well-off families, have not any role in deciding when and whom they will get married. Culturally, marriage denotes the end of childhood, but the reality is that millions of Indian women get married when they are still children, in both the legal and the biological senses.

Politics requires ample time, which entails sacrifice of part of one's private life. This is true for women as well as for men. However, for a woman household work is primarily supposed to be their function whether she is a housewife, professional, salarie or a councilor. During the training program organized by PRIA and its partners many female councilors came forward with the view that in the family they have to behave like docile housewives looking after the household functions. However, in public life we are supposed to act like an active leader. Both type of activity requires different attitude and way of life. Hence once we are women councilors we are compelled to lead a dual life. At times when it comes to priorities between household and the other works it becomes very hard for a councilor to justify which is important. Being a woman and the works associated with her it becomes hard to fulfill all the functions effectively.

Apart from this there are several other restrictions on the part of the family on the elected women which is very clear from our study from various states where the reasons cited were:

(a) Neglect from home

(b) Family Pressure

(c) Politics as social taboo

Violence

Violence defined as physical act of aggression of individual or group against another or others. Violence against women means any gender based violence, which results in, or is likely to result in physical, sexual or psychological harm or suffering. In India the major source of violence is mainly the family, marriage and place of work. Family is the major source of discrimination against the women or the girl child. For the girl child, the family sets the conditions of gender discrimination– be it for food or nutrition, education and work etc. which continues for rest of the life and sometimes it creates situation for physical and emotional violence. Their upbringing in shadow of fear and violence hinder their natural growth and convert them into the passive follower in the patriarchal society.

Generally it is seen that violence is used as one of the tools to restrict entry of persons into politics. However, it is interesting to note that no cases of violence against women have been witnessed in various states at the urban local bodies election. This can be analyzed in the light of the 74th constitutional amendment act. The provision of the 33% per cent reservation to the women at the municipal level has affected the attitude of the male dominant society if not under willingness then under compulsion. Now when the seats are reserved in majority of the cases the women are contesting elections mainly on the ground of the family support, which has political background or linkages. In this case women get families support and in turn party backing which makes the chances of the violence minimal.

Politics as Power

The function of the men and the women in the society has been classified in such a manner that men take all the functions which are related to power and let the women do the subordinate function.

Women hardly get free time to think of politics. Leave alone their effective participation in it. Only in some rich families in which these household works are done by servants, a female can contest election and find time to participate in politics, the husband and in laws grant the permission. The greatest fear which exists in the male dominated society that once their women constitute the majority segment they will have power of legislation that is against the patriarchal society.

Reservation : In Reality

Even after recognition of the fact that women empowerment by providing them representation in the legislature is beneficial for women in particular and society at large, the level of reservation has become a matter of great discussion and debate. Reservation at the local level is being supported on the ground that it would be a level of basic political learning for them and paving away for the state level and the national level representation. Another major reason is that parliamentary sessions takes place in the capital city of the state and the nation and involve long and repeated absence from home, this becomes a major limitation in the Indian family.

Performance Level

Socio cultural factors are also acting deterrent in many cases. The conflict between women councillors role as respectful women and their role as politicians is indeed specially conspicuous when women councillors have to come out of the houses in the night. To do so it involves two kind of dangers in the Indian context: a physical danger, since violence is more likely to happen in the dark; and a more abstract, but nevertheless very real danger, that is putting ones reputation at risk, since respectful women by conviction, is not supposed to be out in the night. For example, at night if any emergency arises, women are mostly not allowed to go to the spot and help. Even during day time many families object to their going out to settle any dispute. Rather, husbands are made to do the job. Apart from attending any official meetings the permission of the parents, in-laws or the husband is necessary to visit any other place. Obviously this is causing serious constraints on their mobility and in discharge of their duties which ultimately affects their performance level.

It was observed from the field that inspite of above all hindrance in the way of women their overall performance level is higher then the male counterpart. This is very much apparent from our field study where women have proved themselves smarter when it comes to making the promises and fulfilling it.

One of the outcomes of the constitutional empowerment is the nomination of Bibi-Bahu-Beti (Lugai, Benani, beti) in the electoral process. At the first instance one can understand that it is that attitude of the patriarchal society to be in the political power but in a long run it has paved the way for other women of the society to enter into the political process. Bibi-bahu-beti is just the first time address from the second time onwards the female will have their own identity and will emerge as empowered political leader of the society.

Even while nominating women contestants, due to the constitutional provision of 33% reservation to the women Bibi-Bahu-Beti (wive, daughters-in-law & daughter of prominent politicians) syndrome plays a vital role. In spite of considering a suitable candidate, strength of the candidate and strength of the rival candidate are taken into account. In the 1995 elections in various states, the proxy battle for ballot was evident as there was a noteworthy reservation for the women candidates and many fielded their wives, daughters in laws, daughters, nieces etc. to fulfill their own political ambitions. (The Hindustan Times 1995:3).

All women candidates were not necessarily formal members of the political parties. So different parties identified female relations of male members and nominated them. The families' perception and role influences the women constant

Promises Made

Commitment to People	*Road*	*Water*	*Sanitation/Waste management*	*Electricity*
Male Promises	43.6	30.7	56.4	30.7
Female Promises	75.8	51.7	75.8	58.6

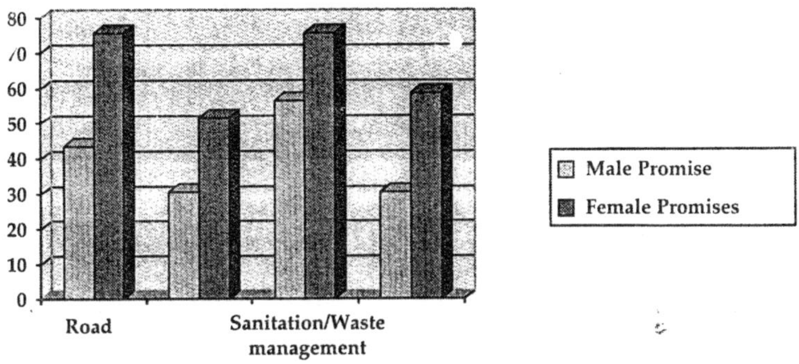

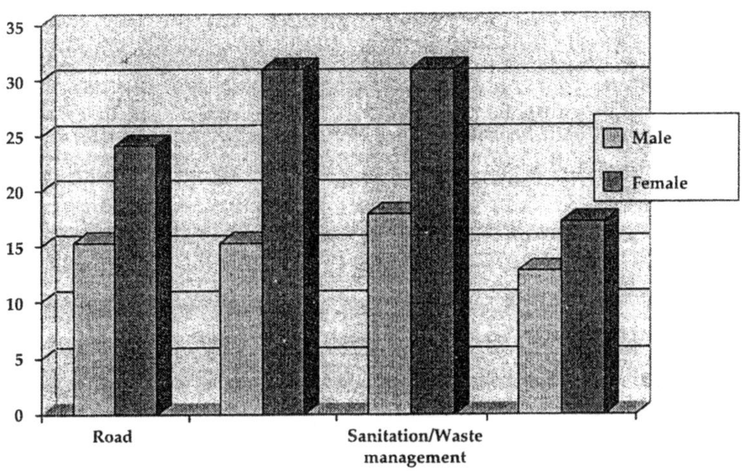

Promises Fulfilled

Fulfillment of Promises	*Road*	*Water*	*Sanitation/Waste management*	*Electricity*
Male	15.3	15.3	17.9	12.8
Female	24.13	31.0	31.0	17.2

Socio–Economic Status of Women and its impact on their Effectiveness.

Bibi-Bahu-Beti–Syndrome (Wife, Daughter-in-law, daughter syndrome) Promises Fulfilled

Fulfillment of Promises	*Road*	*Water*	*Sanitation/Waste management*	*Electricity*
Male	15.3	15.3	17.9	12.8
Female	24.31	31.0	331.0	17.2

Socio–Economic Status of Women and its impact on their Effectiveness.

decision to participate in the electoral process. The women candidates have to take the approval from their husbands and/ or in – laws. The cases of single members were no exception either, in the sense that the approval had to come, in their case, from their parents, even brothers and uncles. Women who have willingly plunged into the fray are mostly those who have had exposure to the political activity within their own families. These are the women who have started with a sure footing and are quite clear about what constructive role they can play, as women in a given setup. True it is difficult to carry out without men's support but women also have a wider role in the total development of the area of her operation.

However, there are large number of members who have been literally pushed into the scene. Many are finding the responsibilities very demanding, some are thoroughly engaged in the domestic responsibilities, some do not maintain good health.

The intervention in selected municipalities reveals that many housewives have come in the election fray after the reservation was given to the women. Majority of the housewives was hailing from those families, which had a political background.

Their Strength as Leaders

Politics is associated with specific systems of values and practices that women find so alienating and daunting that they feel either excluded or reluctant to engage in it. Women as belonging to the male world perceive being adversarial and confrontational politics. These make women choose either to adjust to the milieu and act the man's way, or to assume and impose their different identity. In addition, the current political system is more than often labeled as corrupt and this renders it most unattractive for women. For them, these are probably among the most difficult barriers to overcome.

On the other hand, women benefits from a positive prejudice on the part of the electorate, which tends to place hope in them and to believe that they are not only serious about the job and also honest and can bring fresh values to the world of politics. While this prejudice can be burden it certainly acts a catalyst for women to take office and as an incentive to parties to present female candidates.

The major task of the women of the country in general is to help the new set-up to function properly. This has sown the seeds for women to emerge as the carriers of power and as equal partners in the political process and incoming to power and exercising it. Yet another prospect of the constitutional guarantee of women getting elected to the local bodies is that it will eliminate the dependence of conscious and able women for support and sympathy of the upper cast and the upper class leadership as a part of the politics of co-option. Women now feel that it is their constitutional right to contest for and continue in leadership positions. The reservation will act as a catalyst for higher participation of women in electoral process at the local level and in the longer run at the state and the national level.

The responses from the field level revealed that majority of the stakeholder were of the view that women work more for women related issue.

In many states the second round of municipal election have been held and the women presence have been felt at the elections processes in the way of voting for many years now but even then the women are not getting the right response at every place. The presence of chairman pati is still present and this stops women from voicing their feeling in the municipality. The other problem, which was noted at the municipal level, was the problem of mobility as the women had to depend on the male folks of the houses for doing their ward work and moving out. The women find it hard in the smaller nagar panchayats to attend the meetings as they say it is still male dominated and their voice are not heard. Even in the reserved seats and constituencies the women councilors had to work in accordance to the wish of their husbands and other male member of the party.

Case Study : Ittaunjha Nagar Panchayat, Uttar Pradesh

In Ittaunjha Nagar Panchayat the councilllors are divided on any of the development issues because of the presence of Chairman pati. The present chairman is lady but her husband looks after the work. Husband was the previous chairman and because the constituency was declared as reserved to women his wife contested the election. The husband chairman is even present in the monthly meetings and no one is allowed to meet the wife. We also met the husband chairman only as he is known as the chairman. The chairman (Husband) prefers to do the work of those wards which is supposed to be his vote bank because he is said to be the congress candidate for the coming state elections. Because of this reason The work in the municipality is not going on smoothly and the monthly meeting is not yielding the fruitful results. The women councilors (hailing from other party) are not ready to meet the chairman pati as they say that he never does the work.

Special Support for Women

Even after two rounds of elections in most of the places it is witnessed that the women even after getting the reservations at the local level are not able to fight for their cause. This is mostly because of the reason

- Social Taboos comes in the way
- Family pressure is there
- Male dominance comes in the way of daily functions
- Came in the local level politics just to fill the seats
- Dominance of male party colleagues in municipal functioning

These reasons have become a major hindrance in the way of the women in doing some effective work at the local level.

PRIA Intervention with Various Municipalities Showed Following Results
Women elected Representative Relationship with Municipal Staff

States	*Haryana*		*Kerala*		*Madhya Pradesh*		*Rajasthan*		*Uttar Pradesh*		
	Rati a	*Father dabad*	*Chert halla*	*Kalp etta*	*Seho re*	*Ichh awar*	*Cho mu*	*Bila ra*	*Gazi pur*	*Ittau hjha*	*saidp ur*
Husbands Interference							✓	✓		✓	
Voice is not heard	✓	✓	✓							✓	✓
Difficult to attend the meeting with the males			✓				✓	✓		✓	

It is well known fact the women do not get enough chance to work for the ward and the collective interest of the people but even then people have immense faith in them. The expression of the people shows that women councilors work better for all the issues, as they do not crave for the political improvement. It is necessary that some kind of feeling should be developed in the male councilors also for effective working at the munici al level.

As the people have elected the women candidates also so they come under the review of the people also if they are not able to perform their duties properly. Every one is not ready to accept the male dominance as they say if she is elected she should work for the welfare of the people of their own ward. This is a challenging task for women in the male dominated society.

After further analysis it can be said that women councilors are more concerned with the issues of the municipalities and males are less concerned to the work at the local level because they are guided by other motives. The reasons given for such a trend was

(a) Women are the one who have faced the difficulty of the basic services e.g. water. They have to fetch water from outside if it is not available in the household

(b) Women address the cause of the women better, as they understand better

(c) Males are guided more by political motives as they see it as a chance to enter the state level politics so the patty support and backup is more needed

(d) Most of the women entry into the politics has been because of the reservation at the local level so the women unwillingly came into the political setup because of the compulsion of the male members. Most of the times the male family members do things on their own without the female consent.

Many states has gone into the second round of elections at the municipal, level but even then we see the male dominance

Table Showing the Positive Points of the Women Councilors as Assessed by the Citizens

States	*Haryana*		*Kerala*		*Madhya Pradesh*		*Rajasthan*		*Uttar Pradesh*		
Municipality	*Ratia*	*Fathedabad*	*Cherthalla*	*Kalpetta*	*Sehore*	*Ichhawar*	*Chomu*	*Bilara*	*Gazipur*	*Ittauhjha*	*Saidpur*
Woment Councillors Positive Points											
Women Work more for women related issues		✓	✓	✓	✓	✓	✓	✓		✓	
Women understand Better	✓	✓			✓				✓	✓	✓
Issues neglected by males	✓	✓	✓	✓		✓	✓		✓	✓	✓
Committeed for women upliftment	✓	✓			✓	✓	✓		✓	✓	✓

Table Showing the Negative Points of the Women Councilors as Assessed by the Citizens

States	*Haryana*		*Kerala*		*Madhya Pradesh*		*Rajasthan*		*Uttar Pradesh*		
Municipality	*Ratia*	*Fathedabad*	*Cherthalla*	*Kalpetta*	*Sehore*	*Ichhawar*	*Chomu*	*Bilara*	*Gazipur*	*Ittauhjha*	*Saidpur*
Women Councilors Negative Points											
Works for own interest for political gains									✓	✓	✓
Works on party guidance									✓	✓	✓

in the elections as well as the functioning of the municipality. The male dominance over the female work has been generally seen through three main reasons

(a) Neglect of home and the family if female does the active councilor work

(b) Family pressure to complete the household work as they have to complete dual responsibility

(c) Politics not suited to women of the society, as active participation is not needed for 24 hours.

It was observed from several discussions that within a family as well women have very little say in the decision affecting their own lives. Even among most educated women of well-off families taking independent decisions is not common. For married women it has become difficult to cater to the dual functions looking after the home as well as performing the duties of a councilor. If a women has to move out in the night for attending some meetings in the locality she can not do it alone and she needs some of the male member otherwise comments are passed on her character. These are some of the pretext where male take over the duties.

Important Findings

- Divided on caste and party lines
- Collective thinking lacking
- Municipal staff thinks councilors are not aware of their functions
- Social Structure of the society plays the vital role

Gender and Municipal Functions

Women in India have a definite advantage as compared to the women in developed nations. Domestic help, either paid or within the extended family, is common in India, while it a luxury in developed nations. Also, possibilities for the women politicians to count on the continuing support of the family differ considerably among India and the developed nations. An extended family and grand parents living under the same roof as their grand children are common features in India while in developed nations children come back in empty home. This is one of the major reason why the representation of women at the local level have been very successful at not so at the state and the national level because in the latter case the family is not there to support the women candidates.

Women were always said to have no say in the family life as well as the social life their voice was not considered to be so important in the male dominated world but due the women reservation at the local level now they have a platform to voice their feeling. This was clearly felt when the field level interviews were done with the elected representatives. This was noticed more in bigger center as compared to the smaller one.

Due Scope in Council Meeting to Speak

	Due Scope to Speak in Committes
Male	63.9
Female	36.1

Both male and female have due scope to speak in the meeting but male have a better advantage. Even in the small span to time if women have started to exert their feeling and speak in the meetings this implies that given a right platform and chance they can bring out many a societal problem related to the women.

Issues Addressed

Female are more concerned with the basic issues as it is very clear from the data from various areas of intervention. Women's main area of concern was education, health, pension issues and distribution of other self employment goods for women. Even in the case of general employment their concern was neck to neck that of the male members.

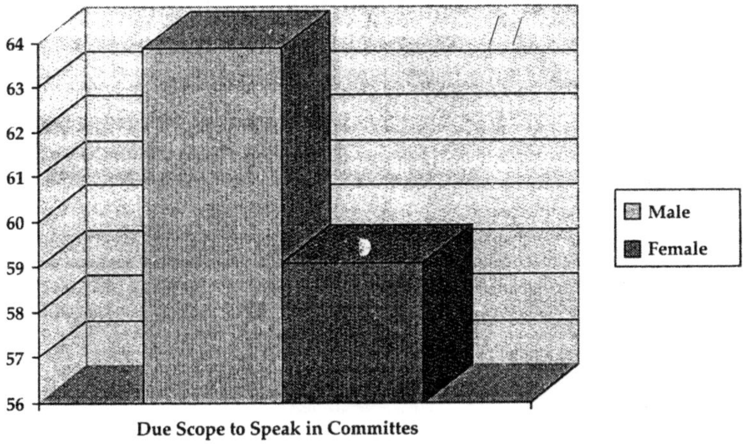

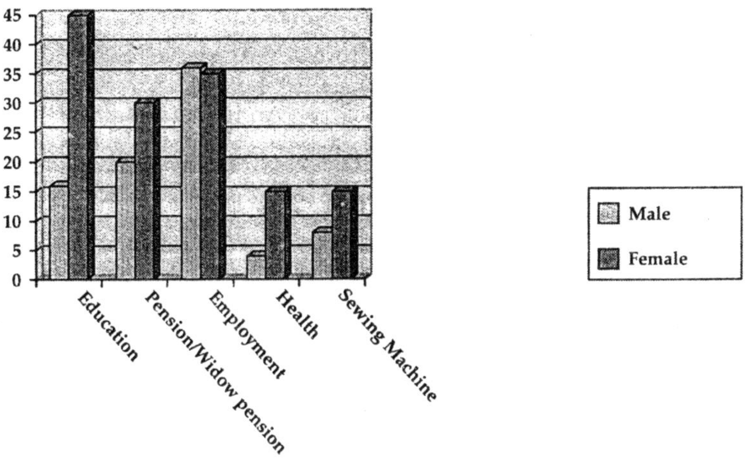

	Education	*Pension/Widow pension*	*Employment*	*Health*	*Sewing Machine*
Male	16	20	36	4	8
Female	45	30	35	15	15

The Problems Faced by the Councilors

It was absorved at the field level that the major problems faced by the female councilors lack of resource followed by bureaucratic apathy and lack of planning.

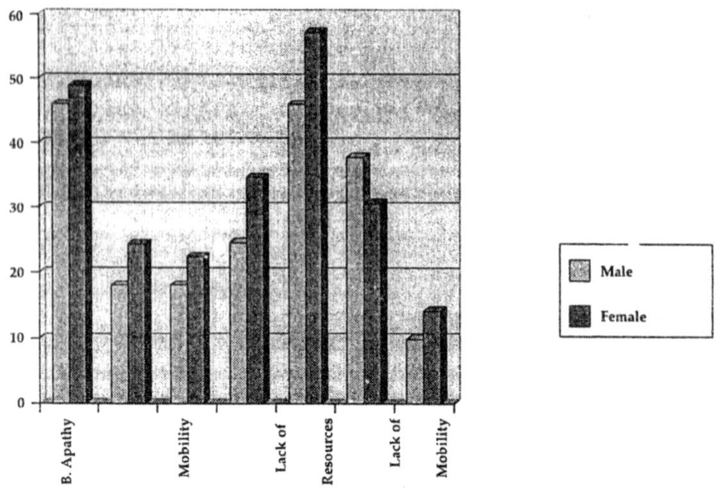

	B. Apathy	*Time cons-traints*	*Mobi-lity*	*Lack of unity*	*Lack of Resou-rces*	*Lack of plan-ning*	*Lack of Mobility*
Male	45.9	18.0	18.0	24.5	45.9	37.7	9.8
Female	48.9	24.4	22.4	34.6	57.14	30.6	14.2

All the facts mentioned in the paper are based on the work done by PRIA and its partners in the states of Haryana, Uttar Pradesh, Madhya Pradesh, Kerala and Rajasthan.

REFERENCES

Women in India How free How equal-UN Report.

Women and Development–The Indian Experience–Mira Nair.

Daughters of 74th Amendment–A study on women elected to municipal bodies in karnal and Delhi-MARG, New Delhi.

Case studies from intervention in the field area.

EMPOWERMENT OF WOMEN : GENDER JUSTICE

Supriya Singh

Women are the vital human infrastructure and their empowerment–economic, educational, social and political would fasten the pace of social development. They are the architect of society. Push the women into the backyards and the society itself will be dragged behind. Unfortunately, even after 54 years of independence, the sensitivity over women's issues are lacking and has still not produced desirable results. Economic independence of women can follow only if they are allowed a larger participatory role in the over all social scenario.[1]

The Department of Women and Child Development under the Ministry of Human Resources Development brought out some facts in its "Platform for Action : Five Years After–An Assessment". It showed that only 49 seats out of 545 seats in the Parliament were held by women in 1999. In 1996, only one out of total 25 judges in the Supreme Court was a woman. Only 3 per cent of the total member of High Court Judges were women.[2] In 1995, the total percentage of woman medical practitioners was 20.8 per cent. The wide variation of women participation in various walks of life indicates that the great potential that is being held on a leash because of several social factors.[3]

---

1. Antony, M.J., Women's Rights 1989 (New Delhi, Clarian Books).
2. Rashtra-Mahila, Vol. 3, October 1999, p. 2.
3. Ahuwalia, Harjeet, Need for Larger participatory Role, Yojana, August 2001, p. 17.

The 1995 Human Development Report pointed out that of the 900 million illiterates in the developing world, women out numbered men, of the 1.3 billion people in poverty, 70 per cent were women. The invisible non-monetised contribution of women to the world output is staggering $ 11 trillion per annum. This can be seen from the following table which shows the picture of GEM (Gender Empowerment Measure) in some countries.

Table 1

Country	*GEM*	*Seats held in Parliament (% women 1994)*	*Administrators (% women 1992)*	*Earners (%)*
Norway	0.752	39.4	25.4	37.8
China	0.474	21.0	11.6	31.2
UAE	0.239	0.0	1.6	6.8
India	0.226	7.3	2.3	19.2
Pakistan	0.153	1.6	2.9	10.2
Sweden	0.757	33.5	38.9	41.6

The table demonstrates conclusively that in all countries women are still unequally placed.[4] Though during the last two decades, the gender gap is narrowed to some extent, the gaps in political and economic participation still remain large.

However, in such a context, the role of the women's self-groups (SHGS) cannot be minimized which are giving examples of micro-level advances towards economic empowerment. Micro Capital Assistance has helped women to free themselves from money lenders. In Orissa, the Agriculture Department is partnering with around 25 NGOs to help women from tribal, landless and marginal families in their food and nutrition security.[5] The success of these prorammes, however, depends strongly on involvement of the participants.

Since seventies the objectives of raising the status of women have also been included in different Five Years Plans. The

4. Human Development Report, 1995.
5. Mahendale Leens, "National Commission for Women–An Appraisal", Yojana, Vol-44, Nov. 2000, p. 33.

Seventh Five Year Plan aimed at human resource development in women. The Eighth Five Year Plan aimed at enabling women to function as equal partners and participants in development The formulation of the National Commission for Women (NCW) and the idea of setting up a National Council for Empowerment of Women are encouraging steps in this direction.[6]

Educational Developments : Goals and Achievements

Empowering women has been a preoccupation with world leaders and conscience keepers over the past so many decades. Education is key to making women self-reliant and giving them the confidence to pursue their goals and achieve success in whichever field they desire.

The fourth World Conference on Women held in Beijing. China in September 1995 emphasised the need to equalize opportunities and status of women vis-à-vis men. A major area where action required, it was felt, was in the promotion of "people–centred sustainable development, including sustained economic growth through the provision of basic education, life long education, literacy and training and primary health care for girls and women".

In urban areas even in India, the mindset has changed to a large extent as cost of living is very high and both the husband and wife have to work to make both the ends meet. In a report brought out by the United Nations called "Women–Challenges to the year 2000", it is remarked that, "Rural societies for their survival are especially resistant to educating them. Rural women tend to have more children, be poorer and in their struggle to survive, have little or no time to spare for adult education. This can be shown from the Census 2001".[7]

---

6. Mazumdar Veena, "Symbol of Power Studies 8th Political Status of Women in India", 1979, Bombay Allied.
7. Jayashuriya Shanti & Jayashuriya D.D., Women & Development–The Road from Beiging, (New Delhi, Har Anand Publications, 1999, p. 19).

Table I : Census 2001

Total Population	–	1,02,70,15,247
Male	–	53,12,77,078
Female	–	49,57,38,169
Boys	–	8,79,11,041
Girls	–	7,59,52,104
Total Literate	–	56,67,14,995
Literate Male	–	33,99,69,048
Literate Female	–	22,67,45,947
Male–Female Ratio	–	1000 : 933

The Government of India has taken numberous measures making honest endeavours to raise the status of women and establish gender equality. It has developed several initiative for guaranteeing education to women, although the size of the population sometimes acts as an impediment. The southern states, which have generally lower population than the northern ones have managed much higher literacy targets. This can be observed from the following table.

Table II : Women Empowerment and Social Development

Women Empowerment Indicators	*Socially Developed State (Kerala)*	*Socially Backward State (Bihar)*	*All India*
Women Literacy	86.20	20.90	39.30
Non-Enrolment of Girl Children	00.00	32.79	29.00
Women Participation in organised Sector	35.58	6.6	14.1
Women Non-Farm employment	58.41	9.11	21.19
Sex-Ratio	1068	956	927
Life Expetancy at birth (Female)	73.80	57.00	59.40

The following steps[8] may help change the socio-economic status of women–

8. G. Khanna & M.A. Varghese, Indian Women Today (New Delhi, Vikas, 1978), p. 91.

1. Universalization of elementary education.
2. Ensuring opportunities to all women for access to appropriate level.
3. Substrantial vocationalization and diversification of secondary education so as to provide a wide scope for employment.
4. Making education an effective means for women's equality.
5. Impetus to enroll in various professional degree courses.

Women's Reservation Bill and the Constitution

The political empowerment of women is crucial not only for the development of women themselves but the availability of their creative potential is socially important and essential for any sustainable development.

While in the urban areas, the post independence, has witnessed the entry of women in the fields of medicine, administration, science and law the life of rural women have not undergone any change. The Constitution's 73rd and 74th Amendments changed the social scenario when they provided for reservation for women in Panchayats and Municipalities. These acts came into force in April, 1993 and mandated not less than 1/3 reservation for women. Reservations have been provided for women not only at the members levels but also at the level of chair person.

The political empowerment of women resulting from the these Constitution Amendments has had impact in two socio-political areas. Firstly, there is a visible impovement in the administration and delivery of services at the grassfoot level mainly, because of greater focus on the felt needs of the people, greater transparency and greater reliance on horizontal linkages. Secondly the Amendments have made possible the creation of political identification which has enabled women to gain social status.

However, women are not adequately represented in the Parliament. It could be remarked that although the recent years have witnessed an increase in women voters, it has not been accompanied by number of women occupying decision making positions. Keeping this in mind, in December, 1999 under the Vajpayee Government, the Union Law Minister introduced the historic 85th Constitution Amendment Bill seeking to reserve 33 per cent seats for women in the Parliament which is considering the issue.[9]

In conclusion of the basis of above survey, we find that until the women get rid of their mental slavery, regain self confidence, get over fear of society and become economically independent, they cannot aspire for freedom. Upliftment of women must be attempted on a global scale.[10] A bill coming from the UNDP paper on human development authored by Dr. Mahbub ul Haq has electrified the human thinking by suggesting that in the present millennium, fully 50 p.c. of all jobs in the organized sector should properly go to women, ending the unfair bias against women.[11]

9. Sharma Roopa, "Women's Reservation : A Crisis of Identity, "The Indian Governal of Public Administration, Vol. KLVII, No. 1, January, 201, pp. 57-66.

10. Gender Guest Laws Bulletin, No. 4, Dec. 1998, p. 10.

11. "Unfair Bias", Times of India, (New Delhi), Aug. 26, 1995.

WOMEN EMPOWERMENT IN URBAN GOVERNANCE

Rashmi Sinha

We have celebrated the year 2001 as Year for Empowerment of Women. This gave us an opportunity to engage ourselves in a serious deliberations to identify the existing system of social, economic, administrative and political support available to the women as a class and in the process several policy intervention, strategy and programme for empowering the women was initiated at various levels. The present venture is a step in right direction to analyse and consolidate this process. The focus, however, is urban administration in the context of political empowerment to women granted under the 74th Constitution Amendment.

At the outset, it is important to have a quick look on the status of women in India. In theory, women have been placed on the highest pedestal of social and religious levels. We, the women, are supposed to be goddess, the incarnation of compassion, provider of food and destroyer of evil. Yes, India is a great paradox and so is with regard to the status of women. Our social mind set has never been free from discrimination against women, right from the birth. I am deliberately not touching the situation before birth as you all know how unwelcome is a female feutus. And yet the paradox is that Indian women running her households have been rated as the best managers as all ingredients of the management principles are imbibed in the Indian housewife.

Ever since the Five Year Plans were launched, the concern for the women has undoubtedly engaged the attention of the planners and the authority as is evident from the thrust it received which from first to fourth Five Year Plans was enforcement of welfare activities with a priority to women education. From Fifth to Seventh Plan period there was shift in the approach from welfare to overall development of women. The Eighth Plan was the most significant as the shift went further from development to women's empowerment. It has been undisputedly accepted now that unless the whole policy making process involves women in the ultimate decision making at all levels and stages, changes in women's social, economical and political status will continue to be marginal.

The political empowerment now being enjoyed by the women under the 73rd and 74th Amendments to Constitution can achieve the desired objectives only when one appreciates the reasons of the chronic blockages of women empowerment and some of these can be counted as:

- Patriarchal social system
- Social and Cultural prejudices
- Financial dependence of women
- Lack of exposure to political power
- Family and childcare responsibilities
- Discriminating attitude
- Criminalisation of politics

In the present context, a persuasive approach through mass communication techniques together with involvement of social and family groups will have to be worked out through collective efforts of all concerned. The 74th Amendment to the Indian Constitution is to promote an effective system of urban local self government. Art. 243W envisages to endow the "Municipalities with such powers and authority as may be necessary to enable them to function as institutions of self-government". The emphasis has now been shifted from "governance" to "good governance" which essentially establishes the relationship of the state with civil society, participation, non-government as well as community based organizations and the focused groups. Good governance entitles participation of stakeholders in formulation and implementation of local plans and policies. Good governance through its participatory approach enhances transparency, effectiveness, efficiency, responsiveness, accountability and equity.

These are the ingredients which represent the bible for the formulation of sustainable developmental strategies and programmes right from the level of urban governance to the requirements of the 1992 Earth Summit through Agenda 21.

Participation, consultation and partnership are ingredients to 'process' which works if there is an appropriate 'structure'. The success of the process crucially depends on the types of functions performed which is the determining factor for empowerment. It is this crucial distinction where the participation of women in the management of Urban Administration is significant. In this context, the empowered women participants are likely to contribute significantly more in certain specific areas pertaining to 12th Schedule such as:

- Planning for economic and social development
- Urban forestry, protection of environment and promotion of ecological aspects
- Safe guarding the interest of weaker section of the society including handicapped and mentally retarded
- Slum improvement and upgradation
- Promotion of cultural, educational and aesthetical aspects
- Prevention of cruelty to animals.

The performance of some states where urban governance under 74th Amendment of Constitution has been enforced for 6-7 years now has shown very satisfactory results. For example, in Andhra Pradesh, where the Municipal Administration Department took the initiative to enable the urban local bodies to entrust some of the basic functions to community based organizations and also to involve women's group in participatory urban governance, the government playing the role of facilitator rather than that of provider. After a survey of all urban poor households in 1998, local governments in 116 towns were facilitated the formation of Community Based Organisations of urban poor women. These C.B.Os. are grass root level organizations and conducting programmes which have far reaching positive impact on Society. They have adopted a 3-tier organizational structure, which are:

1. Neighbourhood group
2. Neighbourhood Committees
3. Community Development Society

All these three levels have different responsibilities and duties. After formation of the community groups, Regional Conferences have been organized to facilitate interaction of women functionaries with the functionaries of Municipal Administration and Local Government. Regular discussions and meetings of community groups facilitate a proper understanding of the objective and philosophy among women. Again, community based organizations formed are also entrusted with social audit functions in their respective towns or localities in the integrated low cost sanitation activities, which involve provision of subsidy and loan.

Such innovative models are required to be developed and implemented in other states including Bihar.

WOMEN EMPOWERMENT : RETROSPECT AND PROSPECT

I.C. Thakur

Women are the creation of God who helped develop this world in present form. According to Hindu mythology Shradha and Manu were the first couple on the earth. Manu alone could not have started the reproductive cycle without Shradha. Without women's active participation this civilization could not have been possible. There are instances where the importance given to mother was more compared to father. Mary gave birth to a child alone, who become Jesus Christ. Most of the religions have given very high position to women—Hindus workship Durga, Parvati, Lakshmi, Saraswati as Goddess, Christians pray to Mother Mary. In society mother is treated as incarnation of God. With mother's blessings every success can be achieved. Women were so important that many literatures were written on them, such as on Padmavati, Mirabai, Ahilyabai etc.

Status of Women in Society

In ancient time the social customs and patterns prevalent in Aryan society tells that women were treated at par with men. They took part in all religious rites. Women were given education and there were women scholars who composed hymns and were well-versed in the secred scriptures. Girls had freedom in the choice of their husbands. Monogamy was the usual practice, though polygamy was also practiced by many people. Women attended all the social functions and gatherings.

There are evidences that in ancient period some women had decision making power in society. Padma, the princess of Kalinga fought a war in 261 B.C. Between the middle of the 7th century, to the end of the 12th century A.D. when Rajput rulers controlled the destiny of India, Rajput women were well known for their lofty ideals with regard to their duties as wives and mothers. They were deeply devoted to their husbands. They possessed tremendous courage and never wavered in choosing death rather than had their chastity and womenhood dishonoured. Sometimes the Rajput women accompanied their husbands to the battlefield to fight against the enemy. They used to fight till they died, instead of surrendering to their foes, such was their courage and valour in battle.

Women in ancient time enjoyed great freedom. They were allowed to chose their husbands. Women received proper education and cultivated excellence in the fine arts like painting and music. Some became great scholars whilst others acquired proficiency in the art of administration and warfare.

In thirteenth century Raziya Sultan (1236-1240 AD) became the ruler of Delhi. However, there was a great change during middle ages. Even common human rights of women were gradually usurped.

In 1857 Rani Lakshmi Bai become the ruler of Janshi and fought with the Britishers.

Social Reforms

Raja Ram Mohan Roy rendered great service in the emancipation of women, by fighting against the prevalent evil practices. In pre-independent India, hardly any laws were passed to ameliorate the condition of women. The British Government deliberately did not legislate in the area of personal or family law on the plea of non-interference. Nowhere laws were passed to improve the conditions of work of working women. Only a few piece-meal legislations were passed in response to social demands and humanitarian consideration. A few such examples are law regarding the Bengal Sati Regulation of 1829 and similar Anti-Sati Laws in Madras and

Bombay. The Hindu Widows Remarriage Act, 1856, was an important social reform legislation which sought to improve the plight of widows. Another landmark legislation was the Hindu Women's Right to property Act in 1937. Actually, The British policy with regard to women and family laws was not one of reform and change.

Government Efforts in Independent India

In independent India, many laws seeking improvement in women's status were enacted. The Constitution of India which seeks to establish India as a democratic and socialist republic, for the first time guaranteed equality for women the addition, fine fear aim also processed women development. During the first Five Year Plan (1951-1956) the Community Development Programme (CDP) was launched. The objective of CDP was to improve the health of women and children. In the year 1954-55 it was observed that women's lack of participation in CDP was, to a large extent, responsible for the programme not having its desired impact. Hence, for the first time women were included in the programmes as target group and women village Sevikas were appointed in each Community Development Block. Women's programmes primarily gave the understanding that the home is the basic unit of the community and women's role is that of the homemaker.

Though the welfare approach to women's issues persisted during the Second Five year Plan (1956-61), but the emphasis was on speedy implementation of the principle of equal pay for equal work and provision of facilities for training which were to be included to enable women to complete for higher jobs. During the Third Five Year Plan (1961-1966), the basic concept of women's development and their role in society remained unchanged. For girls' education a programme was started with the assistance from UNICEF. In the Fourth Plan (1969-1974), the emphasis continued to be on women's education and family planning. Priority was given to immunization of pre-school children and supplementary feeding for children, expectant and nursing mothers. The Fifth Plan (1974-1979), made a marginal departure from the earlier plans. It emphasized the need to train women in need of income and protection. It also recommended a programme of functional literacy to equip women with skills and knowledge to perform the functions of a housewife. The Sixth (1980-85), and Seventh (1986-90) Five year Plans have become a watershed as the question of women's development had been viewed entirely from a new perspective. The shift was brought in by the Declaration of Women's Decade by the United Nation and the excruciating factors revealed by the Committee on the Status of Women in India (CSWI) Report. The CSWI Report led to a debate in Parliament and this resulted in women's role being viewed as critical input for national development rather than a target of social welfare policies. The Seventh Five Year Plan (1986-90), supposedly operationalised the concern for equity and empowerment articulated by the International Decade for Women. The emphasis was slightly more qualitative. Thus it pointed toward the need for inculcating confidence among women, generating awareness about their rights and privileges and the need for training them for economic activity and employment. The Plan emphasized the need to open new avenues of work for women. The Eighth Five Year Plan (1992-97) paid main focus on human (including woman) development, which brought radical change in women's confidence. The ninth Five Year Plan (1997-2002), is known for Empowerment of Women.

As a result improvements are seen in family as well as in the society. Women are performing at par with men. No field is untouched by them. They are working in the field of Science and Technology, Medical Science, Defence, Civil Aviation, Sports etc. In Government bodies their representation is also sizeable. But diversity of achievement in seen on regional basis.

Present Situation

Indian villages are still lagging in facilities like schools, colleges, health centers, tele-communications etc. Many villages are not connected with any road whereas many more are connected with kutcha roads. Due to lack of basic facilities the improvement in condition of rural women is not in equal as compared to urban women. Bihar has always remained a predominantly agricultural state. Even today, in this age of technological and industrial advancement more than eighty per cent of the population depends directly on agriculture and allied activities for their livelihood.

Women constitute about half of the population therefore, their contribution in agricultural activities would have significant share. Their contribution in decision making needs to be reviewed after implementation of so many programmes by the Government both at state and central level.

Role of Women in Agriculture and Their Contribution

Rural women play an important role in agriculture as well as animal husbandry. They perform operations such as sowing, harvesting, threshing, sorting, cultivation of vegetables, raising of nursery, plucking of vegetables, picking of cotton, harvesting of maize, bajra, jowar, storage of grains, cutting and chaffing of fodder, feeding animals, washing of animals and cleaning of sheds treating of sick animals and also milking of animals. Further more, boiling of milk, processing and preparing milk products such as butter, ghee and cheese are also performed by the rural women.

Some historians of agriculture believed that it was women who first domesticated crop plants and thereby initiated the art and science of farming. And till today, Agriculture is largely in the hands of women. Rural women participate in every gainful activities. She spent 30-40 per cent of her working time in agricultural activities in rainy season and nearly same time in her household activities. During harvesting period, she works almost for a whole day in the farm. However, it varies from region to region.

The farming community in India comprises of three groups: male farmers, women farmers and young farmers (both young boys and girls). It has been estimated that second group alone i.e. women farmer perform more than 60 percent of farm activities. Growing marginalization of agricultural holding has further increased their major source of employment and livelihood of majority of rural women in India. The critical role played by rural women in agriculture has gone up manifolds and has become so visible that it cannot be ignored any more.

According to an assessment for one hectare farm, women work on an average 640 hours for intercultural operation like weeding, 384 hours for irrigation, 150 hours for transplanting, organic manures and seed sowing and 984 hours for harvesting and threshing. Her total work of 2158 hours in a year is more than the combined work of man who works for 1212 hours and a pair of bullock which works for 1064 hours.

The majority of the rural women in India, as well as in other developing countries, actively participate in farm related operations, besides fulfilling their responsibilities as homemakers. The extent of participation, however, varies depending on the socio-economic and cultural background of the area. Pearson (1979) has classified the role of the farm women into the following four categories:

1. Independent producer–who manage the farm largely by themselves;
2. Agricultural partner–who share most of the aspects of works, responsibilities and decision making with their husbands;
3. Agricultural helper–who only participate in farm work at busy times when extra help is needed; and,
4. Farm home-maker–who contribute to the farm production indirectly by preparing meals and attending those working in the fields. Women in agricultural families perform many farm-related activities both within and out side the households, in most parts of country. They constitute a large part of the total work force in agriculture, although the pattern of division of labour between men and women varies greatly from region to region, Women are involved in most of the operations in agriculture, including subsidiary enterprises like dairy, poultry, bee-keeping, mushroom cultivation, sericulture, fish culture, rabbit rearing, social forestry, etc.

So far crop husbandry is concerned, women participate in almost all activities, right from preparatory tillage to harvest and even in post harvest tasks like processing, storage and marketing. Ploughing is perhaps the only exception. Seed cleaning, seed grading, sowing, bidding, planting, weeding, harvesting, threshing, shelling, hulling, winnowing, feeding cattle and looking after milk animals and poultry birds are the main jobs attended by women. Activities such as processing and storage at home are performed exclusively by women.

Despite their importance in agriculture production, role of women has not been recognized fully. They are in fact the largest group of Indian labours with little security in case of break up of the family or divorces. The time has come for change in our thinking and we have to provide women they deserve considering their role in agriculture and economic development of the nation.

Women's Status in the Industrial Sector

Women's employment in the industrial sector is low. Manufacturing accounts for a considerable proportion of women's employment. But even here the vast majority of women manufacturing workers are engaged in rural household industry. Women's participation in modern urban industrial sector is quite limited. Even in 1981, 86 per cent of women manufacturing workers were concentrated in food processing, textiles and textile products, wood and wood products and ceramics. Not any women have been able to move into the new sectors of industry. In areas where women's employment may have registered a slight increase, it is confined to areas like silk, wool and synthetic fibre industry or in food processing. Even this has been possible because of the growth of the putting – out system which enables women to work in the household but does not give them the status of full time workers and thus denying of some of the benefits which the full-time workers in the organized sectors enjoy. Several studies on the impact of development policies and modernization on women's economic participation have observed a marked decline in the share of women's employment in traditional economic activities. There

Role of Women in Different Cultivation Operations (Participation of women in different operations whether exclusively or along with men)

Sr.No	*Name of Crop*	*Role of Men(%)*	*Role of Women(%)*
(A)	**Agricultural Operations**		
1	Land ploughing with plough	100	–
2	Land preparation and clod breaking	50	50
3	Sowing with seed drill	70	30
4	Sowing with hand sowing	20	80
5	Gap filing	–	100
6	Transplanting of seedling	10	90
7	Weeding	10	90
8	Interculturing	50	50
9	Irrigation	50	50
10	Fertilizer application	50	50
11	Harvesting of crop	70	30
12	Thresing and winnowing	40	60
13	Plant protection	80	20
14	Seed Storage	50	50
15	Seed treatment	50	50
16	Preparation of seed for sowing	10	90
17	Marketing, selling& purchase of seeds	100	–

Contd....

(Contd...)

Sr.No	*Name of Crop*	*Role of Men(%)*	*Role of Women(%)*
18	Agriculture production drying, cleaning and storages	10	90
19	Manuring preparation	10	90
20	Ficking of vegetables	10	90
21	Preparation of seeding of vegetable crops	10	90
22	Preparation of farm yard manuring	10	90
(B)Animal Husbandary			
1	Cleaning shed	–	100
2	Refuse disposal	–	100
3	Fodder collection for animals	20	80
4	Feeding of animals	10	90
5	Grazing of animals	50	50
6	Milking of animals	10	90
7	Sale of Milk	20	80
8	Animal Health	25	75
9	Breeding of animal	50	50
10	Sale or purchase of new Animal	70	30

has been no increase in their share of participation in the modern sectors of the economy; and there is hardly any evidence to suggest that the relative earnings of women in industry have improved substantially. The attempt to revive the declining village and cottage industries to cope with the effective demand for employment has done precious little.

Women Literacy

According to draft report of census 2001 the average literacy rate for women is 54.16 per cent on national basis. The Kerala is on top with 87.86 per cent where as Bihar is at bottom with 33.57 per cent. Amongst Union Territories, Lakshdwip is on top and Dadra and Nagar Haweli is on bottom. Chandigarh is next to Lakshdwip.

The Empowerment of Women

Commission on Population and Development acting as the preparatory committee for the special session of the General Assembly for the review and appraisal of the implementation of the Programme of Action of the International Conference on Population and Development held on 24, 25, 28 and 29 June 1999 in its Agenda item 3 proposed :

1. Governments should establish mechanisms to accelerate women's equal participation and equitable representation at all levels of the political process and public life in each community and society and enable women articulate their concerns and needs and ensure the full and equal participation of women in decision making processes in all spheres of life. Governments and civil society should take actions to eliminate attitudes and practices that discriminate against and subordinate girls and women and that reinforce gender inequality.

2. Governments should take measures to promote that fulfillment of girls' and women's potential through education, skills development and the eradication of illiteracy for all girls and women without discrimination of any kind, giving paramount importance to the

elimination of poverty and ill-health. Governments in collaboration with civil society, should take the necessary measures to ensure universal access on the basis of equality between women and men, to appropriate, affordable and quality health care for women throughout their life cycle.

3. Governments should take every possible action to remove all gender gaps and inequalities pertaining to women's livelihoods and participation in the labour market through the creation of employment with secure incomes which has been shown to advance women's empowerment and enhance their reproductive health. Legislation ensuring equal pay for equal work should be instituted and enforced.

4. A gender perspective should be adopted in all processes of policy formulation and implementation and in the delivery of services, especially in sexual and reproductive health, including family planning. In this regard, the institutional capacity and expertise of staff in government, civil society, including non-governmental organizations, and the United Nations system should be strengthened in order to promate gender mainstreaming. This should be done by sharing tools, methodologies and lessons learned in order to develop and strengthen their capacity and institutionalize effective strategies for gender–based analysis and gender mainstreaming. This includes the development and availability of gender-disaggregated data and appropriate indicators for monitoring progress at the national level.

5. The differential impact on women and men of globalization of the economy and the privatization of basic social services, particularly reproductive health services, should be monitored closely. Special programmes and institutional mechanisms should be put in place to promote and protect the health and well-being of young girls, older women and other vulnerable

groups. The provision of services to meet men's reproductive and sexual health needs should not prejudice reproductive and sexual health services for women.

6. Governments should give priority to develop programmes and policies that foster norms and attitudes of zero tolerance for harmful and discriminatory attitudes, including son preference which can result in harmful and unethical practices such as prenatal sex selection, discrimination and violence against the girl child and all forms of violence against women, including female genital mutilation, rape, incest, trafficking, sexual violence and exploitation. This entails developing an integrated approach that addresses the need for widespread social, cultural and economic change, in addition to legal reforms. The girl child's access to health, nutrition, education and life opportunities should be protected and promoted. The role of family members, especially parents and other legal guardians, in strengthening self–image, self–esteem and status and in protecting the health and well–being of girls should be enhanced and supported.

Government's Efforts

Development thinking has a perceptible shift towards people–centred programmes. All the Five Year Plans in India gave a special place to women ranging from welfare to development and now from development to empowerment. It is essential that people and communities participate in the process of development and bring about desirable change. They should be in a position to take decisions concerning their lives.

The Ninth Five Year Plan (1997-2002) spells out certain measures as means to women's empowerment. It seeks reservation of not less than one third seats for women in Parliament and State Legislative Assemblies. Existing services, resources, infrastructure and manpower in women specific and women related sectors are to be converged. All schemes and projects of rural development have to have women's component which is not less than 30 percent, so also the benefits that accrue from the schemes should be for women. Organizing self-help groups in order to empower women economically and as development parameters to gets priority in scheme of things.

Equipping women and girls with education and necessary skills and increasing access to credit for women entrepreneurs are also among the strategies for women's development.

There are a number of poverty alleviation programmes with specified women's component designed for rural areas because it is economic empowerment which is a first step towards a developed society. Broadly these programmes have following objectives :

1. Self-employment through credit and training;
2. Wage employment during lean agriculture season;
3. Enccouraging savings habit and facilitating revolving fund;
4. Providing support services and meeting minimum needs like nutrition, health, sanitation, housing and education; and
5. Awareness generation regarding status of women and girl child in society.

Self-employment programmes meant for rural people below the poverty line have 30 to 40 per cent component for women. Swarna Jayanti Gram Swrozgar Yojana (SASY) covers all aspects of self employment like self-help groups, training, credit, technology, infrastructure and marketing. Apart from exclusive women groups, women are encouraged to be part of all self-help groups.

New Goals : New Initiatives

Following are some of the policy missions initiated for empowering the women :

- Year 2001 declared as Women's Empowerment year and various activities and programmes launched nation wide.

- A National Policy for the Empowerment of Women with the objective of bringing about advancement, development and empowerment of women in all walks of life has been formulated.
- Stree Shakti Puraskars named after five eminent women namely Devi Ahilya Bai Holkar, Rani Lakshmi Bai, Mata Ji Jabi, Rani Gaidinliu Zeliang and Kannagi to honour and recognize the achievement and contribution of individual women and institutions who have done outstanding work in social sector have been constituted and presented.
- Guidelines for operationalisation of District Level Committees on violence against women and Helplines for women in distress have been issued.
- A national level committee to monitor Supreme Court's Guidelines on prevention of sexual harassment of women at work place has been set up.
- A tele-conference between parliamentarians and women at the grass roots to establish a dialogue between policy makers and grass roots level functionaries has been organized.
- Training-Cum-Employment Programme for women receive a significant boost during the year 2001. A record number of new projects under Women's Economic Programme (NORAD) were sanctioned and 25650 women were trained in different traditional and non-traditional trades.
- 12 new projects under Support & Training for Employment (STEP) were sanctioned in the year 2001-2002 and 48550 poor and asset-less women were trained in agriculture, dairy farming, handloom, handicraft etc. and subsequent organized in co-operative societies for carrying profitable economic ventures.
- A distance education programme for functionaries working in the field of women empowerment, a

collaborative project between DWCD, IGNOU and ISRO was launched.

- The Department initiated a gender budgeting exercise. For the first time, a chapter on gender inequality was incorporated in the Annual Economic Survey. A gender analysis of the Budget 2001-2002 has been carried out.
- Initiated measures for preparing Gender Developmental Index for the States and Districts.
- For the first time the Finance Ministry consulted women's representatives as part of its pre-budget (2002-2003) exercise.
- Swayamsidha, an integrated scheme for women's empowerment, based on the formation of women into Self-Help Groups (SHG's), aims at holistic empowerment of women through awareness generation, economic empowerment and convergence of various schemes. It is to be implemented in 650 blocks benefiting 9.30 lakh women.
- Swa-Shakti Project, a World Bank and International Fund for Agricultural Development Support Project, is being implemented in 35 districts of 7 States. 91 NGOs have already formed 9000 Women's Self-Help Groups.
- 29 Working Women's Hostels have been sanctioned with Day Care facilities benefiting 61564 women.
- Comprehensive review of legislation affecting women undertaken by sub groups formed under the Task Force on Women & Children.
- India hosted a Gender Training Assessment Meeting for National Machineries of the Asia Pacific Region in November 1999.
- Sixth Meeting of Commonwealth Ministers responsible for Women's Affairs was organized in April 2000.
- India participated in the UN General Assembly Special Session on Beijing + 5 held in New York in June 2000.

- Government has decided to give annual awards to selected anganwadi workers on the basis of exemplary performance.
- A new initiative, 'Kishori Shakti Yojana' is being implemented in 2000 blocks throughout the country.
- Balika Samridhi Yojana has been revised to provide for a post-delivery grant of Rs. 500/- to be deposited in a interest bearing account in the name of girl child. In addition, the girl child will become eligible to annual scholarships for each successfully completed year of schooling.
- A National Session for Women is building consensus against female foeticide and declining sex ratio–by organizing a meeting of religious and community leaders. NCW has launched an ambitious programme to inculcate gender values amongst college students. Laws relating to women are being reviewed. A National Nutrition Mission will be launched shortly to break the intergenerational cycle of malnutrition that affects women and children.
- Rashtriya Mahila Kosh facilitates provisions of micro credit to poor women for income generating activities through a network of social organizations. More than Rs. 104 crore has been sanctioned since inception out of which Rs. 77.8 crore has been distributed benefiting about 4 lack women.
- National Institute of Public-Co-operation & Child Development (NCPCCD) is a premier organization devoted to promotion of voluntary action and research, training and documentation in the overall domain of women and children development and will be developed as a centre of excellence.
- Central Social Welfare Board organizes vocational

training programmes for widows of victims of communal riots and terrorism. It also organizes counseling programmes on pre-marital issues in colleges and universities.

POLITICAL EMPOWERMENT OF WOMEN : MYTH AND REALITY

Tanuja Singh

The year 2001 has been celebrated as the "Year for Empowerment of Women" in India. This has called for a number of determined efforts for the upliftment of the status of women who constitute half of our population. In this regard the 73rd and 74th Constitution Amendments which make provision for reservation for women is a glorious epitome of political empowerment of women at the grassroot level. These amendments envisage the introduction of Panchayati Raj System throughout the country and reservation of one third seats for women in Panchayati and Municipal bodies. Thus it has been tried to ensure democratic decentralization with a step to accomplish gender justice in political participation.

Notwithstanding the fact that there have been important changes in the legislation for women still they continue to be discriminated because many of the acts made for them are bereft of teeth. But the other view is for voluntary commitment rather than legislative coercion. In countries like Sweden and Netherland women are very active specially in local institutions. In Sweden, the Social Democratic Party, the left party and the Green Party have committed themselves to 40 per cent seats for women. In the Netherland, it varies from 26 per cent, in the Christian Democratic Party to 33 per cent in the Social Party.[1]

However, the Indian Bill for the empowerment of women is not flawless. The lottery system of gender based reservation for women is likely to lead a fresh set of constituencies at every election, leading to unpredictability. The rotating constituency for women already implemented at the Zila Parishad level, has resulted in destroying women's incentive to build any constituency. The women will become totally dependent on their political party rather that identifying with any particular constituency for building it systematically. That's why the Indian Election Commission has called for voluntary reservation for women by the political parties.

The recognition of the right of every citizen is the basic requirement of democracy. The cardinal goal of democracy of the people, for the people by the people therefore, can't be accomplished if the fifty per cent of the population remains out of political participation.[2]

Notwithstanding the myth going around "Gods are pleased, If women are worshipped". Women are the objects of faith and devotion, but hardly are equal to men in civic and political matters. In theory women have been placed on the highest pedestal of social and religious levels giving them the three most important departments of Vidya (wisdom) Dhan (wealth) and Shakti (power) to goddess Saraswati, Laxmi and Durga respectively. But India is a great paradox so far as the status of women is concerned. The "Architect of their homes" and "Grih Laxmi" are no better than "Abla Nari". From the very beginning the domain of women was home and her traditional role was home-making as a wife, mother, sister or daughter. Even for educated women family was more natural and fundamental and family obligations were more sanctified for them than men. Unfortunately the Indian mindset is still largely against the progress and advancement of women. Education of urban women, in most of the cases simply amounts to a means of making a better marriage. And the housewives never get the credit for their work.[3] A male presence is deemed essential in women's life as renowned journalist Fatima Narohma has rightly remarked that "the bottom line of our Indian ethos is that woman is worthless without her husband."

So far as the empowerment of women is concerned the political participation of them is crucial not only for the development of women themselves but the availability of their creative potential is socially important and essential for any sustainable development of the society as a whole. However, women's right to vote was first demanded by Mrs. Sarojini Naidu as early as in 1917 itself although women even in England had no such right at that time. The Swiss women got it in 1970 only. The Constitution of India has guaranteed the equal social, economic and political rights to all women along with the men. Yet statistical reality stands against the myth. Women simply have not moved beyond the ballot boxes into local and national life. That too the recorded turn out of women for voting has been increased but even in 1996 it was 47.75% as against 52.25% for men. The women occupying the higher office are generally elites. Representation of women in the parliament has never increased from 8 per cent to 10 per cent. This is not because women are restricted from entering into politics but the reason is that there are some hinderances that blockade the ways to their political participation i.e. social and cultural prejudices, financial dependence on others, lack of exposure to political powers and criminalisation of politics etc.

In Indian society having the patriarchal families, a girl during her childhood, is dependent on her father or brother and is not permitted to develop her own identity. From infancy, girls are taught that they must make a good marriage.

Never is she permitted an identity of her own. Instead she must always be an extension of the male in her life, be it her father, brother, husband or son. In other words, she is secondary citizen. While money is spent on a boy's education, the girl child receives jewellery. Since she is not expected to earn her own living to support herself, serious education is often viewed as a frivolity.

This isn't to say that all women in India besides the privileged few are doomed. India, like the rest of the world, is making progress in terms of securing women's position in society. For example, with the effect of globalisation a middle class has emerged in India. This middle class is the most progressive section of Indian Society. Women belonging to this stratum are normally well-educated and career-oriented.

They are expected to help make a living while juggling the chores at home, including taking care of the children.

These women should be looked upon as role models and admired for what they have achieved. Most offices these days boast of women employees, and unlike in the past they occupy higher positions. It is a struggle for these women to move ahead. But at least they have the opportunity and are striving towards professions outside their homes.

Rural women have also advanced in certain areas. Organisations have been set up to promote cottage industries like weaving and handicrafts which largely employ women. These women are able to work without leaving their homes and villages. It is essential not to ignore this progress of women in India even while looking at the mammoth struggle that still lies ahead for the majority.

There may not be feminist revolution in India but slowly and steadily women are changing their own position in society. It's better to struggle but some day India will truly be a democracy, and not just for the rich and male population, but for every citizen.

The SAARC Decade of the Girl Child, which got ceremonially rolled out in 1991, had its close in 2000 A.D. In what is believed to have been a giant step forward to enhance women's participation in the political process. We in India have already reserved one-third of the seats in local body elections for women, right from the village panchayats to districts panchayats. We are, in fact, all but poised to cap these efforts to enthrone the Eves of our land by reserving one-third of the seats in the Lok Sabha. We even have National Women's Commission. It is no mean achievement that this land of ours has boasted of a charismatic women Prime Minister even before we celebrated International Women's Year. Women have scaled the Mount Everest. Women managers have soared up to no less admirable pinnacles of professional success.

Has the Bharatiya Nari finally arrived? Have we accorded woman her rightful pride of place in society? Do we treat our women at least as human beings, just as much as we consider our menfolk to be? Or do we, in spite of all our platitudinous pronouncements about women's rights, still consider women as objects of sexual exploitation and enjoyment, or as more housekeepers, deep down in the subsconcious recesses of our national psyche?

We have practiced female infanticide right from the time of British rule. More than a century ago, a law banning female infanticide was enacted, and made applicable to the North-West Frontier, Punjab and Oudh provinces. But even today, out of 1.2 crore baby girls born in our country every year, 30 lakhs or nearly 25 per cent, do not live to see their 15th birthday. At least one in six female deaths has been estimated by sociologists to be due to the bias against women. In the Katihar district of Bihar alone, 1,200 newly born baby girls are killed on an average every year. While poor people kill their female infants soon after they are born, the affluent classes determine the sex of the foetus in the womb and resort to female foeticide.[4]

According to the survey conducted in 1988, by the Inter Parliamentary Union in 106 countries, women's representation in National Assemblies was 15 per cent which was reduced to only 11 per cent in 1995. During the period from July 1995 to January, 1997 in 179 countries the general elections to their parliaments were held and in those elections percentage of elected woman parliamentarians was 0.04 per cent only.[5]

In a country like America where they talk much about women status, they have so far not elected any woman as their President. England, which is known as the mother of democracy has 5 to 10 per cent members in the House of Commons. Even during the prime ministership of iron lady Margaret Thacher there was not much improvement in women's representation in the House of Commons. It was the Labour Party of Tony Blair who fielded many women in 1977 elections and the Party got overwhelming support of women voters.

If we examine the political representation of women in different countries of the world the data is very depressing.

In America it is 11.07 per cent, in France it is 6.04 per cent and in Japan, here 90 per cent people are highly educated and the literacy rate is 100 per cent, the representation is only 4.04 per cent. Obviously in a country like India where literacy rate among women is 39.00 per cent only and our literacy rate means to write and read a few sentences only and thus nothing more can be expected from them.

However, after 1993 women's participation in Panchayats and Municipalities have increased (73rd and 74th Constitution Amendments). Further the "Women Reservation Bill" proposing 33 present reservation for the women in parliament could be a landmark in the political empowerment of women but the hard reality is that no political party wants to set aside 33 per cent seats for women even though they show enthusiasm for the Bill.[6]

The matter is now too far politicized, the backward class women in parliament however, have demanded separate quota for MPs. The argument placed by them is that with a blanket reservation the upper caste women would corner all the party tickets and get supremacy in parliament.

Actually the right way of providing more representation to women in parliament will be to nominate more and more women as candidates to parliament election. All the political parties should keep some quota for women when they nominate the candidates, instead of spreading the culture of reservation.

Panchayat Elections and Women in Bihar : 2002

However, the empowerment of women has largely remained an empty slogan in India and especially in Bihar even though it had a woman Chief Minister Mrs. Rabri Devi. Now we must appreciate the 33 per cent reservation of seats for womens in the coming urban local bodies election after 18 years in the state (April 28 and 30, 2002) which carries the potential of bringing women to the forefront of public life.

The state election commission's announcement declaring 19 out of the total of 49 Patna Municipal Corporation wards as reserved for women candidates has effectively ensured that female councillors will grace the newly elected municipal body of the state capital in substantial numbers.

Out of the total 1,075 candidates contesting the PMC poll 389 are women. But can that really ensure the empowerment of women because what the Hindustan Times survey has revealed is that most of the women candidates are a dummy for their husbands or close relatives, who are doing everything from filling up the forms to submitting expenditure details. In fact, an over riding factor is that many of them have had to step out of their homes into the election primarily to accomplish the political aspirations of their close male relatives.[7]

Thus, inspite of a number of constitutional provisions, legislative enactments and amendments, there has not been perceptible change in the status of women in India especially in Bihar. But now things may begin to change if the early promises made by the representatives of democracy are kept alive. Above all everything depends on the willingness, determination, enlightenment and self motivation on the part of women themselves. Late Mrs. Gandhi's slogan of "दूर दृष्टि पक्का इरादा" (foresight and determination) has to be followed strictly. Women with 33 per cent seats reserved in the municipal elections have a golden chance to storm the hitherto male bastion. Will they be able to grab the opportunity or will it remain mere window dressing for democracy only time will tell.

REFERENCES

G. Almond, "Political Participation" in G. Almond (ed.) *Comparative Politics Today*–A world view, 1974, Little Brown and Company, Boston, p. 59.

Usha Narayan, "Women's Political Impowerment : Imperatives & Challenges", *Mainstream,* April 10, 1999, p. 1-2.

Prof. Bishwanath Singh "The Human Rights Covenant and the Indian Social Policy" *The Indian Journal of Social Work,* Vol. XXVI, No. 1, April-June, 1964, p. 57-58.

Wendy Kaminer, "Feminism's Identity Crisis," *The Atlantic Monthly,* (USA) Oct. 1993, p. 51-52.

Kay Mills, "The Media and the year of the women" –*Media studies Journal,* Winter/Spring, 1998, USA 19.

Roopa Sharma, "The Women's Reservation Bill : A Crisis of Identity", *The Indians Journal of Pub. Adm.,* Vol. XLII, Jan. 2001, p. 51.

The Hindustan Times, March 15, 2002, p. 5-6.

DYNAMICS OF EMPOWERING WOMEN IN URBAN DEVELOPMENT

Kumkum Narain & Mira Mridubhashini

Empowerment of Women

Women constitute about 50% of the population in most of the countries. They work 2/3rd of the world's working hours. Even then they earn 10% of the world's income and own less than 1% of world's property. Out of 1.3 bn. absolute poor population of the world, women are 70%. Unfortunately, the number of women living below poverty line in rural areas has doubled in past twenty years. The number of women occupying the top political offices is still rare. Women legislators constitute less than 10.10% of the total parliamentary members of the world.

The status of women in India is similar, may be worse than the world's average. A study conducted in Himalayan region revealed that a pair of bullocks works 1064 hrs, a man 1212 hrs and a woman 3485 hrs a year on one hectare farm. In India the percentage of parliamentary women members was the highest in 1984, i.e. 8.1%. The legislative Assembly did not reserve seats in parliament, or state assemblies because it was felt unnecessary at that time and as such it underestimated the strength of women as equals. May be the low percentage of women in parliament is the result of that faulty decision. Even now, the politicians have efficiently managed to exclude women from politics itself. Women's marginal political presence is attributed to the increasing criminalisation of politics or general stigma associated to political women. Only those women who have a blood relationship with a leader of status can hope for a seat. No attempt is being made by any political party to create a mass awareness to actively involve women in public life.

In spite of these disheartening presumptions and stigma, the South East Asia which is comparatively less developed corner of the world, boasts of the largest women heads of the states, for example India, Bangladesh, Sri Lanka, Pakistan; all had successful women Prime Minister. It is high time, women assert and get their fair share.

Indian women possess human rights as well as rights given by Indian Constitution under articles 14, 15, 16. It ensures the rights of women to contest for places that occupy highest position in the government and participate in all democratic institutions from Panchayat to parliament. But in practice that right has been reduced to almost nothing, because of the tradition that women are inferior to men. Does the law accord full justice to a woman? Do the laws show equality between men and women? Do the laws protect women against discrimination? In India women possess human rights given by the Indian Constitution.

Contribution of Women in Urban Scenario

The contributions of women in the urban development are manifold. Women's tremendous insight and ability are utilized at micro and micro levels. At the micro level, they contribute as sectoral heads or enlightened segments of the society.

At the macro level, elected women councillors or commissioners achieve this magnificent post by several years of input with the people of their constituency. As prospective electorates they share the miseries of the people, women in particular, support them when in need. They fight with them for their common cause and continue to struggle till their goals are achieved. Medha Patkar, Arundhati Roy are examples of such prolonged struggle. They gain recognition by genuine hard work and aspirations of the people.

Once in power the elected representatives certainly benefits their own constituencies first. The development of their constituency is very swift in the beginning, but the leaders generally lack consistency in their loyalty. The same rate of progress is seldom witnessed after two –three years. Reality is, the attention of the elected representatives gets diverted due to many other responsibilities and priority to easy acclaim and recognition.

But it is at the micro level that the net work created by the leaders continues to execute their works. The trained followers at micro level do the actual wonders if united and determined to do so. Generally the small local organizations do this work. Women organizations also play vital role at this level by channelising women in this direction. Women use their hearts, they are more sensitive, motherly and have an eye for details that men lack. In art, hospitality and other creative fields women are born winners. They have the capacity to be the watch dogs of the society. By nature they are the fastest means of transmission of messages. Any organization if assigned, it ensures better functioning of the municipal services like hospitals, schools, parks, cleaning of garbage and drains and supply of drinking water etc. Unless the people raise their voice against inefficiency and negligence in the infrastructure, even the best corporation in the world tends to be complacent and negligent. Thus people contribute to better functioning by being more aware and enlightened. There are many examples where women organizations have ensured proper service by threatening the authorities with their mere kitchen wares. The TV serial "Rajani" should be congratulated for strengthening this move and motivating the womenfolk.

Enlightenment does not come easily. It has long path of struggle, pain, sacrifice, endurance and endeavour. Apart from these self obtained qualities, sharing responsibilities is another method of creating awareness. Unless we entrust responsibilities to the beneficiaries, they never contribute on their own, they just remain recipients. If both men and women share the responsibilities of their locality by willingness or force, what can stop them from scaling heights. Therefore responsibilities have to be trust first, in order to imbibe them in their life as a habit. Women play effective role of teaching the children right from the moment a child is born. A man is actually what he has been habituated in his childhood. It was the insight of a woman, who saw the seeds germinate first, then agriculture became the main occupation of men.

Recent surveys and studies conducted by various organizations, hammer the point that women make better bosses as compared to men sitting in hot seats.

No doubt women do have their inherent weaknesses, due to the dual responsibilities both at home and at their work places. It definitely does not mean they are irresponsible. There is lot of creativity in their work, which again is an innate trait of a woman. Above all, given the adverse circumstances they tend to take assigned jobs as challenge. They have also proved better team leaders than most men around them. They have deeper sense of loyalty and commitment. It is for the society to make best use of this intangible but valuable resource.

Mechanism of Governance

A major landmark in the history of decentralization is the passage 73rd and 74th Constitution Amendment Acts (CAA) 1992. The amendments are said to be given fresh lease of life to the decentralization process of local governance in India. An important provision of these acts relates to reservation of one–third of the seats for disadvantaged sections known as Schedule Castes, Schedule tribes and for women. This radical step has far reaching effects on the social milieu, bringing a vast number of women of rural and urban India to assume active political roles. The need of the hour is to develop cross functional teams to educate the rural and urban women about electoral process and their rights before they enter the political pipeline.

The decentralization process attributes to Panchayat at the village level and Municipal Bodies (Corporations, Councils and Nagar Panchayats) from the core of the local government structure in any urban area of India. Over the years this institution has come to acquire a pivotal position in the management of cities and urban economies. Traditionally the Mayor, the elected representatives and the commissioner, an appointed bureaucrat represent the urban local government. Within urban areas, zonal divisions are based on administrative lines and are further divided into wards to form the basis of political constituency.

By the law the municipal institutions are democratic in character and based on adult franchise. They have directly elected boards (for fringe areas), councils (for small towns), corporations (for metros with a population of 1,00,000 and above). The elected council chairpersons in smaller municipalities share powers of decision making and administration with the councils and the various standing committees. However the management pattern in large cities is based on the principle of separation of powers between the elected body, the standing committees and the bureaucracy which is headed by a municipal commissioner. The elected body deliberates on policies and approves the budget, but the municipal commissioner exercises executive powers. Following the classical definition of decentralization this pattern of local government structure is a combination of devolution and deconcentration.

As far as the functions and accountability of this trio are concerned, theoretically they present a unique combination. As shown in the following sketch, the triangular relationship represents the power dynamics as well as accountability of the three categories of actors.

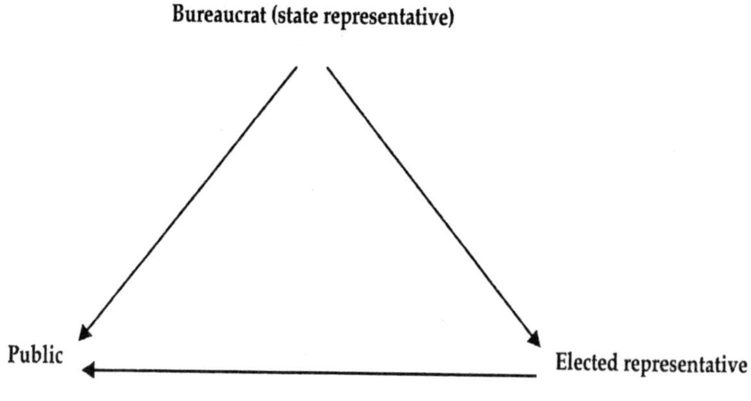

The state represented by the bureaucracy is at the top of the triangle, while the elected representatives and common people form the two ends of the base of this triangle.

More often than not, this level of accountability is the most crucial in the triangular relationship. It is the middle and the lower level of bureaucracy that the citizens have to interact with; that is where the crux of the problem lies. Since the service users are totally dependent on these officers, power dynamics comes into play. Incidence of bribes and other forms of corruption often surface at this stage. The babu's loyalty to the employer and to act as the "middle man" between the boss and the common man presents the biggest hurdle in developing cordial relationship with the concerned people in this system. Most of the time, the procedure to meet an officer in charge of services or simply to register a complaint is so time consuming and long winding that service users find it very inconvenient. Helplessly, bribery and corruption are adopted to take a short cut through this maze.

The second level is represented by the local elected representatives. They have to act more responsibly as, they are now under public scrutiny and cannot bluff their way through a second term. Though the interaction with the councillors is said to have increased over the years, the voters cannot be fooled with promises made under false pretensions. In certain cases some representatives once in power make themselves inaccessible.

Third level is the awareness of the public in exercising their rights and availing the services. More enlightened citizens exercise their rights more effectively and demand accountability from the second and the first levels. In the absence of the enlightened citizens, the upper and the second levels take maximum advantage of their posts. Corruption, cultural and social norms of not questioning the people in authority, granting more importance to a person than a post, all seem to be reason for lack of accountability at various levels of governance.

In order to get rid of this malaise, more and more of women collaboration is desired, as they lag far behind men in corruption and cheating. Even if they indulge in some malpractice, it is not of that magnitude. Women in general have their morality and ethics in place to much greater extent. They display higher degree of sincerity and commitment to their work. Due to these qualities of women there are several companies which have given women an edge over men and not to their disappointment.

While accountability between these three categories takes time to build, simultaneous measures may be adopted to improve intra-sectoral accountability. In fact a few enterprising municipal commissioners have begun to put system in place within the corporation which can improve institutional accountability.

Both the national and the state level decentralization policies do not have any provision built in for improving accountability, transparency or encouraging partnership in their system. However since the state has not taken the initiatives, local NGOs and CBOs, and some women organizations with nodal support from national, international organizations have responded in this direction. They have been working towards creating a space within the state agencies, to institutionalize these mechanisms in order to increase efficiency, equity and improved quality of service delivery.

There is no provision in the 74th CAA, which talks about partnering civic responsibilities. It in fact increased the domain of the municipal functions from what was previously on its list of activities. Five years ago, the local government was not even in position to entertain such a venture, but now it is openly looking forward and inviting tenders for collaborative projects. It will however take a few more years before it actively thinks of engaging the expertise of common people and the voluntary sector in these efforts.

Partnership bridges the gap between the public and private actors, between associations and business dwellers. For example the NGOs help a lot in keeping their localities clean and doing all sorts of odd jobs. Bangalore is a living example of such collaboration. The NGOs help to train the rag pickers and also the residents in recycling and marketing the products. The municipal authorities provide garbage trucks and land for composting. Every resident is responsible for keeping his premises clean and plants alive planted by the corporation. That is how Bangalore is supposed to be the most beautiful, clean and green city of India.

Empowerment of Women for Urban Governance in Bihar

So far we have discussed the mechanism of urban governance and the role of women to be contemplated. Now let us manifest the urban electoral scenario in Bihar.

The government of Bihar amended the Bihar and Orissa Municipal Act 1922 and the Patna Municipal Corporations Act, 1951 in commensurate to the provisions of the 74th Constitution Amendment in the year 1994. Since no follow up was taken after the 1994 amendment, no municipal elections were held for adeeade. The highlights of this amendment act are as follows:

1. Representations of women in the urban local bodies are symbolic till date.
2. No provisions for reservation or proportionate representation existed in the Patna Municipal Corporation (PMC) Act till 1983.
3. A provision was made in the Act, in the year 1983, through which a woman may be co-opted in the Municipal Board if any woman has not been elected as Municipal Councillor.
4. First time in the year 1993 a constitutional status was granted to the Urban Local bodies through the 74th CAA 1992.
5. Specific provision was made in the Constitution through Article 243-T(3) as reproduced below:

"Not less than 1/3rd (including the number of seats reserved for women belonging to the schedule castes and scheduled tribes) of the total number of the seats to be filled by direct election in every Municipality shall be reserved for women and such seats may be allotted by rotation to different constituency of a Municipality."

6. Accordingly the PMC Act 1951, and Bihar and Orissa Municipal Act 1922, was amended in the year 1994 through an ordinance which became law in the year 1995.

7. It is a matter of great satisfaction that out of total 2179 wards of Urban Local Bodies of Bihar, 1/3rd wards have been reserved for women representation.

8. But no representation for women chairpersons has been made in the Act or Rules.

9. Apart from non-reservation of women for chairpersons of urban local bodies, if one third ward commissioners of women community consolidate themselves, they may be in a commanding position. They may even snatch the chair in most of the municipal boards.

10. For the implementation of municipal functions a provision for constitution of committees exists in the Municipal Act. But no provision for 1/3rd reservation of women representation in these committees so far has been made.

11. In the present circumstances, occasion may arise when only male members of the board may grab these implementation committee membership and women will have no saying in these implementation committees/

12. As such statutory provisions of 1/3rd women representation in each committee should be made in Acts and Rules for these municipal Function Implementation Committees.

The fresh election of municipal councillors were held recently. It is very encouraging to note that out of 378 nominations filed, 146 nominations were filed by women aspirants. Out of 804 nominations filed for different local bodies in the city of Patna 257 were women contesting from various wards. Whatever be the final results of municipal elections, at least women are appearing more conscious, aware of their rights and are willing to undertake the responsibilities.

Legislative reservation is imperative in the initial stages of women empowerment. It is necessary to overcome the imbalance of history, custom and tradition. We can cite example of Norway. The country of rising sun passed an Equal Status Act that stipulated 40% women in all public boards and councils. Media campaign funded by Norwegian government encouraged women to stand for elections. With women in elected posts of power, Norway has been able to make magnificent changes in social policies. In India election campaigns are very expensive and unless a woman is wealthy she does not stand a chance.

What ever be the circumstances when we are talking of urban development the second half of the society i.e. the women folk should be given equal importance if not more. Any corner of the world can be glorified by building a positive image of women by recognizing their contributions to society, polity and economy. Both the government of the day and the society as a whole have moral responsibility to strengthen the other wheel of the social chariot i.e. women and oil of the chariot is empowerment.

REFERENCES

Urban India–Vol. XX, Jan-Jun 2000. A journal of the National Institute of Urban Affairs, New Delhi.

Urban India–Vol. XX, Jul-Dec 2000. A journal of the National Institute of Urban Affairs, New Delhi.

Roshni–Feb-Jun 2000. A journal of the All India Women's Conference, New Delhi.

Roshni–Apr-Jun 1998. A journal of the All India Women's Conference, New Delhi.

Times of India–Supplement (Patna edition) 8-3-02.

Hindustan Times Patna edition (Patna live) 8-3-02.

EMPOWERING WOMEN THROUGH RESERVATION IN URBAN LOCAL BODIES– DIFFERENCE BETWEEN THEORY AND PRACTICE

S.M. Haider Rizvi

Introduction

The importance of local self-government lies in sustaining democracy because it satisfies the basic tenets of the democracy and conceives a society free of bias and domination, which can function democratically with every individual's (caste, creed sex and religion) voice being heard and grievances being redressed. The most essential attribute of local government is its representative and responsible nature. Here elected or nominated representatives who are responsible to the local community control the executions of local administrative powers. It is commonly understood as the administration of a locality, a village or a town, a city, or any other area smaller than the state by a body representing local individuals. It possesses a fairly large amount of autonomy to raise at least a part of its revenue through local taxation and spending of income on services, which are regarded as local and make them distinct from central government.

The local governments play an important role in the social and cultural life of a nation. The efficiency and success of local administration can lead to the health and overall progress of that region, because it provides a range of services to the local people and performs functions of great variety and magnitude.

Thus, it helps the state and national government in reducing their responsibilities. Here the concept of democracy can be practiced locally where the social, economic, political and administrative changes can be introduced to see its impact. Local self-government forms a sub system of the political system of the state and national level, which has got several dimensions such as social, economic, geographic, legal and political. Constitutionally it has been given a legal status in the eyes of law to survive and act as per the given local circumstances. It is subordinate to the state government to represent the interest of local citizens as per the power delegated to it. The local self-governments are expected to behave as an organised entity, possessing organization and powers of autonomy to raise revenue, preparation of budget and management of local human fiscal and material resources. It has characteristics of a government as an agency of people, because the persons to whom it is accountable, choose it. As a local government it has right to enter into contracts and to own and dispose property. The beauty of the concept of local self-government lies in its political character as it exists in every country irrespective of the dominant political philosophy and form of government.

The essential features of local government are: its statutory status, its power to raise finance by taxation in the area under its jurisdiction, participation of the local community in the decision making in specified subjects and their administration, the freedom to act independently of central control and the general purpose of it instead of single purpose character.

The Legislation of 74th Constitution Amendment Act and its Importance

The undue interference by government from time to time and curtailment of the powers of municipal bodies hindered their smooth functioning. Government did not bother to bring any change as per the changes occurring in the socio-economic scenario in the society; rather the local governments were superseded from time to time. All this led to growing unrest among the citizens, which was felt by the central government. Since the pressure on the central government was at its height now it was imperative for the government to bring certain changes to improve the conditions of urban local bodies in the country, so that the citizen can have a feel of democracy locally and participate in the decision making process at local level for their own affairs. More or less same kind of discontentment was prevalent in the area of rural local self-governance (Panchayats) and to counter this, the Government of India has brought out two legislations to improve the conditions of the local governance. These two legislations were passed in 1992 known as 73rd Constitution (Amendment) Act, 1992 and 74th Constitution (Amendment) Act 1992 (74th CAA) for the rural and urban areas respectively.

Salient Features of 74th CAA

- 74th CAA has broadened the domain of urban local governance by devolving the responsibilities of planning for economic and social development, safeguarding the interests of the weaker sections, slum improvement and urban poverty alleviation.
- As per the Article 242-T of the CAA, one-third seats have been reserved for women as members and chairpersons in the Municipal bodies. The Act has ensured the entry of weaker and marginalized sections in the Municipal bodies.
- Article 243-U pertains to the 'right to exist' of Municipal bodies. In the case of demand of their dissolution, they will be heard and if dissolved, fresh elections must be held within six months.
- Formation of District Planning Committee (DPC) has been made an obligatory provision in the Act {Article 243ZD(1)}. This is meant to encourage the participation of elected representatives both from rural and urban areas for the planning and development of their areas. Four-fifth of the total number of members of the DPC shall be elected by and from amongst the elected members of Panchayats at the district level and of the Municipalities in the district. Similarly, provision of

forming Metropolitan Planning Committees has been made for the Metropolitan areas.

- Provision of 'Ward Committees' for the Municipalities having more than three lakhs population further decentralizes the power and encourages interaction and dialogue between citizens, civil society and elected members at the ward level.
- Formation of State Finance Commission by the state government to make recommendations to govern sharing of state taxes, duties, tolls and fees between the state governments and the Municipalities is one of the very noteworthy features of 74th CAA.
- Article 243 W envisages the addition of Twelfth Schedule in the powers, authorities and responsibility of the Municipalities to empower them to take decisions for the holistic development of their areas.

There seems no doubt in it that the 74th CAA has become the basis for the present reformed municipal government system in India. Although it continues to be the subject of several debates and discussions, it is generally accepted as the turning point in the development of urban local self-government in India. Because the philosophy behind the formulation of this Act was that the municipal institutions should be given a number of basic situations for its smooth functioning. It must have a constitutional recognition with a strong spine. There should not be undue interference from the state and national government, which has the capacity to create and regulate it. The expenses for the maintenance and desired developmental works should be met from the financial resources of the local institutions. The elections of the local bodies should be made mandatory at regular interval and the power of abrupt suppression by the state government should be checked. The working of elected council should be regularized and they should be given sufficient power to perform their duties.

Powers, Authorities and Responsibilities of Municipalities

Article 243(G) of 74th CAA deals with the powers, authorities and responsibilities of the municipalities. It has sought state legislatures to provide by law the municipalities powers and authorities to enable them to function as institutions of self-government by devolving powers and responsibilities. This should empower the municipalities to take decisions in the preparation of plans for economic development and social justice and in the performance of functions and the implementation of schemes as may be entrusted to them the matter listed in Twelfth Schedule (Article 243W). The areas included in the jurisdiction of the municipality through the Twelfth Schedule are as follows:

1. Urban planning including town planning.
2. Regulation of land use and construction of buildings.
3. Planning for economic and social development.
4. Roads and bridges.
5. Water supply for domestic, industrial and commercial purpose.
6. Public health, sanitation, conservancy and solid waste management.
7. Fire services.
8. Urban forestry, protection of the environment and promotion of ecological aspects.
9. Safeguarding the interests of weaker sections of society, including the handicapped and mentally retarded.
10. Slum improvement and up-gradation.
11. Urban poverty alleviation.
12. Provisions of urban amenities and facilities such as parks, gardens, and playgrounds.
13. Promotion of cultural, educational and aesthetic aspects.
14. Burials and burial grounds, cremations, cremation grounds and electric crematoriums.

15. Cattle ponds, prevention of cruelty to animals.
16. Vital statistics including registration of births and deaths.
17. Public amenities including street lighting, parking lots, bus stops and public conveniences.
18. Regulation of slaughter houses and tanneries.

In the above background the urban local bodies can be viewed as institutions of local self-governance with autonomous and integrated development responsibilities within their jurisdictions. It is also visible that the 74th CAA has ensured constitutional safeguards to women's rights in urban governance and it may be used as an important and powerful tool for women empowerment. It has tried to seek effective participation of women in the functioning of local government to improve the quality and add new dimensions in the style of governance.

The Representation Vs Participation

The accountability of Municipal governance is of critical importance to the concerns of the poor including women and socially disadvantaged sections. Citizens' participation in local governance must be strengthened in order to ensure transparency and accountability of elected representatives and appointed functionaries in municipal bodies. Because it is now widely recognized that the poor and marginalized specially women are important contributors to the city's life. Yet they continue to be dealt with on the periphery. They are bound to live in high density informal settlements and to struggle for shelter, water and services that enable daily life. The women and children face the brunt of the problems in keeping the fragile lives of their family going. Even employment opportunities in the form of informal employment run the constant risk of disruption, uprooting and harassment.

This paper is based on the observations, experiences and data available on the status of women representatives in urban local bodies in U.P. in general and the studies carried by Sahbhagi Shikshan Kendra, Lucknow on the Status and

Functioning of Ghazipur and Itaunja Municipalities of Uttar Pradesh in particular. The provisions for reservations for women/weaker sections provide an opportunity for strengthening the voice and leadership roles of such groups in urban governance. The tables given below depict that the participation of women has been ensured in the municipalities of Uttar Pradesh as per the provisions in the 74th CAA and U.P. Municipalities Act, 1994.

Table 1 : Reservation of Seats in Urban Local Bodies (1995 Municipal Election)

Particular	*Nagar Nigam*	*Nagar Palika Parishad*	*Nagar Panchayat*
Chairman/President	11	226	444
Scheduled Caste women	–	8	23
Schedule Caste	1	15	47
Scheduled Tribe Women	–	–	–
Scheduled Tribes	–	–	–
OBC Women	1	20	36
OBC	1	41	84
Women (General)	2	47	86
General	6	95	168
Total Women	**3 (27.27)**	**75 (33.18)**	**145 (32.66)**
Ward Members/Corporators	830	5744	5074
Scheduled Caste women	40	313	439
Schedule Caste	66	391	324
Scheduled Trible Women	–	3	5
Scheduled Tribles	–	3	7
OBC Women	64	607	517
OBC	111	828	806
Women (General)	174	1134	947
General	375	2465	2029
Total Women	**278 (33.49)**	**2057 (35.81)**	**1908 (37.60)**

Source : U.P. Election Commission, Lucknow.
Figures in parentheses do note per cent.

Table 2 : Reservation of Seats in Urban Local Bodies (2000 Municipal Election)

Particular	*Nagar Nigam*	*Nagar Palika Parishad*	*Nagar Panchayat*
Chairman/President	11	225	446
Scheduled Caste Women	–	9	21
Schedule Caste	1	17	42
Scheduled Tribe Women	–	–	–
Scheduled Tribes	–	–	–
OBC Women	1	20	40
OBC	2	40	80
Women (General)	2	46	88
General	5	93	175
Total Women	**3 (27.27)**	**75 (33.33)**	**149 (33.41)**

Source : U.P. Election Commission, Lucknow.

Figure in Parentheses do note per cent.

Representations of women councillors were ensured in the Municipality as per the criterion given in Act. In 1995 election they have got more representation i.e. 33.49 in Nagar Ngams, 35.81 in Nagar Palika Parishads and 37.60 in Nagar Panchayats, as against 33% of their due share council. In 2000-2001 election, too, their representations in Nagar Nigams, Nagar Palika Parishads and Nagar Panchayats were 27.27, 33.33 and 33.41 respectively.

Though representation of women was as per the provisions but their participation was limited to participate in the monthly meetings only yet they were very excited about their being as the representatives of their words. Women councillors reported that due to their domestic liabilities and many other hindrances they were not able to ensure their participation in the meetings and other affairs of the Municipality.

Status of Representation and Participation Caste Study of Women in Ghazipur Municipality

As per the provision made in 74th CAA and respective changes made in the UPSMA the Municipality has been divided into 25 wards. One councillor has been elected from each ward. Out of 25 councillors 9 were women. The representation of SC and OBC women has also been done as per the given criteria 1-SC, 5-OBC and 3-General.

Reservation of Seats

Elected Representatives/Chairman	*Category*			
1995 Election				
Members	*General*	*SC*	*OBC*	*Total*
Men	7	2	7	16
Women	3	1	5	9
Chairman			1	1
	Total			**26**
2000 Election				
Men	7	2	7	16
Women	3	1	5	9
Chairman			1	1
	Total			**26**

Source : Survey of Municipality by SSK in 1999-2000.

Participation of Women

Representations of women councillors are 36% in the Municipality in both the elections 1994 and 2000. Generally their participation is limited to participate in the monthly meetings only. Those who have been elected for the second time are more articulate than the new ones.

The representation of women in this municipal council is due to the provision made in 74th CAA. The 74th CAA certainly has encouraged the participation of members from women and weaker sections in the area of urban local self-governance. The women have got more representation than as mandated in the Act i.e. one third of the total seats reserved for women. It should be certainly regarded as a positive development in the area of women emancipation and empowerment because earlier the women were confined to the four walls of their homes only. The participation of women used to be almost negligible in the urban local bodies before the 74th CAA and UPSMA. Only few women from the politically active and affluent families could get entry in the municipalities. As far as the weaker sections (S.C., S.T. and O.B.C.) were concerned, it was certainly a boost for them because after 74th CAA onwards at least the share in the Municipal Councils in proportion to their population in the Municipality has been ensured.

In Ghazipur Municipality the participation of women was not still as meaningful as it was visualized in the 74th CAA and UPSAMA, because they have not reached the stage where they can express their concerns about the problems, articulate their demands and have say in the decisions making process as yet. But it cannot be generalized for all the women councillors; some of them were found to be very articulate and it can be hoped that this gradual development would certainly lead to the empowerment of women in local governance.

Hindrances to the Participation

At Personal Level

- As far as urban local governments are concerned most of the women elected representatives are either first or second timers to the municipality. Hence they are not having experience of municipal functioning and are unable to participate effectively in the decision making.
- Generally they were forced to come to this area because of the pressures created by their respective husbands, children and relatives. Their capacity of decision making is also hampered because of their financial dependence on their husband and children. Hence are supposed to abide their dictates which are generally decided by them as per their permutation and combinations.
- As far as the domestic chores are concerned there has been no concession in these even after becoming the elected representatives in the urban local bodies. The social norms and taboos associated with the women folk affect adversely the participation of women in the affairs of urban local government.

At Municipal Level

- When the male elected representatives are asked separately about the provisions of women reservations in the municipality they speak very high and positive about it. But in practice their attitude towards their women counterparts remains the same. They generally are given second class treatment in the municipal functioning such as planning, decision making and implementation of the development programmes.
- If a woman representative is found to be more articulate and confident as leader and tries to put forward her concerns in the meetings she is not allowed to speak. Creating various kinds of disturbances by male members is restricting their participation. As against the purpose of 74th CAA, which tries to enhance the confidence and encourage leadership qualities in them, they are being suppressed morally as well as psychologically.
- In general it has been found that the information on the provisions of 74th CAA, various policies and programmes to the elected representatives are low but as far as women representatives are concerned it is even lower which deters their increased participation in the meetings.
- Rough attitude and abusive languages used by male counterparts finds the women representatives in an uncomfortable situation. All these make them speak very less or only when they are asked to speak.
- Women elected representatives are divided on the political lines because they have contested under the banner of various political parties. So in the process of confirming the political ideologies and commitments of the political parties they belong they are not able to get themselves united on the women cause.

Empowering Women

As per the provisions given in the 74th CAA and inclusion of Twelfth Schedule in the jurisdiction of urban local bodies now almost every possible areas come under the purview of municipal functioning. If these areas are taken properly to work upon by the local governments it will certainly lead not only to the availability of the basic civic services to the citizens rather also to the economic and social upliftment of the poor and the marginalized such as SC, OBC, poor, women and slum dwellers. Following may be some of the ways through which urban local governments/municipalities may help in generating income and creating employment opportunities to empower the poor and marginalized especially women.

Capacity Building of the Municipalities

The elections of the municipalities in UP was held in 1995 and 2000 on the basis of the changes made through 74th CAA, and UPSMA, 94 in terms of the reservation for the SC, ST, OBC and women, election of the chairman, addition of Twelfth Schedule etc. But after the election and formation of municipal councils no efforts were made to get the municipal staff–appointed as well as elected-familiar with the new arrangement. Insensitivity was shown both on the part of the government as well as voluntary organizations towards the problem of urban government. None has taken it as an issue of remote or immediate concern and it remained getting the step brotherly treatment. Hence no efforts were made for the awareness building of the citizens and capacity building of the elected representatives. It is imperative to conduct workshops, training sessions, seminars etc. for capacity building of elected representatives in general and women elected representatives in particular on 74th CAA and U.P. Municipalities Act. The provisions made in the 74th CAA and UPSMA should be used as tools to enable the poor and marginalized especially women, in developing leadership in them and encouraging their participation in the decision-making processes. It will help them to raise their voice and negotiate their demands on one hand and build the capacity of local government to be more accountable, on the other.

Engagement of Women in Municipal Functioning

The municipalities are always overburdened with the work and generally it is not possible for the municipalities to perform these activities by their own. Hence they are engaging people on ad-hoc and contract basis to get these work done. These works are allotted on the basis of personal relations and to those who have influence on the municipality of some sort. If these works are given to the women, this may be a great help to them. The municipalities give a greater say to the women representatives, which will not only develop a sense of responsibility and confidence in them rather they in turn will help greatly to the women in general.

Encouragement of Region/Caste Based Professions and Allied Activities

Every city is having some of its speciality; these may be in terms of their culture, food habits or professions. Some of the professions of an area depend on particular characteristics like weather, land or culture and women generally engaged in these professions and activities. Efforts should be made by the local government to encourage and regularize these professions by providing them adequate conditions and facilities. This may be beneficial to both-the local government and the people who are engaged in these. The municipalities can generate revenues through taxes whereas the people will identify with the profession and can excel in these fields. Some of the professions in this regard may be regulation of riverbanks, goat and sheep rearing, leatherwork, basket and mat making, bidi and agarbatti making, match making, potteries, chiken and embroidery, terracotta woks, papad and pickle making, toy making, bangles making etc.

Regularisation of Bazars and Melas

Almost every municipality has some weekly markets, evening markets and melas on various social and religious occasions. These not only contribute to the economy of the local government rather they also provide quality goods to the inhabitants on reasonable prices. But chaos is generally found on the places where there is no regulation, no discipline is maintained. The municipal employees, police and the local goons have an undue control of these places by harassing the shopkeepers and taking money from them. In return the shopkeepers instead of getting some benefit out of it loose their capital money, too.

If the local governments take a genuine interest to the problems of these people by setting some rules and regulation and control the corrupt practices of their employees and minimize the influence of local goons, these will be a respite for the shop keepers and will help the poor in engaging themselves in income generating activities and employment opportunities.

Access to Market and Formation of Co-operatives

To provide market for the domestic goods and products and regularize its prices the local government should form co-operative. This will help in getting the right prices of the goods and materials and will reduce the exploitation of the people from the intermediaries. Many successful attempts have been made in this regard, which can be replicated by other local governments.

Establishment of Linkages Between the Women and other Government Agencies

Apart from the municipalities man other government departments work in the urban areas for the development of the area with various programmes and policies for women, poor and marginalized. But generally due lack of co-ordination between local government other agencies the real purposes of the programmes are not achieved and ultimately the interests of the women and poor hamper. The local governments instead of clashing for their ego should see the thrust of the programmes are not achieved and ultimately the interests of the women and poor hamper. The local governments instead of classing for their ego should see the thrust of the programme and to programme and try to link the women, poor and marginalized with the programmes. They should also provide conducive environment and infrastructure facilities for the realization of the goal. Some of the government agencies for example District Urban Development Authority (DUDA), State Urban Development Authority (SUDA), District Industry Centre (DIC), District Administration etc. have many policies and programmes for the poor, the municipalities should interact with these department and try to extract as much as possible benefits for the citizens of their area.

Formation and Regulation of Self-Help Groups

The women ward members should be encouraged by the local government mobilizing and motivating the women to form self-help groups. These groups may or may not be called as self-help groups. The purpose of such groups may be multi-dimensional. The groups may act as pressure groups and will help the local governments in their functioning. At the same time they can save some money in the name of the group which can be utilised for the development of their respective locality and may be given to the needy as loans to start some activity for their economic betterment. Here the role of the local government and the elected representatives of the wards may be very crucial who can help the groups in linking with the bank or any such organization, which helps these kind of endeavours.

Regularisation of Street Vending/Hawking

As a result of migration from rural to urban areas and the ill policies of industrial and business houses and the government there is a large bunch of skilled, semi-skilled or unskilled workers, majority of them being women in the cities known as the street vendors. The street vendors are generally perceived as the burden on the social and economic fabric of a city creating problems for the common citizens. But the facts go against this notion and show the importance of street vendors in a city. They not only provide goods and services on the prices to the citizens but also contributing immensely to the economy of a country. As per a latest survey the contribution of street vendors in the economy of Mumbai city alone is about Rs. 6,000 crore. Actually, the street vending and hawking must be regarded as a boon for economic system of our country specially the urban areas because they don't create a burden on the government (national, state or local) by asking employment for themselves rather they contribute socially and economically to the system.

But they meet with several problems created by the police and the local government. They always live in an environment of threat and uncertainty because of not having any legal status to their profession and place for practicing it. The local governments should recognize the rights of street vending and hawking by giving them licenses for the professions and place, regularize the services and employment of these people by declaring the vending and hawking areas in each and every locality. They should be a part of the planning and decision for the area where they can put their grievances. These will certainly lead to the economic up-liftment of these poor lots.

Organisation of Professional Courses/Training

The municipalities should also plan in advance for the youths and marginalized by running professional courses and organizing professional training. This may help them in starting income generating activities as per their own professions.

Transparency of Information and Accountability

Getting information regarding the development programme and functioning of the Municipalities was found to be a very difficult task. Though after the acceptance of the recommendations of the State Finance Commission by the state government the budgeting for the Municipalities could be regularized yet there was found to be no system of accounting of income and expenditure. There was no standard format for it. There was no culture of asking for information from the Municipality regarding their budgets, income, expenditure etc. by the citizens. The non-awareness about the functioning of the Municipality unlike Panchayats, led to the non-accountability of the government staff towards the citizens who did not have any check on them. If at all somebody was interested to get information on the function of the Municipality, the person had to face a lot of hardship to get the same due to complex procedure and bureaucratic intricacies.

It is not that the accountability was from the appointed staff; rather the elected representatives also did not bother to the queries of the citizens because of their casual behaviour, non-seriousness towards their duty as the public representative and lack of information the accountability will also help the poor get benefited from various policies and programmes at the local government level.

Conclusion

The provision of reservation for women is certainly a positive development in the area of women emancipation and empowerment at local level with help of local government. It has helped the women who were confined to the four walls of their homes to join the mainstream. Though the participation of women is still low and does not go as per the desired goals of 74th CAA, now it is certainly better than pre-74th era where the participation of the women used to be almost negligible in the urban local bodies.

There is urgent need on the part of the government and civil society organizations to take this issue seriously and practice what they preach through various legislations, policies and programmes. It is only then, the real empowerment of women could be realised.

BIBLIOGRAPHY

Bhargawa, A. (1996), Gramin-Nagariye Sanrachna. Printwell, Jaipur.

Joshi, R.P. (1998), Constitutionalisation of Panchayati Raj–A Reassessment. Rawat Publications, Jaipur.

Mehrotra, S (2000), Strengthening Participation of Women Urban Governance : Barriers and ways Forward. Participation & Development, Vol. 7, No. 19 November 2000.

Mohanty, B (1993), Municipal System in India : Citizens' Involvment. Ashish Publishing House, New Delhi.

Prasad, P. (1995), Urban Slums : Health, Education and Development Delta Publishing House, Delhi.

Rajyon Ke Panchayati Adhiniyam–A Alochnatmak Samikcha (1995). Voluntary action Network India, New Delhi.

Rizvi, Dr. S.M. Haider (2001), Role of Urban Local Self-Governance in Promoting Income Generating Programmes and Employment for Weaker Sections. Contemporary Social Work, Vol. XVIII.

Rizvi, Dr. S.M. haider (2001), A Participatory Study on the Status and Functioning of Ghazipur Municipality as an Institution of Urban Local Self-Governance. Sahbhagi Shikshan Kendra, Lucknow.

Roy Burman, B.K. (1997), Seventy Third and Seventy Fourth Amendments of the Constitution–Public Discourse and State Response, PRI Occasional paper No. 1. Society for Participatory Research in Asia.

Roy, K.K. (1998), Uttar Pradesh Nagar palika Adhiniyam. Alia Law Agency, Allahabad.

Singh S. (1993), Constitutional Safeguards to Enhance the Status of Panchayati Raj Institutions. Journal of Rural Development, Vol. 12(1), pp. 77-88.

Singh, H.S. (1998), Financing Urban Local Bodies in Uttar Pradesh. Urban India, Vol. XVIII, No. 1.

Singh, S. (1999), The 74th Constitutional Amendment Act : Conceptual Premises and Public-Private Partnership. Quarterly Journal of all India Institute of Local Self-Government, Vol. LXX, No. 1-2, January-June.

Status of Municipalities in Gujrat–A Participatory study of four Towns. UNNATI, Ahmedabad.

Subzwari, Arshad (1999), The U.P. Municipalities Act, 1916 [Act No. II of 1916], Law Vision, Allahabad.

United Province Municipalities Act, 1916 with Short Notes (1994), Eastern Book Company, Lucknow.

Uttar Pradesh Municipal Corporations Adhiniyam, 1959 with Short Notes (1994), Eastern Book Company, Lucknow.

Uttar Pradesh Shasan, Nagar Vikas Vibhag Ka Karya Vivran, 1998-99.

EMPOWERMENT OF WOMEN IN URBAN ADMINISTRATION IN MADHYA PRADESH BEYOND THE CONSTITUTIONAL MANDATE

M.K. Dixit

Introduction

The concept of women empowerment in the broader sense implies a process of creating conditions and taking measures which provide opportunities to women for their development in its different manifestations–physical, economic, political, legal, socio-cultural and psychological. There has been more debate and discussion in the country regarding women empowerment in general, but less in respect of different aspects of empowerment and their interaction, coordination, and integration, their prioritization, sequencing, pacing and implementation. Even the National Policy for Women Empowerment, 2001 which is considered to be a comprehensive document, enlisting the goals, objective, policy prescriptions, operational strategies and institutional mechanism for women empowerment, does not spell out priorities, inter-relations between different components of policy, their co-ordination and integration, and ways and means of implementation of programmes and policies. The Madhya Pradesh Government Policy on Women, though more specific and time–bound, touching different aspects of women's life suffers, more or less, from the same deficiencies and shortcomings. Despite these policy pronouncements and some steps taken thereunder, more particularly in respect of reservation of jobs in government service and of seats in local bodies and other institutions, there is a wide hiatus between the goals of gender quality enshrined in the Constitution and the ground realities regarding the status of women obtainable in the country.

It is not possible to cover all the aspects of women empowerment in a single paper. The scope of this paper, therefore, is very much limited to focus on women empowerment in regard to strategies and programmes in the field of urban administration and the ways and means of making them successful and fruitful, beyond the constitutional provision of reservation for women. Because of linkages between different components of urban administration and also between different issues concerning women empowerment, some transgression into other areas outside the legitimate domain of this paper becomes inevitable.

The impact of political empowerment of women in urban administration, as envisaged in the Constitutional amendment, can be studied with considerable interest and profit, if the study is buttressed by empirical evidence collected through field survey of sampled municipalities in the state. But this task seems to be time consuming and can be taken up by some Research Institutes and not by the present paper.

Good Urban Governance

Considered in a broader sense, good urban governance implies a continuous process of raising the level of performance of urban government in its different manifestations, forging harmonious relationship between different stakeholders, evolving institutions and techniques for better governance, improving the capacity of the city government to meet demands, challenges and pressures imposed by changes taking place within the city as well as externally. In this task of good urban governance all stakeholders, including women, have to play their respective roles. The key issues of good urban governance do not stand alone, but are inextricably linked to each other. These linkages are not automatic but contrived, and the inadequacies and imperfections of one have the potential of impacting on others.

Recent trends in decentralization, a major issue in urban administration, suggest four types of reforms. These include, (i) political empowerment which includes creation of elected bodies with adequate powers devolved to different bodies in the hierarchy and adequate representation of women and weaker sections on these bodies, (ii) functional empowerment which includes devolution of functions and concomitant powers, (iii) fiscal management which includes optimization of expenditure and mobilization of financial resources and also their devolution from higher levels of government to local bodies, and (iv) urban planning which implies bottom-up planning of different aspects of urban government and involvement of different stakeholders in the process.

Madhya Pradesh has been a pioneer in adopting participatory governance structure in response to the constitutional amendment which intends to entrust decisive role to local bodies as institutions of self-governance. The State has created a three-tier system of urban governance, consisting at present of 14 municipal corporations, 85 municipal councils and 235 nagar panchayats. The new functions assigned to urban local bodies (ULBs) in respect of planning, welfare and development, in addition to the traditional ones, have yet to be taken up by a majority of ULBs, since with the present level of revenue and expenditure, even all the obligatory functions are not being performed.

The central and the state governments are no less responsible for slackening the process for decentralization, by not acting in the direction ordained by the 74th constitution amendment. Most of the subjects intended to be devolved to ULBs under the amendment are also being handled by the central and the state governments through central and state programmes and centrally sponsored programmes and, therefore, the emerging functional decentralization may not be of the type which may give ULBs the status of units of self-governance, as envisaged in the Constitution.

Some Facts About Urbanization Relating to Women in Madhya Pradesh

Madhya Pradesh is a comparatively less urbanized state of India, with 26.67% of its population being urban as against 27.78% in India in 2001. The female population of the state constituted 47.32% of total population and the female/male ratio comes to 899:1000 in urban M.P. as against 901 in urban India. The urban female literacy rate has recorded a higher growth rate compared to that of male literacy rate from 51.74% in 1991 to 70.62% in 2001, as against 80.98% and 87.78% for urban males in respective years. This rapid growth of female literacy rate in urban areas holds promise for larger and effective participation of women in urban administration. There is heavy concentration of urban population in class I cities, each with a population of one lakh and above (55.77% of total urban population), nearly 28% of urban population in living in medium sized towns in the population range of 20,000 and less than one lakh, and 16% of urban population living in small towns, each with a population of less than 20,000. The urban problems are more pressing and acute and of larger magnitude in bigger cities, but non-availability of basic services is more pronounced in these small towns. Nearly 25% of urban population in the state lives in slums where urban amenities are either not available or are very scanty.

Reservation of Seats for Women in the ULBs in Madhya Pradesh

The conformity legislation enacted by Madhya Pradesh Government makes provisions for the reservation of seats for the marginalized and weaker sections of society, such as SC and ST and OBCs and also for women, so as to give them their due share in urban administration. As per provisions of the state legislation, not less than 1/3 of total number of seats are to be reserved for SC, ST and OBCs and not less than 1/3 of the total number of seats so reserved, shall be reserved for women belonging to these classes. The other provision is that not less than 1/3 of the total number of seats filled up by direct election in every ULB (including such reserved seats for women belonging to SC, ST and OBCs) shall be reserved for women and allotted by rotation to different wards in respective municipalities in the prescribed manner. Similarly, 1/3 of the total number of seats of Mayors/Presidents, shall be reserved for women (including number of seats reserved for women belonging to SC, ST and OBCs).

In the ward committees to be constituted in urban areas which have population of 3 lakhs and above, women shall get 1/3 representation. These ward committees are intended to ensure closer proximity of citizens and elected representatives and thereby widen the process of participatory governance. These ward committees provide the necessary linkages between the citizens and the civic administration. The people are more confident of bringing local problems to the ward committees as they believe that proximity will get more attention. Different aspects of day-to-day civic life, such as water supply, drainage, maintenance of local roads, solid waste disposal, street lighting, neighbourhood parks and environmental pollution, can be handled and supervised in a better way at this level. Women have much greater role to play in these ward committees since they are more aware of the problems of the households in their respective wards. But in no case, the status of these ward committees is to be reduced to the level of ineffective advisory committees.

We regret that these ward committees have not yet been constituted in the state. The state government must remove hurdles in the way of constitution of these committees. It is suggested that, as in Kerala, in Madhya Pradesh also ward committees should be constituted in ULBs with population of one lakh and above and there can be ward sabhas for towns with less than one lakh population.

The legislation relating to the constitution of District Planning Committees, which have a constitutional status, also makes a provision for reservation of seats for women. It is expected that the participation of women in the DPCs would help in effective tackling of problems of women and children in their respective jurisdictions.

Since the implementation of 74th Constitution Amendment Act, women representation has increased considerably in municipal administration and district planning. From an insignificant level prior to the amendment, women representation in ULBs in M.P. has increased to more than 33% of total number of seats. To be more specific, out of 6866 urban wards in the State, in which elections to ULBs were held, 2300 wards were reserved for women and the number of wards in which women were elected constituted 34.6% of total number of wards. Similarly 1/3 seats of Mayors and Presidents have gone to women. This is reckoned as a big force in urban administration provided it is channelised in right directions through right type of motivation, awareness and training.

Beyond the Constitutional Mandate

Reservation of seats for women, which is constitutional mandate for the state government, does not mean the end of the process of empowerment of women. It may be the beginning and not the accomplishment of the task. Much lies beyond the mandate to make women participation in urban governance, as well as outside, more meaningful and effective.

Though the domain of ULBs has been broadened with more financial resources made available to them through devolution from the central and the state governments, they have seldom attempted to include programmes relating to women in a big way and allow women to take up leadership, more particularly in small and medium towns. Mostly, the ULBs are getting these programmes tailor-made along with necessary funds from the central and then state governments, with little involvement of local bodies in their formulation.

The basic needs of the poor pose a challenge to the urban administration and city planners. The human settlements in the congested conglomerations are having abysmal infrastructure. The women in urban areas have to bear the brunt of the burden at all stages, water taps, washing points, polluted drainage often go through the trauma when their children play in dangerous and unhealthy environment. The poor women are deprived of their fundamental rights to live in peace and dignity. The conditions under which a sizeable number of poor women live and work are really deplorable. More serious problems include exposure to water borne diseases, fatigue and risk of miscarriage during pregnancy. Added to this is the problem of alcoholism encouraged by the location of liquor shops within the proximity of slums. Their make-shift jhuggies, with no facility of lavatories, remain under the constant fear of demolition by anti-encroachment squads of the local body.

A number of problems facing the urban population can be better understood and tackled by women decision makers, managers and planners. They have the experience of facing such problems in their day to day activities. Even illiterate women belonging to SC and ST have some awareness about cleanliness, sanitation and environment. What they lack is confidence and initiative which can be created and developed through proper orientation, training and change in attitudes.

We agree that it is difficult to draft literate and vocal women for the tasks, particularly in slum areas and small towns. What is lacking is awareness among women about their rights and obligations. In bigger cities, there is no dearth of educated women even with specialized knowledge, to take up assignments in the ward committees and other committees of the municipal corporations or council. In due course of time more women would pick up courage and determination to solve people's problems. Considerable responsibility lies with different political parties to train women workers for taking up responsibility, particularly on reserved seats. It has been reported that women Mayors/Presidents are more sensitive and responsive to peoples' problems than their male counterparts, though this needs empirical evidence for substantiation.

Non-government organizations (NGOs) can play an important role in organizing women and creating awareness about problems facing women in urban areas. In the rural areas of some states, the well-known NGO, Action for Welfare and Awakening in Rural Environment (AWARE), started in 1975, has played a significant role in providing the alternative strategy of development and empowerment of women that begins with awareness generation, psychological empowerment, motivation and sensitization and involvement in participation in programmes rather than mere economic empowerment. Information and awareness about what they can do legally, peacefully and constitutionally to fight against their exploitation are very essential. In this sense, awareness is empowerment. The efficacy of legislation protecting women interests largely depends upon the level of information disseminated among the members of the community about their legal entitlements.

The strategy for empowering women has to focus beyond economic restructuring to include restructuring of social relations. Experience shows that even programmes of economic amelioration have not improved their status in the family and society because of lack of awareness about these programmes and their entitlements.

It is observed that state sponsored programmes generally adopt a top-down approach, without much participation of beneficiary groups, both in decision-making and implementation. Even massive outlays in five year plans have not brought about desired social change to ensure a sustainable process of development. We agree with the approach of the AWARE that a massive programme of psychological awareness generation, information sharing and motivation, backed up by economic assistance can bring about multi-dimensional transformation which financial assistance alone cannot bring about. Awareness can be created even before the spread of literacy, though the process would become more accelerated if women become literate.

The NGOs working in the field of social development can be entrusted with the task of providing necessary forum to women working in the field of urban administration for sharing their failure and success stories. The women representatives in local bodies need to be made aware of programmes of different departments, their implications and the nitty-gritty of urban administration, with a view to making women office-bearers more independent and confident in performing their functions and duties.

For better implementation of urban schemes, it is proposed that the Andhra Pradesh pattern of community-based organization may be adopted in Madhya Pradesh, for the dissemination of information about different programmes and for providing women participation in their formulation and implementation. The initiative taken by the Andhra Pradesh Government in all the urban local bodies of the state in respect of involvement of women in urban governance is commendable. The most striking feature of the programme is the role of 'facilitator' adopted by municipalities. In all the towns, community-based organizations of urban poor women have been created and entrusted with all the works under Swarn Jayanti Shehri Rojgar Yojana (SJSRY) along with maintenance and improvement of community sanitation. A three-tier organizational structure has been constituted at different levels. This includes (i) the neighbourhood groups (NHG) at the lowest level consisting of 10 to 40 women, representing urban poor or slum families, to identify the felt-needs of the people, (ii) the neighbourhood committees (NC) at the ward level to prioritise the needs in accordance with the availability of funds, (iii) Community Development Societies (CDS) at the municipal level, with a view to identify availability of basic services and missing services in poor neighbourhoods, to provide links with agencies and departments for promoting action for meeting the needs, to prepare community plans proposals, to moblise resources of men and materials and to explore the possibility of borrowing funds for financing the projects. The urban local bodies, instead of entrusting the works to registered civil contractors, assign such works to community groups and involve the community in every stage of development, from selection of works to execution and participatory good governance. The government has also taken up the task of capacity building of women to empower them with required knowledge and skills to carry out their responsibilities effectively. These community-based organizations are also entrusted with the function of social audit in their respective areas. This scheme for women in participatory urban governance introduced by the Andhra Pradesh government may be taken up in other states, including Madhya Pradesh, after thorough examination of the scheme to suit local conditions.

Conclusion

The constitutional safeguards for women in terms of reservation of seats may not be taken as the end of women empowerment. A lot has to be done to involve women in urban governance. In this task, NGOs and womens' organizations can play a catalytic role. What is needed the most is awareness about programmes of different departments in respect of women empowerment. Within the framework of National Policy for women empowerment and the state policy, we have to set goals and objectives, determine priorities, lay down sequence and the pace of different programmes, promote coordination and integration between different programmes and ensure participation and involvement of women in their formulation and implementation.

The strategy of Womens' Component Plan adopted in the IX Plan and to be continued in the subsequent plans, ensuring not less than 30% of benefits/funds flowing to women from all ministries and departments, can succeed only when there is proper coordination between different departments and programmes prioritization of programmes and sufficient awareness among women and their organizations and involvement of NGOs and womens' organizations in their formulation and implementation. Mere strategy of reservation of seats and funds for women, by itself, cannot deliver the goods.

EMPOWERMENT OF FEMALE SCAVENGERS: LIBERATION FROM SOCIAL AND OCCUPATION BONDAGE

Awadhesh Kumar Singh[*]

Women empowerment is the key term that defines and determines the direction of diverse discourses on women. The Beijing Conference (1995) was the most significant milestone in the journey towards ensuring gender equality and enriching pragmatic insights into issues concerning women's empowerment. Moreover, under the New Women Policy (2001), Government of India has emphasised an action plan for empowerment of women. Significantly, the series of world and national conferences on women over the last two decades have contributed to the progressive strengthening of legal, economic, social and political dimensions of gender equality through women empowerment. The dynamics of gender disparity and women's abuse and exploitation have attracted the attention of policy makes to reconsider the strategies, approaches and programmes for women's steady march towards their all-round development. Importantly, a lot of progress has been made all over the country towards the goal of equality, development and empowerment, at the levels of awareness, advocacy, formulation of policies, programmes and plans and enactment of laws.

Moreover, government, non-government, private and voluntary sectors have done significant work to operationalize these. It is high time that vigorous efforts are made at the level of plan formulation and implementing these policies, programmes and plans into action and making women's empowerment a reality. Educational empowerment of women holds the key to their economic and political empowerment. It is the first step towards ensuring equality, justice, human rights concerns and entitlements. Importantly, economic empowerment of women is a necessary condition for enabling women to seek justice and equality. Without economic strength women cannot be able to exercise their rights and entitlements. Therefore, it is necessary to seek participation of women as equal partners with men in all fields of work, equal access to employment, equal opportunities for work related training and full protection of women at work place. Economic empowerment of women including reduction of female poverty requires programmes that focus on identifying, developing and promoting alternative approaches to increase women's access to and control over the means of making a living on a sustainable and long term basis. Moreover, economic empowerment necessitates supporting their existing livelihood, widening their choices and building their capacity to take advantage of new economic opportunities (Srivastava, 2001). Economic empowerment strategies advocate that the government undertakes legislative measures to speed up women's participation in economic life, including the rights of equality in property ownership and inheritance and access to credit, financial services and assistance in entrepreneurial development.

Scavengers are predominantly found in cities to remove night soil and clean latrines. Scavening as an occupation for women is still predominant among the *"Bhangi"* , though the heinous practice has been legally banned in India. Despite the Constitutional and legal provisions which direct the state to promote the educational and economic development of scavengers, they remain marginalized in the Indian society because they are still engaged in sanitary services specially in carrying the night soil. The attempts at improving scavenging conditions and empowerment of scavengers through national scheme of liberation and rehabilitation of scavengers and their dependents (1991) has no doubt paved the way of liberation from occupational and social bondage but the existing sanitary conditions in cities and towns simply demonstrate that progress of integrated low cost sanitary scheme is beyond satisfaction. Moreover, the efforts for liberation and rehabilitation of scavengers particularly female scavengers and sweepers are inadequate and the execution of the scheme is also found to be ineffective. Against this backdrop, present paper attempts to review the scavenging conditions in urban India, status of scavengers and efforts for their empowerment, perspective of liberation of scavengers from social and occupational bondage and also presents a package of recommendations for policy imperatives.

Status of Scheduled Caste Women

It is rightly observed that the struggle for gender equality is one of the hallmarks of the 20th century. Much progress has been achieved, but the agenda remains unfinished in all societies. Gender continues to be a powerful barrier shaping the rights, capabilities, and opportunities of an individual from birth throughout life-time. Fairness and social justice cannot be attained if women are violated, and if they do not have equitable control over resources and decision making (Action for Gender Equality, a group formed at Beijing conference, 1995). The Action Plan further stated that we believe that the empowerment of women, equitable access to resources, power and decision making is essential to gender equality. We recognize that such a process requires a realignment of power in decision making at the household, institutional and all levels of society. The ultimate goal, we believe, should be an equitable partnership between women and men built on the strength of shared knowledge, energy, creativity and skills. Such a partnership is of intrinsic value. It can also bring positive benefits to society as a whole, and contribute in solving many of the world's most pressing problems. The role of women in development is most intimately related to the goal of comprehensive socio-economic development. Any development strategy which perceives women as a specific interest issue and designs programmes to generate income or meet their basic needs will not serve the purpose, until and unless the multi-dimensional and multi-sectoral process and structures that marginalise women are examined and tackled. For this we need to observe development as human development with the direct involvement of women through participation and empowerment (Pinto, 1995).

The plight of women in India is no better than that of women in other developing countries. Importantly, the status of women in a complex society is not uniform. Within the Indian subcontinent, there have been infinite variations of the status of women, differing according to the cultural milieu, family structure, caste, class, occupation, property rights etc. All these factors are significant determinants of variations in her position in different groups. The Scheduled Caste women who constitute a sizeable population of India is subjected not merely to gender bias, but also to indignities arising out of the age old tradition of untouchability from which, incidentally the entire social group of Scheduled Caste suffer. The deep rooted social discriminations have compelled this section of India's population to lead a life of bare subsistence level, both in economic terms and human values (NCW, 1998).

Of the 407 million total women of India (1991 census), 66.29 million i.e. 16 per cent belong to the Scheduled Caste communities constituting a sizeable percentage of rural peasantry and labourers. Having occupied the lowest rank in the social hierarchy, these communities, generation after generation, have been the victim of age old practice of untouchability. Because of the consequential social and economic disabilities, the development problems of the Scheduled Caste women get compounded, the various prejudices and discrimination, against them coming in the way of their personality development. The Scheduled Caste women thus form a category of their own which is more deprived of access to development resources, social, economic and political than their counterparts in the general population needing special attention in the empowerment programmes for women (NCW, 1994).

The Scheduled Caste women are prone to occupational health problems associated with degraded working environment, mental stress, long hours of work, lifting a heavy weights, contact with hazardous and infected material, inconvenient postural conditions of work etc. Besides they suffer from malnutrition, anaemia, post delivery complications, tuberculosis, chronic eye problems and general delibrity due to low level of food intake, child bearing and constant deprivations. The general debility and occupational health problems result in constant ill health among this class of women. Maternal mortality is much higher among Scheduled Castes than the average national rate and one of the main reasons for this has been found to be unhygienic and primitive parturition practices. The Scheduled Caste children suffer from disadvantages of low immunity and low birth weight resulting in high infant mortality rate (NCW, 1998).

Urban Sanitation

Till recently, standard of living of a country and particularly of a region was judged primarily by its Gross National Product and of its people by per capita income. Increasing concern about the environment, air quality and health had led to the conclusion that there is more to life than mere growth for growth's sake; merely being rich in terms of material good sans clean air, safe water and healthy environment is not a fair measure to determine the quality of life. Now acceptable indicators reflecting quality of life are as follows (Shafi, 1995) : (1) availability of safe drinking water; (2) quality and quantity of food intake; (3) shelter and delivery of basic services and facilities within a habitat; (4) medical and health care services; (5) basic/primary education, literacy levels; (6) environmental sanitation : air and water quality; solid waste (garbage) collection and disposal.

A convenient supply of safe water and the sanitary disposal of human waste are essential, although not the only ingredient of a healthy, productive life. Water that is not safe for human consumption can spread disease, water that is not conveniently located results in the loss of productive time and energy of the water carrier usually women or children and inadequate facilities for excreta disposal reduce the potential benefits of a safe water supply by transmitting pathogens from the infected to the healthy by various direct or indirect routes. Invariably it is the poor who suffer the most from the absence of safe water and sanitation, because they lack not only the means to provide for such facilities but also information on how to minimize the ill effects of the insanitary conditions in which they live. As a result, the debilitating effects of insanitary living lowers the productive potential of the very people (Singh & Singh, 1999).

Plight of Scavengers

In India today, scavengers and sweepers still carry out the basic sanitary services in cities and towns. While many are employed by urban local authorities to clean the sewers and sweep the streets, a significant number still work in their traditional occupations. This means that scavengers are still cleaning latrines by hand and carrying night soil in baskets/ buckets on their head or waists. As their occupation renders them permanently polluted, scavengers are treated as untouchable, even by other Scheduled Castes. Again, scavengers are not limited to urban areas only. In rural areas also they are engaged in cleaning of service (dry) latrines as well as safe disposal of wastes including lifting and flaying of fallen carcass (dead animals) and also processing, tanning and manufacturing of leather goods. These activities are performed by a specific caste or community in the rural areas. In Uttar Pradesh *'Chamar'* and Jatav (Scheduled Castes) are engaged in this job while in some parts of state a sizeable number of lower castes of Muslims and lower castes of Hindus are engaged in this job. This means that scavengers have extremely limited job opportunities than other sanitary work that they live in acute poverty in segregated communities and have extremely low level of literacy and job mobility (Chaplin, 1997). Such socio-economic conditions for scavengers still persist despite various provisions in the Indian Constitution which stipulate that the state should promote the economic and educational interests of Scheduled Castes and protect them from discrimination and exploitation.

Interestingly, in 1993 Employment of Manual Scavengers and Construction of Dry Latrines (Prohibition) Act 1993 was implemented in the country to abolish scavenging and rehabilitate scavengers. It was estimated that the dehumanising practice of scavenging still continues in 2587 towns, involving 7,00,000 scavengers (Jayanti, 1995). Though accurate figures of scavengers, including sweepers is not available however it is estimated that in India more than 150 million untouchable are engaged in lower job viz. Cleaning latrines, streets, sewers and handling municipal solid wastes including industrial wastes; lifting and flaying fallen carcass; handling hydes and collecting trash. They are marginalized and living in sub human conditions (Apaeth,1996).

Characteristics of Scavengers

In generalised terms, the existential reality of scavengers could be described as under (Pathak, 1998) : (i) Scavengers constitute an underprivileged social group treated as 'impure' and consequently socially ostracized and ritually avoided; (ii) Like "Pariah" groups, they are treated as inferior and often regarded as less than human. They live on the fringe of society, often excluded from social contact, though their services are accepted as highly valuable; (iii) They are socially ostracized because of practising a polluting profession, as also for certain peculiar and objectionable habits; (iv) They are backward, and often oppressed, not because they are racially, socially and culturally inferior than others, but simply because they have been assigned the lowest of the low status in social hierarchy; (v) As outcastes and rejects of the Indians society, scavengers have suffered condemnable human indignities throughout the ages; (vi) They have been treated like dreaded contagious disease calling for a disdainful distance and the most minimal social contact; (vii) Because of their degradation, scavengers have been compelled to live their life as socially disadvantaged persons reluctantly resigned to accepting their social degradation and discrimination as part of their fate; (viii) Besides social backwardness, scavengers are economically backward too. Most scavenger families therefore live in poverty because of both structural and personal factors. Structural factors being the low family income on account of engagement in low paying occupations, and personal factors being their

Table 1 : Statewise Status of Sanitation in Urban India

State	*Percentage of population served by safe drinking water (1991)*	*Percentage of population covered by sewerage (1989)*	*No. of scavengers (1997-98)*	*No. of scavengers liberated (2001)*	*No. of conversion and construction of latrines (2001)*	*No. of community toilets*
Andhra Pradesh	73.8	11	7453	3136	604448	150
Assam	64.1	16	16873	1881	90340	—
Bihar	73.4	23	40249	—	9465	—
Gujarat	87.2	38	62842	—	—	—
Goa	61.7	13	—	—	45500	—
Haryana	93.2	28	25279	7982	200224	—
Himachal Pradesh	91.9	14	4760	—	—	—
Jammu & Kashmir	N.A.	8	4150	1900	61845	—
Kanataka	81.4	38	14555	3227	177689	117
Kerala	38.6	28	1339	726	14540	—
Madhya Pradesh	79.5	8	80072	3361	113216	—
Maharashtra	90.5	40	126691	2998	199466	2089
Meghalaya	75.4	N.A.	607	30	5290	—
Nagaland	45.5	N.A.	1800	—	—	—
Orissa	62.8	10	19103	856	51597	10

Contd....

Table 1 : (Contd....)

State	*Percentage of population served by safe drinking water (1991)*	*Percentage of population covered by sewerage (1989)*	*No. of scavengers (1997-98)*	*No. of scavengers liberated (2001)*	*No. of conversion and construction of latrines (2001)*	*No. of community toilets*
Punjab	94.2	49	31290	15353	223777	—
Rajasthan	86.5	10	57736	11506	423947	—
Tamil Nadu	74.2	48	35561	4393	155561	372
Tripura	71.1	13	—	—	18788	—
Uttar Pradesh	85.8	14	246916	43404	775113	100
Uttranchal	—	—	—	2415	4092	—
West Bengal	86.2	20	30000	8996	299820	420
Chhatisgarh	—	—	—	210	6194	—
Delhi	—	—	17420	—	—	—
Jharkhand	—	—	—	—	1771	—
Sikkim	—	—	400	—	—	—
Urban India	81.4	28	825572	112460	3492955	3966

Source : India Infrastructure Report, 2001, OUP, Delhi, 2001.

Urban Infrastructure Finance Wing, HUDCO, Delhi, 2002.

large-family size and male members' indulgence in smoking, drinking and gambling; (ix) Most scavengers are illiterate and thus educationally backward. In spite of the facilities for their free education, children are not sent to schools in an overwhelming number of cases, and female education is not considered to be at all important; (x) The economic and educational backwardness has deprived many scavenger families from advantage of the Constitutionally concerned privileges meant for the welfare of the dispossessed; (xi) Politically too, scavengers are little organized as compared to people of other low-born sub-castes.

Liberation and Rehabilitation of Scavengers

The objective of this scheme is to liberate them from their existing hereditary, obnoxious and inhuman occupation of manually removing night-soil and filth and to provide for alternative and dignified occupations within a period of five years.

The Scheme had the following components :

(i) Time-bound programme for identification of scavengers and their dependents and their aptitude for alternative trade.

(ii) Training in identified trades for scavengers and their dependents in the nearest local training institutions/ centres of various departments of State Governments, Central Government and other semi-government and non-government organizations.

(iii) Rehabilitation of scavengers in various trades and occupations by providing subsidy, margin money, loan and bank loan also.

The responsibility of rehabilitation of municipal scavengers in the service of local bodies has been entrusted to the local bodies themselves. The scheme proposes to provide rehabilitation training to private scavengers and their dependents, including the dependents of scavengers employed by local bodies. The scheme arranges for training of all the scavengers whether they are partially or wholly engaged in the said occupation.

The rehabilitation of scavengers thus freed from the traditional work of disposing night soil as head load, is the responsibility of the Ministry of Social Justice & Empowerment. This is the 'soft core' work of the entire scheme of liberation and rehabilitation. To meet this objective the scheme evolved three time bound programmes of identification of scavengers and their dependents at the national level in different state/union territories and up to the level of village and a survey of aptitudes of scavengers for alternative jobs or trades and a comprehensive training programme for identified trade or job. (Chandra, 1989). Further an expenditure of Rs. 5000 per month and a stipend of Rs. 150 each for identified liberated scavengers and their dependents was envisaged. For their rehabilitation sum of Rs. 50,000 has been fixed as financial assistance to the project for each beneficiary. It includes 50 per cent of subsidy subject to a ceiling of Rs. 10,000 of capital, margin money loan of 15 per cent of the project cost at a nominal interest rate of 4 per cent. Remaining portion of fund requirement is to come from commercial banks. However, the entire amount of subsidy on training is to come from the Central Government while the outlay on margin money is to be shared by respective state and the Central Government in the ratio of 49 : 51.

Ever since the inception of the scheme of liberation and rehabilitation of scavengers in 1991-92 with total fund of Rs. 50.50 crore as Central assistance, there has been an upward steady increase in fund allocation. The cumulative assistance of Central Government under liberation and rehabilitation of scavengers during 1991-92 to 1999-2000 has been reported to be Rs. 531.07 crores. The states which got the lions share in Central assistance are Uttar Pradesh (41.87 per cent) and Madhya Pradesh (20.27 per cent). Importantly, Government of India has established National Scavenging Employees Finance And Development Corporation and Rs. 2164.97 lakh has been released to the states during 1997-98 to 1999-2000. The corporation has sanctioned 6149 units which will benefit to 6344 beneficiaries. Moreover, sanitary marts have been established in the areas of 20,000 to 100,000 population of scavengers for the production of sanitary materials to convert dry sanitary units into flush units.

The HUDCO, under Integrated Low Cost Sanitary Scheme has sanctioned 836 schemes with the project cost of Rs. 141716.78 lakh. The subsidy component of sanctioned project cost was reported to be Rs. 47864.12 lakh. In the state of Uttar Pradesh too, this scheme is being implemented in 59 towns and is progressing in 10 another towns. Under the scheme Rs. 3626.97 project cost of units was sanctioned by HUDCO. By the end of Dec., 2001 48653 units were completed in 59 towns and 69984 units were likely to be completed in 10 towns (Table 3). Importantly, 3492955 units were converted and constructed under the scheme and 112460 scavengers under liberated. In the state of Uttar Pradesh too, 4622 scavengers were liberated in 59 towns and 1175 scavengers were likely to be liberated in 10 towns. During the Eight Plan Period (1992-97), Rs. 464 crore was set aside for this purpose. During the 1991-92 to 1995-96, 104122 scavengers were trained while 223573 were rehabilitated.

Interestingly, out of total identified scavengers in India (736114) a large chunk of scavengers were reported in Uttar Pradesh (30.72 per cent) followed by Maharashtra (17.21 per cent), Rajasthan (11.95 per cent) and Madhya Pradesh (10.88 per cent). Importantly, in western states of Gujarat, Rajasthan and Maharashtra, work of rehabilitation has been slow. In none of these states has the training component covered more than 3.15 per cent of the identified scavengers, and rehabilitation accomplishment is about 11.00 per cent. In Delhi, where the abolition of scavenging was announced by former Prime Minister Shri Rao from the raqmpart of Lal Quila, out of 17420 identified scavengers only 153 where offered training in alternative vacations and 701 were rehabilitated by 1994-95. Situation at the national level is far from satisfactory as out of the total number of identified scavenges (736114) only 13.29 per cent could be trained and 25.74 per cent could be rehabilitated until 1995-96. Since 1991-92, central assistance of Rs. 601.07 crore has been released upto 1999-2000 under the scheme towards assisting 1,38,155 scavengers for training

Table 2 : Funds Released by Central Government for Rehabilitation of Scavengers (1991-92 – 1999-2000)

State	*Central Government Assistant*		*HUDCO Infrastructure Schemes*			
	Funds released (1991-92 – 1999-2000)	*Percentage*	*Urban sanitation (low cost) schemes No.*	*Project cost (Rs. Lakh)*	*Loan Amount (Rs. Lakh)*	*Subsidy anctioned (Rs. Lakh)*
Andhra Pradesh	13.45	2.53	78	25124.57	15711.33	7861.06
Assam	2.15	0.40	27	3908.27	1501.63	1284.50
Bihar	11.27	2.12	3	242.60	118.88	106.75
Gujarat	15.26	2.87	—	—	—	—
Haryana	18.37	3.46	85	4730.90	2357.41	2034.94
Himachal Pradesh	3.13	0.59	—	—	—	—
Jammu & Kashmir	1.03	0.19	7	1707.75	—	215.99
Karnataka	13.30	2.50	67	8054.02	5693.70	1119.98
Kerala	0.55	0.10	2	309.50	213.45	69.93
Madhya Pradesh	107.67	20.27	19	2055.51	1020.30	863.57
Maharashtra	24.87	4.68	58	8245.34	2528.40	2206.42
Orissa	16.76	3.16	63	1218.92	613.33	476.40
Punjab	6.63	1.25	77	5906.33	2065.11	2257.73
Rajasthan	27.86	5.25	158	13393.37	455.74	5149.60

Contd....

Table 2 : (Contd....

State	Central Government Assistant		HUDCO Infrastructure Schemes			
	Funds released (1991-92 – 1999-2000)	*Percentage*	*Urban sanitation (low cost) schemes No.*	*Project cost (Rs. Lakh)*	*Loan Amount (Rs. Lakh)*	*Subsidy anctioned (Rs. Lakh)*
Tamil Nadu	25.27	4.76	87	6590.44	4354.02	1713.51
Uttar Pradesh	222.38	41.87	69	37463.94	12493.71	16850.02
West Bengal	5.63	1.06	14	16578.64	5747.68	5097.37
Delhi	5.28	0.99	—	—	—	—
Nagaland	0.11	0.02	—	—	—	—
Meghalaya	0.03	0.001	3	172.93	71.57	66.67
Pondicherry	0.08	0.01	—	—	—	—
Uttaranchal	—	—	6	116.27	53.20	44.89
Jharkhand	—	—	1	45.40	22.25	19.98
Chhatisgarh	—	—	3	101.86	50.63	44.14
Total	531.07	100.00	836	141716.78	58351.90	47864.12

Source : Report of Ministry of Social Justice & Empowerment, Govt. of India, Delhi, 1999-2000.
Urban Infrastructure Finance, India, HUDCO, Delhi, 2002.

Table 3 : Progress for Integrated Low Cost Sanitation Scheme in Uttar Pradesh

Sl. No.	*Particular*	*59 Towns*	*10 Towns* (Dec., 2001)*
1.	Project cost (Rs. Lakh)	3626.97	18478.51
2.	Amount released (Rs. Lakh)	1558.73	2309.80
3.	Amount utilized (Rs. Lakh)	1464.25	2865.47
4.	Percentage of utilization	93.94	—
5.	Total unit sanctioned	160278	415438
6.	Total unit completed	48653	69984
7.	Physical progress (%)	68.52	—
8.	Percentage completed against sanctioned unit	30.36	16.85
9.	HUDCO Loan	752.91	—
10.	Scavengers liberated	4622	1175

• Banda, Badaun, Moradabad, Mathura, Agra, Muzaffarnagar, Allahabad, Bareilly, Jhansi, Aligarh.

Source : SUDA, Uttar Pradesh, Lucknow, March, 2002.

Table 4 : Number of Scavengers Benefited Under Scavengers Liberation Scheme (1992-93 – 1996-97)

State	*1992-93*		*1993-94*		*1994-95*		*1995-96*		*1996-97*	
	T	*R*	*T*	*R*	*T*	*R*	*T*	*R*	*T*	*R*
Andhra Pradesh	710	1083	153	1406	313	1937	202	1315	—	519
Assam	—	—	—	—	37	61	—	—	571	—
Bihar	—	—	—	—	—	—	—	—	—	—
Gujarat	—	33	—	873	790	1221	—	1681	44	1606
Haryana	—	—	833	1295	1993	1411	827	4735	482	1790
Himachal Pradesh	115	10	123	151	127	158	241	200	604	353
Jammu & Kashmir	20	—	273	7	—	40	—	—	—	—
Karnataka	—	166	166	431	469	987	264	234	83	146
Kerala	—	—	144	116	12	25	—	—	—	—
Madhya Pradesh	11395	10194	10892	12383	8717	15661	7274	14854	4566	7216
Maharashtra	1248	1675	644	2792	3170	3481	2031	3094	1440	1442
Orissa	209	26	1080	872	705	888	422	1060	901	991

Contd....

Table 4 : (Contd....)

State	*1992-93*		*1993-94*		*1994-95*		*1995-96*		*1996-97*	
	T	*R*	*T*	*R*	*T*	*R*	*T*	*R*	*T*	*R*
Punjab	130	—	4102	1138	291	375	—	308	—	552
Rajasthan	528	178	2147	1543	2181	2096	3007	3622	999	2374
Tamil Nadu	—	—	500	2556	3461	4987	625	4094	471	2048
Uttar Pradesh	1865	4620	10651	4213	2692	29665	11556	43006	10396	37416
West Bengal	—	—	103	—	—	—	—	—	100	3000
Delhi	—	505	13	196	121	303	44	825	222	1112
Nagaland	—	—	—	—	—	—	—	—	—	—
Meghalaya	—	—	—	—	—	—	—	—	—	—
Pondicherry	—	93	—	93	—	—	—	—	—	—
Sikkim	—	—	—	—	—	—	—	—	—	—
Total	**16220**	**18583**	**22238**	**41165**	**25079**	**63296**	**26493**	**79028**	**20879**	**60565**

T = Trained, R = Rehabilitated.

Source : Annual Report (1997-98), Ministry of Social Justice & Empowerment, Govt. of India, Delhi.

and 3,56,146 for rehabilitation (Annual Report of MOSJ & F, 2000-01). It is to be noted that central assistance is also extended for the providing scholarship to the children belonging to scavengers.

Conclusion

Scavengers remain marginalised in Indian society even today despite the constitutional provisions which direct the state to promote their educational and economic interests. They remained marginalised because their communities are still predominantly employed to carry out the country's basic sanitary services. Lacking the necessary literacy skills to take advantage of government reservations in education and employment, scavengers have not been able to participate in the job mobility associated with living in rapidly growing urban environment. Moreover, scavenging remains a complicated socio-economic problem, which not only requires adequate funding for its redressal, but needs a radical change of mental outlook. Further, it requires improving scavenging conditions in the urban areas by involving local NGO's in construction of low cost sanitary latrines as well mobilizing scavengers and sweepers for their rehabilitation. The prospect of changing social attitude to scavenging which is an unclear and polluting job also appears distant. The prospects of social transformation of scavengers and sweepers lies in economic empowerment ensuring social justice and adequate representation in government job and political bodies.

A close look at the present trends unmistakably points out the stark reality that the new millennium is unlikely to bring about qualitative improvement in the economic and social postures of women in our country. Unfortunately, Indian women still continue to be crowded in a limited number of low paid, low productivity and uncertain jobs which hold out little prospects for advancement and career building. The reason for this sad state of affairs is that so far none of the potential agents of change, that is the, women's movements, the state or the market forces have seriously challenged the house-hold based patriarchal control over women's labour and family.

Suggestions for Advancement

1. From the point of view of gender equality, there is an imperative need for direct involvement of women in the development programmes in terms of plan formulation and its execution. There is a need to introduce gender sensitivity at the project formulation stage as well as project implementation, both at the governmental and non-government levels.
2. It is the need of hour to design and implement programmes for women through community based organizations. Non-government organizations may be helpful in better targeting of the poor women by creating an environment in the community for sustainable development.
3. In the participatory development process supported by various voluntary organizations, organizing as well as strengthening of women's groups may generate a new sense of dignity, confidence and economic independence to some extent.
4. A societal reorientation for gender friendly society would require a radical transformation through awareness on gender issues and sustained efforts of imparting training and education on various developmental activities. Women's own perceptions about themselves also need to be changed, besides a positive role played by media and other related organizations.
5. Developing first generation entrepreneurs, strengthening existing support system, and improving the performance of women entrepreneurs are some of the crucial points that should be focused.

This can be successfully achieved through sustained support of various organizations for developing infrastructure and imparting training, skill and other EDPs. However, these programmes must focus on the following areas : (a) identifying and selecting the right type of women entrepreneurs; (b) developing entrepreneurial behaviour/qualities to ensure better management of the unit; (c) linking viable projects with timely supply of production/raw materials and marketing channel and the area in which the project is to be set up; (d) preparation of project plans best suited to the entrepreneurial concern and the area in which the project is to be setup; (e) equipping the woman entrepreneurs with managerial competence to ensure effective m..nagement of the units; (f) to organize finance, infrastructure and implementation support to ensure successful running of business; (g) post-supervision of projects established to ensure proper understanding of problem being faced and their appropriate solution (Sengupta and Singh, 2001).

6. The contribution of women to many subsistence, home based, non-traditional and viable economic activities should be upgraded through programme inputs, like training, credit, marketing etc. There is a dire need of appreciating and understanding the links between the different roles of women and hence for a conscious articulation and policy to promote employment of women as well as the links between technology and work opportunities.
7. An effective support mechanism is needed at the grass-root level to ensure that policies of rights, entitlements and ownerships are made sustainable.
8. Guaranteeing equal employment opportunities; providing preferential treatment and positive discrimination are essential for economic empowerment of women. Moreover, ensuring adequate welfare services, social security, and providing equal access to financial assistance and credit is needed to make the women competent successful entrepreneurs.
9. Organizing women's groups and promoting female leadership to encourage women-entrepreneurship and other self reliant activities, particularly in the formal sectors should be ensured through active involvement of NGO's and voluntary sector.

10. The programme of liberation and rehabilitation of scavengers should be made more gender sensitive and integrated strategies should be formulated to rehabilitate female scavengers in India on the priority basis.

11. To educate people about the Reservation Policy and its benefits. It is imperative that the policy and its benefits should be made known in clear terms to the target group. The governments at different levels and their instrumentalities have a special duty to educate the concerned people to reap the fruits of Reservation Policy available to the concerned castes. The respective local bodies, Directorate of Local Bodies, State Government and the Central Government have an obligatory duty to carry the benefits of Reservation Policy to each the every individual. To this effect they must launch special awareness drives and other campaigns including audio visual aids so that the scavengers could be made aware of the benefits accruing to them.

12. For the education of scavenger's children, separate schools with modern syllabi, equipped with all facilities should be opened by the state, urban local bodies or by N.G.Os. It should be preferably residential, so that children could be brought up and educated in a modern environment. To discourage the scavengers from making their children work and earn meagre wages to supplement family income, vocational institutions should be opened for their children only, so that their wards could be trained in some trade which might be helpful to earn substantially and they might make the trade their profession.

13. To mitigate the acute problem of accommodation employer should invariably provide accommodation on official rate of rent. The houses should be such as to accommodate their cattle and live-stock. Special colonies should be constructed by the employers to accommodate the scavengers and their families.

14. The payment of salary should be regularly made on time. This will ease out the money-lender who always demands his pound of flesh on the pay day itself. It may be suggested that the payment be made through cheques to overcome this problem. To overcome the practice of taking loans and advances in the name of marriages and festivals, it is suggested that some mechanism should be designed to ascertain that the money has actually been spent on the purpose for which it was taken. In this sphere the community and the society can do the maximum to assist the organization giving loans and advances.
15. Proper system of performance appraisal should b e developed whereby the better performance is rewarded and worse is punished. This would deter the superior's bias in favour of males and give female workers incentives to perform better. About changed duty hours leading to dissatisfaction original time schedule of the working hours should be reinforced but it should be strictly fixed working hours with definite period which should not be changed arbitrarily.
16. The promotional avenues should also be opened for the scavengers in the service. This will enhance their morale and sense of commitment to the service. Their promotion as beat incharge and superior should be time-bound subject to the rejection of unit. Their mobility to the job outside the present service would automatically increase if they are provided facilities of education.

REFERENCES

Chandra, Ramesh, Rehabilitation By Scavengers, *Economic & Political Weekly*, Sept., 11, 1999.

Chaplin, S.E., Scavengers : Still Marginalized, *the Administrator*, Vol. XIII, January-March, 1997.

Jayanthi, C., The Sewage Problem, *the Pioneer*, 14 Dec., 1995.

NCW, Report on Development of Female Education; National Commission on Women, Delhi, 1994.

NIUA, Report on Urban Sanitation, National Institute of Urban Affairs, Delhi, 1997.

Pathak, Bineshwari, Liberation of Scavengers From Social and Occupational Bondage in Social Justice and Development of Weaker Sections (Ed.) Pathak, B., Inter India Publications, Delhi, 1998.

Pathak, Bineshwari, Road to Freedom : A Social Study on the Abolition of Scavengers in India, Motilal Banarsi Das Pub., Delhi, 1992.

Pinto, M., Development Through Empowerment of Women in India, *Kurukshetra,* August, 1995.

Sengupta, A.K. and Singh, A.K. Women Empowerment : Some Issues and Suggestions in Gender Equality Through Women's Empowerment : Strategies And Approaches (Ed.) Surendra Singh and S.P. Srivastava, Bharat Book Centre, Lucknow, 2001.

Shafi, S.S., Quality of Life and the Indian Metropolis, *Mainstream,* Sept., 9, 1995.

Singh, S.K., Dalit Women : Socio-Economic Status and Issues, New Royal Book Comp., Lucknow, 2000.

Singh, U.P. And Singh, A.K., Human Ecology and Development in India, APH, Delhi, 1999.

Spaeth, Anthony, Society, *Time,* March 25, 1996.

Srivastava, S.P., Gender Justice and Human Rights of Women in Gender Equality Through Women's Empowerment : Strategies and Approaches (Ed.) Surendra Singh and S.P. Srivastava, Bharat Book Centre, Lucknow, 2001.

Time, The Fighting Back, *Time,* Oct., 20, 1997.

U.P. Government, Ninth Five Year Plan (1997-2002) and Annual Plan, 1997-98, Vol. I, SCP, For SC, U.P.

URBANIZATION AND DEMOGRAPHIC BOTTLENECKS IN UTTAR PRADESH

(Role for Urban Local Bodies)

M.K. Agarwal

Pattern of development among today's developed nations suggests that urbanization is the panacea of socio-economic development of a developing nation or its region. Urbanization is considered to be accompanied by improved quality of life, better income and employment opportunities. The quality of life might include better access to consumption and expenditure, better civic amenities like road, transport, housing, schooling, higher and technical education, drinking water, medical facilities, etc. Thus, it is hoped that urbanization helps the population to avail of better socio-economic opportunities. However, the accompanying features in a developing society might not be as rosy considering the fact that the urbanization might not be in a position to be so good to the rapidly increasing population size. Considering the Indian scenario, in can be offered that despite efforts for more than five decades in improving the socio-economic conditions of the people, results have not been up to the mark. Hence, the Government of India came out with the third tier of government through the 74th Constitution Amendment that bestows more powers to urban local bodies also.

In the present paper, an attempt is being made to analyze the pattern of urbanization in Uttar Pradesh and its impact on demographic variables in the State. In Uttar Pradesh, it is widely held that demographic variables have been at highly uneatisfactory levels. It has been made out in the National Population Policy–2000 that the control of growing population and other improvements in demographic features is now to be accomplished through active involvement of the local governments. Moreover, it is to be appreciated that more than one-fourth of the national population and more than one-fifth of the Uttar Pradesh population lives in urban areas. Therefore to make any policy successful, urban population cannot be ignored. The pace and degree of urbanization in Uttar Pradesh has been very low. The rate of urbanization in the State has been 14.0 per cent in 1971, 18.0 per cent in 1981 and 19.8 per cent in 1991. Even the latest census of 2001 shows that in the total population of 166.05 millions, the urban population was 34.5 millions, i.e., just around 21 per cent. Still, it can be argued that despite relatively low level of urbanization in Uttar Pradesh, overall conditions of urban population and urban infrastructure have been unsatisfactory on many counts.

If we look at the demographic level alone, it is obtained that urbanization in the State has not been helpful in increasing the growth process of the economy nor in curbing poverty and unemployment. Regarding poverty, it might be argued that the incidence of poverty was 60.1 per cent in 1973-74. This declined to 35.4 per cent after two decades in 1993-94 and now as per the latest estimates, the incidence of poverty could not be reduced much in the urban areas. During 1999-2000, the urban poverty rate has been 30.9 per cent whereas the total poverty ratio of the State was 31.2 per cent. Thus, the scenario of urban poverty is not much different in Uttar Pradesh. However, due to high pace of population increase in the State, the absolute size of poverty has gone up instead of being pegged down in the last three decades. There were 8.57 million persons below poverty line in 1973-74. It has been increasing ever since. The number swelled to 10.83 million in 1993-94 and further higher at more than 11 millions in 1999-2000. Thus, whatever be the level of economic development and the pace of urbanization in Uttar Pradesh, the absolute size of poverty has been increasing throughout even though the incidence of urban poverty has been halved between 1973-74 and 1999-2000. Besides the poor economic performance, the important and chronic villain of development has been the poor show in terms of demographic achievements despite increasing urbanization. Even the records of urban segment of the State, in this regard, have not been satisfactory.

Literacy

The literacy rate has been very low in Uttar Pradesh. It was only 57.4 per cent as per 2001 census. The urban literacy rate has been 70.6 per cent. But even in urban areas we find the female literacy rate at 62 per cent as against male literacy rate of 78.1 per cent. This suggests that even in the urban segment of the State spread of literacy has been unsatisfactory. We can also find with the help of district level analysis (presented in Table-2) that the coefficient of variation for urban literacy rate, urban male literacy and urban female literacy has been very low as compared to the coefficient of variation for district wise urbanization. This suggests that the urbanization has poor impact on improving literacy rate in Uttar Pradesh. It is further confirmed through regression estimates presented in Table-6 also for district level urban literacy for males and females and the level of urbanization in 2001.

Impact of Urbanization on Demographic Variables

It is hoped that urbanization helps in improving vital statistics like birth rate, death rate, and infant mortality rate so the stage of population stabilization is reached early. However, the scenario in Uttar Pradesh is not much helpful in this regard. It can be seen through Table-5 that the crude birth rate in the State has declined faster than in the urban areas. Though the urban areas reported lower birth rate than the entire State, the gap between the two has become narrower in 1998 in comparison to the 1980s. This implies that the rural segment has taken a lead in bringing down the birth rate. For the crude death rate, it is found that the crude death rate has almost stopped declining in the urban areas. During the 1990s, there has been a sort of stagnation in the

CDR. Thus, one may derive that the urbanization has no effect in cutting down death rates in the urban segment. In the case of the infant mortality rate also there is an edge for the urban sector. However, the notion of stagnation is more obvious in the 1990s as the IMR has just been lower at 65 in 1998 in comparison to 67 in 1990 and 66 in 1993. Thus, during the decade of the 1990s, urbanization could not show its impact on improving the demographic scenario at least in the urban sector itself.

These points are further analyzed with the help of regression estimates using district wise trend of urbanization and its impact on demographic variable. The results are contained in Tables-4 & 6. Very peculiar types of results are obtained regarding impact of urbanization on total fertility rate and sex ratio in the districts of Uttar Pradesh. If we go though the results contained in Table-4 for 1991, the increased urbanization seems to reduce total fertility rate as well as under-five mortality rate (that is, child morality). However, poor explanatory capacity of the equation does not allow anyone to draw the conclusion that urbanization helps in improving the demographic features of the State. Even regression estimates of the seventy districts of Uttar Pradesh based on 2001 census (given in Table 6) show similar trends. Although the situation seems to be slightly better in 2001 as unlike in 1991, the value of R^2 has been higher at 0.34 with respect to impact of urbanization and TFR among the districts.

However, one thing is there that has been another source of worry to the urban planners and demographers alike. It is in terms of adverse impact of urbanization on the sex ratio in urban areas of Uttar Pradesh. What has been more puzzling is the probability that 0-6 years sex ratio is higher than the over all sex ratio in the urban areas. Therefore, it suggests that urbanization in Uttar Pradesh does not mean any improvement in the sex ratio in favour of females. Rather there seems to be adverse situation obtaining in the urban areas for leadings secure a better life even in the urban areas.

Table : 1 District Wise Demographic Features of Uttar Pradesh : 2001

State/District	*CBR*	*TFR*	*Urbanization*	*Urban Literacy Rate (%)*			*Urban Sex Ratio*	
				Persons	*Males*	*Females*	*All Ages*	*0-6 years*
Uttar Pradesh	31.4	4.4	20.78	70.61	78.13	62.05	879	880
Saharanpur	29.5	4.0	26.15	69.34	75.06	62.79	873	857
Muzaffarnagar	31.9	4.4	25.52	66.64	74.74	57.58	887	853
Bijnor	33.0	4.6	24.33	62.12	68.07	55.51	904	917
Moradabad	34.5	5.0	31.03	57.10	62.78	50.67	887	917
Rampur	35.5	5.1	24.97	52.20	58.18	45.58	906	927
Jyotiba P Ngr	34.1	4.9	24.64	54.30	62.09	45.60	899	919
Meerut	27.7	3.9	48.54	68.02	75.47	59.50	873	861
Baghpat	27.5	3.9	19.72	70.00	79.81	58.73	865	837
Ghaziabad	28.7	3.9	55.20	75.94	83.90	66.76	862	838
G B Nagar	31.1	4.4	36.79	73.99	82.19	64.07	826	823
Bulandshahar	29.8	4.4	23.05	64.61	74.56	53.54	893	862
Aligarh	30.7	4.5	28.87	66.38	75.15	56.37	871	880
Hathras	30.6	4.4	19.88	70.51	79.71	59.73	875	873
Mathura	32.0	4.6	28.14	72.04	83.89	58.46	853	846
Agra	28.3	3.8	43.12	68.48	76.04	59.87	866	819
Firozabad	34.1	4.8	30.36	65.12	72.80	56.42	877	882
Etah	34.1	4.9	17.34	75.27	82.26	67.43	884	892
Mainpuri	31.1	4.4	14.45	54.08	61.46	45.78	889	872

Contd....

Table : 1 (Contd....)

State/District	CBR	TFR	Urbanization	Urban Literacy Rate (%)			Urban Sex Ratio	
				Persons	Males	Females	All Ages	0-6 years
Budaun	37.7	5.5	18.16	58.11	64.77	50.64	889	887
Bareilly	34.1	4.9	32.59	61.24	69.10	52.32	893	892
Pilibhit	33.9	4.9	17.89	54.98	65.81	42.85	885	910
Shahjahanpur	33.7	4.8	20.66	68.26	74.13	61.52	850	678
Kheri	32.8	4.7	10.78	67.39	73.85	60.23	875	904
Sitapur	33.0	4.7	11.94	66.52	73.94	58.05	903	912
Hardoi	33.8	4.8	11.98	70.09	76.85	62.56	881	906
Unnao	29.5	4.1	15.25	77.20	81.82	72.00	897	885
Lucknow	24.2	3.1	63.62	74.14	81.44	66.16	890	903
Rae Bareli	31.6	4.3	9.53	71.64	77.95	64.40	913	906
Farrukhabad	29.8	4.3	21.61	66.91	74.37	58.31	870	858
Kannauj	30.7	4.4	16.74	77.61	83.91	70.47	895	878
Etawah	29.5	4.0	23.06	82.86	88.95	75.98	881	878
Auraiya	30.0	4.1	14.31	75.68	82.30	68.14	885	886
Kanpur Dehat	29.0	4.2	6.78	81.52	83.05	79.76	882	899
Kanpur Nagar	20.7	2.6	67.00	73.60	82.29	63.54	869	829
Jalaun	27.0	3.7	23.39	78.06	86.53	68.29	865	882
Jhansi	26.2	3.4	41.08	76.02	85.97	65.00	868	873
Lalitpur	36.1	4.9	14.51	72.84	83.73	60.14	901	894

Contd....

Table : 1 (Contd....)

State/District	*CBR*	*TFR*	*Urbanization*	*Urban Literacy Rate (%)*			*Urban Sex Ratio*	
				Persons	*Males*	*Females*	*All Ages*	*0-6 years*
Hamirpur	30.0	4.2	16.64	68.11	78.97	55.70	861	884
Mahoba	32.3	4.5	21.84	73.65	83.31	62.23	878	893
Banda	32.4	4.6	16.27	78.74	88.20	67.68	855	901
Chitrakoot	36.5	5.2	9.55	72.00	79.75	63.35	869	937
Fatehpur	31.8	4.5	10.29	75.98	85.52	65.72	898	913
Pratapgarh	31.5	4.2	5.29	61.89	72.19	50.30	923	890
Kaushambi	34.7	4.8	7.09	80.71	86.20	73.87	902	966
Allahabad	30.2	4.2	24.56	62.39	69.18	54.79	813	900
Barabanki	33.1	4.7	9.27	75.57	82.10	67.78	897	918
Faizabad	29.6	4.0	13.47	73.00	79.82	65.59	851	935
Ambedaker Ngr	31.5	4.2	8.92	79.49	86.44	71.70	925	940
Sultanpur	32.3	4.4	4.77	65.96	70.62	60.63	894	903
Bahraich	36.0	5.2	9.98	58.24	67.38	47.93	886	958
Shrawasti	34.0	4.8	2.84	63.05	70.52	54.66	902	972
Balrampur	34.2	4.9	8.03	73.34	79.16	66.35	898	947
Gonda	33.1	4.7	7.09	70.15	80.22	58.97	846	924
Siddharthnagar	36.1	5.1	3.81	79.01	85.89	71.22	908	942
Basti	32.4	4.7	5.57	67.37	78.01	55.69	886	896
St Kabir Nagar	34.4	4.9	7.10	72.36	84.14	59.41	906	889

Contd....

Table : 1 (Contd....)

State/District	*CBR*	*TFR*	*Urbanization*	*Urban Literacy Rate (%)*			*Urban Sex Ratio*	
				Persons	*Males*	*Females*	*All Ages*	*0-6 years*
Maharajganj	36.2	5.0	5.09	78.65	86.19	70.15	912	928
Gorakhpur	29.9	4.3	19.57	71.16	80.99	60.18	893	927
Kushinagar	33.7	4.7	4.58	74.40	83.87	64.07	901	930
Deoria	31.1	4.4	9.89	48.26	55.30	41.23	920	934
Azamgarh	33.1	4.5	7.63	74.19	82.60	65.15	987	915
Mau	33.8	4.6	19.36	68.94	77.33	59.62	936	956
Ballia	28.4	3.8	9.84	73.90	82.32	64.67	903	928
Jaunpur	32.1	4.3	7.39	73.48	82.52	63.53	913	913
Ghazipur	31.8	4.3	7.64	76.09	85.61	65.29	913	941
Chandauli	32.7	4.5	10.58	71.25	90.04	49.76	887	915
Varanasi	30.1	4.1	40.30	68.25	79.14	55.77	879	906
St Ravidas Ngr	32.6	4.4	12.77	70.71	79.45	55.77	879	904
Mirzapur	33.5	4.7	13.56	70.71	79.45	60.63	875	919
Sonbhadra	35.3	4.8	18.91	83.58	91.39	73.95	824	903

Source : Census of India : 2001.

Table 2 : Some Statistics About Inter-District Demographic Analysis in U.P. : 2001

Variables	*Total Dists*	*Min.*	*max.*	*Mean*	*SD*	*CV (%)*
Crude Birth Rate	70	20.70	37.70	31.82	2.97	9.32
Total Fertility Rate	70	2.60	5.50	4.45	0.49	10.97
Urbanization	70	2.84	67.00	19.18	13.69	71.39
Total Urban Literacy	70	48.23	83.58	69.93	7.54	10.78
Urban Male Literacy	70	55.30	91.39	78.04	7.79	9.98
Urban Female Lit.	70	41.23	79.76	60.69	7.99	13.17
Urban Sex Ratio	70	813.00	987.000	885.70	26.27	2.97
Urban 0-6 Sex Ratio	70	678.000	972.00	896.60	42.64	4.76

Source : Based on data released by the Census of India : 2001.

Table : 3 Trends in Literacy Rates in Uttar Pradesh

Census	*Total*			*Urban*		
Year	*Persons*	*Males*	*Females*	*Persons*	*Males*	*Females*
1971	25.4	36.4	12.5	50.5	59.7	99.1
1981	31.4	44.5	16.3	52.5	62.0	41.0
1991	41.6	55.7	25.3	61.0	70.0	50.4
2001^	57.4	70.2	43.0	70.6	78.1	62.1

Note ^: It shows literacy rate for divided Uttar Pradesh.

Table : 4 Regression Estimates of Urbanization and Demographic Parameters : 1991 (District wise Analysis)

TFR	=	5.683	–	0.016 Urbanization
		(9.537)*		(3.078)*
				$R^2 = 0.135$
UFM	=	137.636	–	0.603 Urbanization
		(4.968)*		(2.518)*
				$R^2 = 0.096$
Log SR	=	3.021	–	0.063 Urbanization
		(113.142)*		(5.5175)*
				$R^2 = 0.336$

Note : Figures in parentheses are t-values. * : Significant TFR-Toatal fertility rates among districts;

UFM : Under-five mortality; SR: Sex Ratio.

Table 5 : Some Vital Statistics in Uttar Pradesh

Year	*Crude Birth*		*Crude Death Rate*		*Infant Mortality Rate*	
	Combined	*Urban*	*Combined*	*Urban*	*Combined*	*Urban*
1980	39.4	33.0	15.1	10.4	159	99
1990	35.6	29.3	12.0	8.8	99	67
1993	36.2	31.1	11.6	8.0	94	66
1995	34.8	28.8	10.3	8.3	86	66
1997	33.5	27.9	10.3	8.2	85	66
1998	32.4	27.2	10.5	8.1	85	65

Table 6 : Regression Estimates of Urbanization and Demographic Parameters : 2001 (District wise Analysis)

TFR	=	6.329 – 0.0212 Urbanization – 0.0210 ULR (14.868)* (6.517)* (3.542)* $R^2 = 0.44$
Log UML	=	81.538 – 1.285 log Urbanization (21.530)* (0.953) $R^2 = 0.013$
Log UFL	=	64.820 – 1.518 log Urbanization (16.712)* (1.099) $R^2 = 0.017$
Log USR	=	931.606 – 16.840 log Urbanization (80.932)* (4.110)* $R^2 = 0.199$
Log UCSR	=	985.369 – 32.595 log Urbanization (55.735)* (5.180)* $R^2 = 0.283$
TFR	=	4.846 – 0.021 Urbanization (58.423)* (5.847)* $R^2 = 0335$

Note : Figures in parentheses are t-values; *: Significant.
TFR : Total fertility rate among districts; ULR : Urban literacy rate;
UML : Urban male literacy rate; UFL : Urban female literacy rate;
USR : Urban sex ratio; UCSR : Urban 0-6 sex ratio.

Conclusion

From the above analysis, it can be derived that the pace of urbanization has been very slow in Uttar Pradesh. Still, it can play a crucial role in not only improving economic development but also better quality of life. However, given the scenario it is very difficult to highlight the positive role of urbanization in Uttar Pradesh in terms of many socio-economic variables. We find with the help of inter-district analysis in Uttar Pradesh, urbanization has so far not been able to show its impact effectively in improving literacy rate and sex ratio in favour of females. The slow pace of urbanization has also not been helpful in bringing down the total fertility rate, infant mortality rate, and child mortality rate. But in the changed scenario, the urban local bodies cannot escape from their role in improving such situations. Now even the Central and State governments are looking at the urban local bodies to intervene in socio-economic issues like population control, better health care, literacy, etc. Therefore, the urban local governments have not only to do better in terms of their traditional responsibilities, but also through new measures like above.

REFERENCES

Guilmoto, Christophe Z. & Rajan, Irudaya (2002) : 'District Level Estimates of Fertility from India's 2001 Census'; *Economic and Political Weekly,* February 16.

Government of India : *Economic Survey : 2001-2002.*

Rajaram, S. (2000) : 'Fertility and Child Mortality in India : A District Level Analysis Using Simultaneous Equations'; *Demography India;* Jan.-June.

Singh, Ajit Kumar (2001) : *Uttar Pradesh Development Report : 2000;* New Royal Book Company, Lucknow.

I.I.P.S. & PRC (1994) : *National Family Health Survey : 1992-93 (Uttar Pradesh).*

I.I.P.S. (2001) : *National Family Health Survey : 1998-99 (Uttar Pradesh).*

Government of India : Year Books for various years; Ministry of Health and Family Welfare, Dept of Family welfare.

Government of India : http://www.census of India.net

WOMEN EMPOWERMENT IN URBAN ADMINISTRATION : ROLE OF NGOs

Renu Shankar & Suman Lal

Arise ! Arise ! Arise !
The creator of this world
You ! women !

Wake up ! yet up !
Don't loose time
The preserver of human kind
You ! women !

Hurry up ! drops the veil
Don't look frail,
Buck up ! come up !
You ! women !

The health of a nation is fudged not by its economic development but by its human resource development. If the health of the fifty present of its population is poor and one-third of this half times under abject poverty, how healthy the nation is, one can well imagine.

The process of dis-empowerment of women was achieved not in one day, but over quite a long period of time. Women have been subjugated to slavery and have been treated as a second rate citizen not only in India but all over the world. Men, great or small, since the very beginning have been hatching a conspiracy against women in order to subject her to exploitation, slavery and submission. Manu/ the first father of man has been the forerunner in declaring that a women should live all her live all her life under the guardianship of her father, husband and son.

In modern times the famous psycho- analyst Frend's theory of biological determinism that anatomy is destiny and many more such hypothesis are deep-rooted obstacles in the analysis of women's exploitation. But the fact is just the opposite. It is not women's biology but historical process unbroken form the storage to the present, which has created asymmetrical relationship between men and women.

The Gene Equation that shapes individuals rather than environment or the social conditioning with regards to gender relation in society, has always been a contentious issue: Sex is biological and gender is its social ramification. There are indeed biological differences between men and women, which may even lead to some differences in their roles but that can't become the basis of a sexual hierarchy in which men are dominant.

During the Mesolithic age or food hunting and gathering stage, women used to hunt and gather food. She participated in the economy of the age that greatly enhanced her reproductive role. In such societies female sexuality was not a threat and did not have to be managed.

It was after the Aryans established control over large tracts of land, subjugated the indigenous takes that women retreated into household and no longer associated directly with economic production. Religion completed the process of female subjugation. Male dominated institutions like the church (religious) and state (politics) laid down rules regarding women's reproductive capacities. She had to have no control over her own body. She could not get unwanted child (conceived by rape) aborted out of shame and ignoring that was attached to female sexuality. Their dress, behavior and mobility have been carefully monitored by family according to social, cultural and religious codes.

She was further alienated from the intellectual society by being forced to live behind the veil. Her freedom was defined and confined to the domestic space, in complete isolation from the external world. Her movement was restricted to the interaction with her own sex within the four walls of her house. Thus she was kept away from education, religious discovers and the development and modernisation in the field of science and technology. She accepted her status and position gladly and even justified their condition and castigated those women who would try to raise voice against such inhuman treatment. Thus, this male conspiracy was completed to serve the interest.

Through history is full with example of women who enjoyed a privileged place due to their erudition in the society of intellectuals right from the Vedic age down the modern age; their number can be counted on finger tips and this they could achieve by a pre-ordained destiny called inborn qualities or luck. Their examples can't be generalised and cited as the prevalent norm of the society.

Women even in the technically most advanced European and American societies are not given equal opportunity in governance and politics. Not even in senior administrative fields. Therefore, it is not surprising to find women in the developing third world still languishing in the dark age. Women enjoy a privileged position in those countries where their share in politics is maximum. In this regard Sweden stands at number one with 43% women representation in its parliament, followed by Denmark, Netherlands and Germany. Where about 30% of the parliamentarians are women. The Industrialized most affluent nation of the world i.e. USA, France and Italy give somewhere between 11% to 14% representation to women in the national politics while in Japan it is the lowest at 7% even lower than that of India where women's share in the national politics is 7.9%

The end of the 20th and the beginning of the 21st century has seen an unprecedented upsurge in activities revolving around women's development and 'women empowerment' has become the most widely used 'phase' by every tongue. Therefore, there is a necessity of defining 'What women empowerment' means?

According to a United Nation Population Information Network (POPIN) report, "women empowerment has five components:

1. Women's sense of self-worth
2. Their rights to have and to determine choices
3. Their rights to have access to opportunities and resources
4. Their rights to have power to control their own lives, both within and outside the home
5. And their ability to influence the create a more just social and economic order, nationally and inter nationally.

The 1990's have seen increasing recognition of the centrality of women's empowerment to the success of development programmes. The empowerment of women was essential to the declaration and platforms for action of the 1990 world conference on education for all, on environment and development, the 1995 world summit for social development and regional preparatory conference for the 1995 Fourth world conference on women.

The programme of Action of the International conference on population and Development stresses that the empowerment and autonomy of women and the improvement of their political, social, economic and health status is both a highly important end itself and necessary for the achievement of sustainable human development. It states further that "Advancing gender equality and equity and the empowerment of women and, the elimination of all kinds of violence against women, and insuring women's ability to control their own fertility are priority objectives of the international community" (principle of the ICPI) programme of Action.

Thus, on the issue of empowerment not only of women, but human beings as a whole, in any society. I believe the best and the surest method is to empower them with the knowledge of their rights, duties and responsibilities, which would be possible only through the process of EDUCATION has much as it is the panacea to all the social decease that infest a society.

The second method of empowerment is by getting Economic Independence. No one can deny the fact that an economically dependent man is also in the same position as that of a woman. Therefore, the two "Es" 'Education' and 'Economic Independence' are the only method of women empowerment, when these two are achieved then only the dream of having women politicians and parliamentarians in a country can be achieved. Without these two, no number of bills on resolution of seats in politics would make any woman empowered politically in essence. Even through the 73rd and 74th Amendment of the Indian Constitution have ensured 33% seats for women in local governance, the fact remains that it is the father, brother, husband and son, who call the shots and not the actual representative. And very few women have got a seat cast for themselves by their personal merit; as most of them (these who have been elected to the various local administrative bodies) have got it because they are the 'Bahu, Beti or Patni' of great politicians.

We do not find either the culture or the environment conducive enough for the upliftment of women. We must modify our attitude towards women issues. We must shed away "Shaw" from our policies on women empowerment as a whole and women empowerment as a whole and women empowerment through politics should not be in mere talks. Let us all join our hands and work together in unison in achieving our targets and goals.

Ours is a small organisation, I very humbly, repeat, we have small organisation called Prayas Mahila Audhyogik Shayog Smiti, small not because we have not much fund, small not because we have not much space, small not even because we have not many hands, small not because property of ideas; but small because whatever, we do for the upliftment of women and children is very little compared to their size, number and volume.

We, at Prayas Mahila Audyogik Shayog Samiti, work for the women empowerment social, economic, and political.

In the social empowerment sector we impart education and training in human rights specially child rights and women rights, we launch awareness campaign and organise meetings and seminars on health issues, dowry property rights, legal rights and political rights . Besides organising seminars and meeting, we actually help needy girls and women's in getting social justice in our society. Prayas concentrates on atrocity and trafficking of women and children. It has developed resource material to spread awareness among the masses about what trafficking is? How it is done? For what purpose it is done and what is its modus operandi.

In the economic empowerment sector Prayas is trying to establish itself as a training resources centre. We impart training in about forty technical and non-technical vocational fields. Prayas women have even began a small food joint "PRAYAS RASOI " and catering services. We are trying to institutionalize the domestic helper services into an organized industry, for this planning and processing is in the pipeline.

Prayas has made arrangement for display and sale of products manufactured by women groups. It organizes Mela, exhibition in Patna, participates in all such market for their produce.

On the environment front, its conservation and protection and for its gainful economic utilization, it has adopted vermiculture and vermicompost production in Samastipur district. This programme is being organized for the women SHGs of the mentioned area.

Vermiculture helps in solving the problem of urban garbage utilization, thereby helping in controlling pollution and keeping our environment clean.

For helping women in getting political power, PRAYAS helped women in the Panchayat election and three of its members are contesting in the municipality election going to be held in April 2002.

ROLE OF WOMEN IN NATURAL DISASTER MANAGEMENT

S.K. Sinha

Introduction

The definition of Natural Disaster is "an over overwhelming ecological disruption, which exceeds the capacity of the community to adjust and consequently requires assistance from outside". This ecological disruption suddenly disrupts the normal pattern of life within the community and the consequential effects are that the people are plunged into suffering and helplessness. This calls for urgent need for food, clothing, shelters, medical attention, restoration of life sustaining requirements etc followed by relief and restoration activities.

Natural Disasters also have a socio-economic dimension, in as much as on the one side they vetard the development process in the disaster-affected as well as neighbouring area/ region and on the other side, the poor and socially disadvantaged groups are the worst sufferers and are economically the least equipped to cope with the sufferings.

Natural Disasters have generally been grouped as follows :

- Wind-related : storm, cyclone, hurricane, storm surge etc.
- Water-related : flood, cloud burst, drought etc.
- Earth-related : earthquake, landslide, avalanches etc.

All these Disasters suddenly destroy the life and property, housing stock, the physical and social infrastructure, heritage items, and the economic activities of the area/region, where the Disaster occurs, as well as in the neighbouring area/region.

Natural Disaster Management

During the last two centuries along with radical advancement of Science and Technology, there has been tremendous growth in different socio-economic sectors viz., agriculture, industry, business, utility services etc. These have resulted into pursuit of better productivity and amenities is all parts of the world and emergence of a global consciousness for protection of Environmental Degradation, Natural Disaster Management and Adoption of Sustainable Development Strategy in various developmental activities. This Strategy aims to meet the needs of the present generations without compromising the ability of future generations to meet their own needs.

Natural Disaster Management has emerged as a scientific system for Pre. Disaster preparedness and Post-Disaster Response with five basic objectives, namely :

(i) Reduce/Avoid Physical and Economical Losses,

(ii) Reduce/Minimise Personal Sufferings,

(iii) Fasten Recovery Process (Rehabilitation, relocation and reconstruction),

(iv) Provide Rescue operations to ensure survival of maximum number of victims, and,

(v) Provide Emergency Supports like Relief, medical and security measures.

The *three key perquisites* to understand the nature of any disaster phenomenon and thereby assess the chances of its occurrence have been identified as *Prediction, Forecasting and Warning*. The Inter relationship among these three key perquisites are briefly as follows :

- Earthquake : None of the three exist at present, hence maximum damage.

- Cyclone : Systems have been developed to Predict Cyclones and thereby Forecasting and Warning have been successful.
- Flood/Drought : Very Scientific systems have been developed to Predict Floods/Drought and thereby Forecasting and Warning have been successfully implemented.
- Landslide/Avalanches : Predictability of less intensity have been possible and thereby Forecasting and Warning have also been possible commensurate with this intensity.

Some Aspects of Natural Disaster management

Natural Disasters are a natural phenomenon caused due to geo-climatic conditions and India has been traditionally vulnerable to natural disasters on account of its unique geo-climatic conditions. In other words, we have to face the natural disasters and with the advancement of Science, Technology and Management Techniques, we are now in a position to *Mitigate* the seriousness of the damages, losses, sufferings and socio-economic crisis arising out of these disasters.

Some of the *initiatives launched in the direction of Mitigation* are briefly mentioned in the lines hereinafter.

- *Hazard Analysis :* This technique involves an assessment of the intensity, frequency and location of the natural disasters. It depends on historical records available (written and memory) as well as data on regional and local physical characteristics, and scientific analysis. This enables the Government and the community to prepare and implement Preparedness planning.
- *Preparedness Planning :* This basically comprises of two components, viz :

  (a) Prediction, Forecasting and Warning to understand the nature of the disaster phenomenon and thereby to assess the chances of its occurrence.

(b) Preparedness for mitigation of the disasters, which are bound to occur. A Disaster preparedness Plan essentially spells out the measures to be taken before, during and after the disaster occurs. It also identifies on inventory of what materials are available where and with whom, and the system of delegation of responsibilities among the various government departments and their officials.

The Plan also identifies Rehabilitation and Reconstruction Strategy and spells out the guidelines in respect of partnership of government with NGOs, social workers and international agencies.

- *Government Initiatives* : In India, the institutional and policy mechanisms for carrying out response, relief and rehabilitation measures have been well-established since Independence. This mechanism comprises of the following :

1. *A the national level the Ministry of Home Affairs is the Nodal Ministry for all matters concerning disaster management.* The central Relief Commissioner (CRC) is the Ministry of Home Affairs the *Nodal Officer* to coordinate relief operations for natural disasters.

The CRC is assisted by the following in receiving information relating to natural disasters on a continuing basis :

(i) Information relating to forecasting/warning of a natural calamity from India meteorological Department (IMD);

(ii) Central Water Commission of Ministry of water Resources.

In addition to the above the following Ministries/ Departments/Organizations of the Government of India assist the CRC with respect to primary and secondary functions relating to the management of disasters :

(i) Ministries : Home Affairs, Defence, Finance, Rural Development, Urban Development, Health, Water

Resources, petroleum, Railways, Information and Broadcasting, Social Justice, Environment and Forest,

(ii) *Departments* : Communications, Agriculture & Cooperation, Civil Supplies, Surface Transport, Women and Child Development, and Food.

(iii) *Organizations* : Central Water Commission, Planning Commission and Cabinet Secretariat.

The Institutional Framework comprises of

(i) Each Ministry/Department/Organization nominating their Nodal Officer to the *Crisis Management Group Chaired by the CRC;*

(ii) The Nodal Officer is responsible for preparing Sectoral Action Plan/Emergency Support Function Plan for managing disasters.

(iii) The Crisis Management Group (CMG) reviews every year the contingency plans formulated by various Ministries/Departments/Organizations required for dealing with the natural disasters in their respective sectors;

(iv) The CMG also coordinates the activities of the Central Ministries and the State Governments in respect of disaster preparedness and relief as also obtains information from the Nodal Officers on measures relating to above; and,

(v) In the event of a natural disaster, the CMG meets frequently to review the relief operations and extend all possible assistance required by the affected States to overcome the situation effectively. At all such review meetings, the Resident Commissioner of the affected State is also associated.

2. Control Room of the Nodal Ministry of Home Affairs : An Emergency Operations Centre (Control Room) functions round the clock to assist the CRC in the discharge of his duties.

The main activities of the Control Room are the following :

(i) Collection and transmission of information relating to natural calamity and relief;

(ii) Keeping close contact with the governments of the affected States and interaction with the other Central Ministries/Departments/Organizations in respect of relief;

(iii) Keeping up-to-date records in respect of all relevant information relating to action points and contact points in the Central Ministries etc. and details of all concerned officers at the Central and State levels.

3. Contingency Action Plan and Funding Mechanisms : A National Contingency Action Plan (CAP) has been formulated by the government of India to facilitate the launching of relief operations without delay with the initiatives by various Central Ministries/Departments and in keeping with the procedures laid down by the Government.

The institutional arrangements and funding mechanisms for Response and Relief in respect of Natural Disasters are well established and have been functioning effectively in the following forms :

(i) A National Calamity Contingency Fund (NCCF) has been created at the Central Government level to support the State Governments in such situations where the calamity is of such proportion that the funds available in the Calamity Relief Fund (CRF) will not be sufficient for provision of relief.

(ii) A Calamity Relief Fund (CRF) has been set up in each State which operates under norms spelled out by a State-level Committee under the Chief Secretary of the State. The Government of India contributes 75% of the corpus of the CRF in each State and 25% is contributed to by the State.

The *Finance Commission* plays a significant role in management of these Funds, firstly by reviewing every five years their performance, and secondly by making recommendations regarding the division of tax and non-tax revenues between the Central and State governments and also regarding policy for provision of relief assistance and their share of expenditure thereon.

4. *At the State level, Response, Relief and Rehabilitation are handled by the Departments of Relief & Rehabilitation* and the Mechanism at the State level comprises of a *State Crisis Management Committee* set up under the Chairmanship of the Chief Secretary. All the concerned Departments and Organizations of the State and Central Government Departments located in the State are represented in this Committee.

A *Control Room* functions at the office of the Relief Commission to coordinate the functioning of relief and rehabilitation activities.

5. The district level is the key level for disaster management and relief activities. *The District Collector/Deputy Commissioner* is the focal function *any in the district* for preparation of district plans and for directing, supervising and monitoring calamities for relief & rehabilitation.

For effective functioning a *District level Coordination and Relief Committee* is constituted under the Chairmanship of the District Collector and comprises of representatives from all related government departments and non-government agencies (NGOs).

To receive/supplement the efforts of the district administration in the rescue and relief operations the collector is required to maintain close liaison with the State Government as well as with the nearest units of Armed Forces/Central Police organizations and with other relevant Central Government organizations live Ministries of Communication, Water Resources, Drinking Water, Surface Transport etc.

6. *State Relief Manuals:* Each State Government has Relief Manuals/Codes which identifies the role of

each Officer in the State for managing the natural disasters. These are reviewed and updated periodically based on the experiences in respect of disaster management and the need of the State.

7. International Assistance in Natural Disaster Reduction and Development Process : This Assistance is presently being provided by UNDHA (UN-Department of Humanitarian Affairs), FAO (Food and Agriculture Organization), UNDP (United Nations Development Programme) UNESCO, WHO, World Bank etc. for providing assistance in Pre-Disaster State, Response Operations, Recovery Programmes as well as for future development.

The process of Assistance depends upon an understanding between the Agencies and the National Government of the country seeking Assistance.

Role of Women in Natural Disaster Management

The Community is the most significant partner in all activities of Disaster Management. The Women in the Community can play a purposeful and effective role in the following specific areas :

- *Creating Public Awareness* amongst senior citizens, school children the youth and housewives in respect of DO-S and DON'T's during occurrence of Natural Disasters. This can successfully be achieved through lectures, orientation progammes, exhibitions, and interaction meets etc. The Media and IT can play a significant supporting role to the Women Groups Community Groups, NGOs etc. in creating the awareness though Disaster Education Training and Information Dissemination.
- *Capacity Building, Training and Education* in respect of ways to better respond to and mitigate disasters to the responders go a long way in building the capacity and resilience of the community to reduce and prevent

disasters. While such training facilities exist for government functionaries, there is urgent need to *Identify and Train Volunteers* from the community towards first response measures as well as mitigation measures.

A programme of periodic drills should be introduced in vulnerable areas to enable prompt and appropriate community response in the event of a disaster, which will enable to save valuable lives.

- *Incorporating Community based Approach in the Disaster Management System* wherein the NGOs and Community Based Organizations should be made to function more effectively with government functionaries.
- *Providing Special assistance in terms of evacuation, relief, aid and medical attention to the Vulnerable Groups* within the community like women and children, aged and infirm and physically challenged people who need special care and attention especially during disaster situations.
- *Education and Research* are two important tools to provide stronger base for future development and welfare of human beings. Studies/Research by *Women Academicians* in respect of major lessons learnt from past experience of each disaster will enable Disaster Management System to initiate concrete steps to tackle the situation in future. Government should sponsor such Studies/Research.

WOMEN EMPOWERMENT : A CASE STUDY OF AN URBAN COUNCIL IN URISSA

K.S. Padhy

Introduction

Women, who constitute half of the human race, can certainly play a key role in influencing the course of history as well as shaping the destiny of mankind. Gifted with talents and skills, they can achieve their goal and accomplish their mission. No doubt, nature has made them physically weak, docile, tender, innocent, tolerant, charming, simple, graceful and beautiful. But this does not mean that they are helpless, incapable, inefficient, ineffective and good for nothing. And, therefore, they should depend upon others for their survival on the contrary, their weakness itself is their strength, their tolerance their capacity, their grace their ability, their charm their effectiveness; their beauty their power. A saying in Sanskrit, that 'Vinasraye Na Bartante kavita, Vanita and Lata' (Poetry, Women and shrubs can not survive without depending upon others). They have an ability and capacity to deliver the goods, in fact, they have (though their number is less), over the years, proved themselves to be able administrators, effective ministers, dedicated parliamentarians, devoted legislators, committed jurists and self-less workers. As competent decision makers, they have rendered significant contributions to the socio-economic and political development of a society. But despite this, they are denied of an opportunity to participate in decision-making, deprived of their dues and made subject to torture and suffering. They have become the victims of lost greed, jealousy, anger and violence perpetrated upon them and this can be prevented if they are empowered.

It may not be unpalatable to observe that compared to their contributions towards human development, they get little or much less in return. The United Nations in its report (1980) has, therefore, very rightly observed :

Women constitute half of the world population, perform nearly two-thirds of work hours, receive one-tenth of the world's income and own less than one-hundred percent of world's property.

It is because of their discrimination and deprivation, they do not have the same privileges and opportunities as men have in a society. As a result, wide disparities persist between women and men.

Women's Movement

There is no dispute that women, notwithstanding their contributions and achievements, sacrifices and sufferings, have been physically tortured, psychologically humiliated, economically discriminated, politically marginalized, socially suppressed and culturally dominated. The inhuman conditions in which they live (d), the untold sufferings they suffer (ed), the formidable difficulties they face (d), the challenging problems they confront (ed) in a society have forced them to launch struggles to acquire a rightful place for them.

The struggle launched by them for their rights entered a new phase in the 19th century. England had to reform laws governing marriage, France had to recognize women's rights to divorce, China had to allow women to hold office. In 1893, New Zealand became the first country to extend the right to vote to women. In the first decade of the 20th century women's movement gathered much strength and acquired a new dimension in several countries, including China, Japan, Iran, Korea, etc. In the first half of the 20th century the right to franchise was granted to women in countries like Austria,

Germany, Turkey, Uruguay. It was during this time Margaret Sanger in the US, Allen Key in Sweden and Shizue Ishimoto in Japan launched campaign for reproductive rights for women.

Women's Issues Internationalized

It is distressing to note media paid little or least attention to the women's issues till 1975. She was presented as a house holder, her stereo-typed image. However, after the declaration of Women's Year and Women's Decade in 1975, suddenly their issues and concerns acquired a new dimension as these were highlighted extensively by the media.

Following the Nairobi Conference held in 1985, to make an assessment of the Women's Decade, media have started laying much emphasis upon their problems like gender discrimination, their role and importance, health and education, etc. Earlier, these issues were discussed as problems of individual women's. Now they are being seen within the socio-political structural context. They were discussed only in the privacy of homes, they were considered matters of individual misfortune, personal tragedies, gossip for neighbours, relatives and friends. Their issues have become news.

Suddenly the personal became political, individual cases seemed to fit into a pattern, a pattern that was discernible through the application of an ideology–the feminist ideology. What had seemed to be stray cases of suicide by married women or accidental deaths by the explosions of stoves became suddenly explicable as "dowry deaths". The anger and militant protests of small groups of middle class women at a couple of such deaths snowballed into a campaign. A new era ushered in: an era of women's emancipation and empowerment.

Status of Women in India

"It is pertinent to note that India is a great paradox. Nowhere is this more evident than the situation with regard to the status of women in India. They have been treated in the scriptures as the Goddess, the incarnation of compassion, the embodiment of virtues, provider of food for sustenance and destroyer of evil. The deities of learning, wealth and valour, Saraswati, lakshmi and Durga have been categorized as women. Shakti has been prominent from the days of yore". Manu[1], the Ancient Indian Law-Giver, has told about women thus :

PRAJANARTHAM STRIYAH SRUSTAH
SANTANARTHANCHA MANABAH
TASMASAT DHARANO DHARAMAH SUTOU
PATNYA SAHODITAH
KSHETRABHUTAH SMRUTA NARI
BIJA BHUTAH SMRUTAH PUMAN
KSHETRABIJA SAMAYOGA SAMBHABAH
SARVADEHINANM

This means for the continuance of human race female possessed the sacred field for conceiving and male was made responsible for such conception being the possessor of the seed. According to Vedas both Stridharma and Purasha Dharma stood on equal footing. Thus between Male and Female there was mutual respect, cooperation and understanding irrespective of the relations like husband-wife, father-daughter, brother-sister, etc.

Even women were respected more in the family and society. Attempts were never made to ignore them, neglect them, undermine them. The idea of torturing them mentally a physically was unthinkable. The ancient Indian scriptures have said :

Yatra Naryastu Pujyante Tatra Ramante Devata[2]

It means where women are worshipped God resides there.

It is significant to note that a woman's presence as wife was a must in every social function. This shows her importance in the society. The "Ram-Gita[3]" mentions about the variegated roles that she placed in her life :

Karyesu Mantri Karanesu Dasi
Bhojyesu Mata Sayanesu Rambha
Dharmanukula Kshyamaya Dharitri.

The aforesaid has also been put in a different way which is as follows :

Karyesu Dasi Karanesu Mantri
Rupeicha Lakshmi Kshyamaya Dharitri
Bhojyesu Mata Sayanesu Veshya
Sata Dharmayukta Kula Dharmapatni.

This means that a woman should serve like a slave to her husband and others; advise them like a minister, feed them like a mother; gratify her husband sexually like a prostitute; be his life-partner with all virtues.

However, her position and status began to decline with the conquest of India by the foreign forces. During the regimes of Khililis[4] (1290-1320 A.D), Tughlaqs[5] (1320-1414 A.D), Moghuls[6] (1526-1765 A.D.), Christians (1765-1947 A.D), etc. she was treated as an object of pleasure or as a robot intended to serve men, family and the society without any expectation, without any hope and to tolerate injustice meted out to her without any protest. She was forced to play a subservient role within the four walls of the house. There might have been some exceptions, but, by and large, the social mindset has been that of inhuman discrimination against them right from the birth. From cradle to grave their life style has been controlled : during their childhood stage by their patents, by the husbands after their marriage and by their children when they grow old. In other words, they were made dependent upon others; parents, spouses and children. For a majority of them, from womb to tomb, life itself is nothing but a continuous, ceaseless, hard and painful struggle, both within and outside the family. They do not get even minimum guarantees and safeguards in life. Bride burning, torture, rape, kidnapping seem to be the lot of women today in India as elsewhere. The criminal law also is loaded against women. In case of adultery the wife alone can complain and in cases of rape open obscene interrogation in courts has become the order of the day. So many prefer to die with their humiliations and sufferings rather than seeking justice since "medicine is found to be more dangerous than the disease itself". This situation can be changed if they are empowered by law and Constitution[7].

Empowerment : A Conceptual Framework

Empowerment, which is ensured through participation, includes, not only integration into formal institutions and channels but also extends to any collective action directed towards any type of justice. It encompasses much more than formal 'legal' right, extending to the recognition and assertion of 'human right' of the minorities and weaker sections. It aims at conferring rights upon an individual and the rationality of it lies in his commitment and belongingness to the system as opposed to his alienation from it. He empowers him through his awareness, participation, group identification and collective action which further increases his awareness. It is a circular path with a cyclical movement.

Empowerment promotes one's awareness about his rights and this helps him to participate in socio-economic and political process; identify his in-group and out-group with similar experience and attitudes and act with them in order to define the need and exert pressure through collective action to fulfil it. Through collective action, he finds out his identify and knows his power and strength. Again empowerment makes him aware to claim his right. The cyclical process goes on. Any social, economic or political (in a formal sense) process may serve as a catalyst for the cycle. The cycle which consists of awareness (of right), participation, group identification, collective action and empowerment, brings about changes in civil, criminal and constitutional laws, in socialization process, and helps in building the self-image and the institutions, formal and informal, political parties and mass media.

Participation, which fosters social integration, creates a sense of community which gives meaning to human existence. It is only through participation, one realizes his identity, personality and status in society.[8] It means different things to different people. A project administrator means it implementation, a political scientist considers it people's involvement in decision-making[9], while an economist treats it as sharing of benefits of development programmes. Now participation includes all these things; implementation[10] of programmes, sharing of power and benefits. It broadly means people's involvement which enhances their well-being.[11]

In the context of development, participation means two things; an input in development; and empowering the target groups to play key role in development.[12] It is an intrinsic part of the process of development rather than being merely a facilitator; an educational process; increases the value of one's freedom by enabling to (and remain) his own master; creates a sense of awareness, a sense of involvement, a sense of belongingness and a sense of possession or ownership; develops self-reliance, self-confidence, competence and managerial capacity; enables one to discover his innate potential, increases his aspiration level and mobilizes his resources for productive purposes. Participation makes people, thinkers, decision-makers, doers and implementers.[13] In short it has three roles : educative, integrative and empowering. It brings people to the core from periphery, to activeness from possessiveness and to be thinkers, decision-makers, doers and implementers from acceptors.

Women Empowerment : A Need

Women's participation, which implies involvement[14] and empowerment in decision-making and developmental process, is a must as it helps them in giving direction to social change. Change, which is brought about by sharing of an effort and social participation, possesses democratic vitality and is also realistic. Self-imposed changes have a permanence as compared to those imposed from outside and above.

Women must learn participatory skills in democracy because, unless they themselves share responsibility and participate in fulfilling their demands they do not strengthen their cause, nor the democratic structure of the society. They should learn to solve their own problems. Nothing should be allowed to prevent them from playing their participatory role in the direction of social change as this will inhibit and impede personal development. They are to be organised to reach their goal.

Women's empowerment has two goals : short term and long term, the former deals with their involvement in the current pogrammes and development activities, and the utilization of resources, while the latter seeks to make them morally strong, self-reliant and confident so that they can initiate their own proposals and manage their own problems. It is, in fact, a continuous process of democratization.

The society, the state, the government and the people (men in particular) should have their trust and faith in the capacity of women, give them an opportunity to play their role, take their ideas and views seriously, channelize and integrate their energies and resources for improving the quality of their life.

Women Empowerment : Principles

Any attempt to empower women should give due importance of the following principles :

(i) Equality of rights between women and men must be treated as a fundamental principle and enshrined in the statues or constitutions. Steps should be taken to remove all the barriers, legal, political, economic, social and cultural–that prevent the exercise of equal rights, and remove these obstacles through comprehensive policy reforms and strong affirmative action.

(ii) Women must be regarded as agents and beneficiaries of change and empowered to exercise their choices as this will strengthen their capabilities, promote economic growth and bring an overall development.

(iii) The engendered development model, though aims at widening the choices for both women and men, should not predetermine how different cultures and societies exercise their choices. What is important is that equal opportunities to make a choice exist for both men and women.

Women Empowerment : Steps Taken

(A) Political Empowerment

As stated above, women in India, as elsewhere, have been subject to unbearable onslaught by the other half of the human race. However, after Independence in 1947 the scenario underwent a change following the adoption of certain measures by the Government of India to improve their socio-economic conditions. It is however, significant to note that the wheels of development started rolling even in the pre-independence days.

In fact, during this pre-independence period the social reformers like Raja Ram Mohan Roy, Isswar Chandra Vidya Sagar and others did their best to reform the society by getting rid of social evils like "Sati" (widow-burning), child marriage, etc. Mahatma Gandhi's clarion call to Indian women to join the national stream by taking an active role in the freedom struggle had a tremendous impact on them. The Sharada Act, 1952 raised the age of marriage to 15. After Independence, steps are taken to ensure equal status for women in every sphere of life. And this is enshrined as one of the main objectives in the Indian Constitution.

The principle of gender equality is enshrined in the Indian Constitution which has not only granted equality to women, but also empowers the State to adopt measures of positive discrimination in favour of women. Besides, adoption of laws, development policies, plans and programmes have helped in bringing an all-round development of women in different spheres.

In recent years the empowerment of women has been recognized as the central issue in determining the status of women. The National Commission for Women was set up by an Act of Parliament in 1990 to safeguard the rights and legal entitlement of women.

Women's representation in the Parliament increased from 4 per cent in 1952 to 8.9 per cent in 1999. This development may not be significant. But, at the village and the district levels, nearly one million women are heads and members of the local self-government institutions changing the destiny of their own and also that of others–thanks to the 73rd Amendment to the Constitution.

The 73rd and 74th Amendments (1992) to the Indian Constitution have served as a breakthrough towards ensuring equal access and increased participation in political power structure for women. The rural and urban government will play a central role in the process of enhancing women's participation in public life. They will be actively involved in the implementation and execution of the national Policy for Women adopted by the Government of India in 2001 at the grass root level.

India has also ratified various international conventions and human rights instruments committing to secure equal rights of women, the most important among them is the ratification of the Convention on Elimination of All forms of Discrimination Against Women (CEDAW) in 1993.

The Government of India has also endorsed without any reservation the following with a view to promote the well-being of women : The Mexico Plan of Action (1975), the Nairobi Forward Looking Strategies (1985), the Beijing Declaration as well as the Platform for Action (1995) and the Outcome Document adopted by the United Nations General Assembly Session on Gender Equality and Development and peace for the 21st Century, titled "Further actions and initiatives to implement the Beijing Declaration and the Platform for Action".

(B) Economic Empowerment

It is pertinent to note that right from the First Five Year Plan (1951-1956), attempts have been made to provide equal status to women and involve them in the process of development. While emphasis was laid during the first four Five Year plans (1951-1974) on organizing welfare activities and giving nigh priority to women education, the Fifth (1974-1979) and the Sixth (1980-1985) Plans witnessed a shift in approach from welfare to their overall development with a three pronged thrust on their health, education and employment.

During the 7th Plan period (1985-1990) beneficiary-oriented programme for women was identified and promoted with an intention to extend direct benefits to them. The 8th Plan (1992-1997) made a further significant shift from 'development' to 'women's empowerment'. It recommended 30 per cent reservation for women in different sectors of the Government, besides stressing that benefits of development from different sectors did not neglect or ignore them.

The 9th Plan (1997-2002) aimed at ensuring a minimum of 30 per cent of benefits or funds to flow to women from all ministries and departments. Real empowerment of women has been a serious commitment of the 9th Five Year Plan through creating an enabling environment where women can freely exercise their rights both within and outside their homes, as equal partners alongwith men.

It is significant to note that economic empowerment of women is one of the dimensions of development, which cannot be dismissed or overlooked, in any developing society. Through Rashtriya Mahila Kosh[15] (RMK) the Government of India has, therefore, launched several new initiatives and tried to strengthen the micro credit programme for gender development. Unless access to resources is ensured economic development would not he complete. It is with this motive the Ninth Plan (1997-2002) specifically stipulated identifying "Women Component Plans"[16] for which at last 30 per cent of funds should flow to women development schemes. There are women specific welfare schemes/programmes that receive funds under the annual budgetary allocations such as Mahila Samridhi Yojana, Balika Samridhi Yojana, Working Women's Hostels, Swashakti Project, and other projects–twenty-nine identifiable women specific schemes that received Rs. 856.64 crore allocation in 2000-2001 Central Government budget as against Rs. 605.46 crore in 1999-2000.

(C) Social Empowerment

The Government of India has also taken steps to make women socially empowered. So that they can be a force in the development of the country. A task force on Women and Children has been constituted to review the existing legislation and the government schemes for improving the asset base of women to improve their social status. It is very significant to note the impact of welfare measures on women :

- Expectancy of life for females at birth rose from 31.6 years in 1951 to 40.6 years in 1961-71 to 58.1 years during 1981-1991 and the projections for 1991-2001 put it at 62 years;
- The infant mortality rate (IMR) for females declined from 151 in 1951 to half in 2000-2001. The IMR has been reduced from 152 during 1982 to 97.6 during 1998 and in case of female, the IMR has been reduced from 124 during 1982 to 96.9 during 1998;
- Similarly, the sex differential which was quite high in the 1970s has now been bridged;
- Maternal Mortality Rate (MMR) in rural India still continuous to be uncomfortably high at 324 per 1,00,0000. It showed a declining trend from 468 in 1980 to 324 in 1989;
- Also the total fertility rate has come down from 5.97 in 1951-1961 to 3.3 in 1997 signaling a comparatively greater acceptance of family planning and late marriage norms;
- There is a considerable improvement in the female literacy which went up to 54.97% in 2001 from 8% in 1947. The enrolment of girls in primary schools has also improved; and
- In the field of employment, the women's participation has grown from 19.7% in 1981 to 22.3% in 1991. Similarly the number of women in the organised sector has also risen from 12.2% in 1981 to 15.4% in 1995. Further, employment of women in the Central Government has also been rising steadily from year to year. Women's share has grown from 3.6% in 1981 to 7.58% in 1991, reflecting a further women's participation in the government. It also indicates a remarkable breakthrough after reservation of 33% of posts for women in the government services.

The Protection from Domestic Violence Bill–2001 if enacted will empower women to a great extent.[17]

(D) Disturbing Trends

While the foregoing are the redeeming features and positive indications, there are some disturbing trends as well. In 1991, the sex ratio in 0-6 age group between men and women was 1000 : 945. But it further declined and it is now 1000 : 927. This disheartening trend speaks of a systematic bias and unhealthy use of ultra-sound prenatal test devices. According to the 1991 census, of the 324 million illiterate, 197 million i.e. 61% are girls and women. According to an estimate for 1995-96 only 43.2% girls attended primary schools, 39% at middle level and 35.3% at secondary stage signaling a considerable number dropouts.

The percentage of women labour to total workforce has declined from 28.98% in 1951 to 26.8% in 1996. Women comprising 94% of the work-force in the unorganized sector (working in the fields, construction and other such sectors), find themselves at a loss in the organised sector. Their share in paid employment in industry and service stands at a mere 15%. In the decision-making capacities (IAS, IPS and IFS), the number of women, though increased from 311 in 1985 to 501 in 1996, still needs to be improved. Their placement and postings, too need a review. To top it all, girls are still considered as a financial burden in the Indian homes. Nowhere this indignity is more apparent than at the time of marriage and even after marriage. Problems of dowry and subsequent ill-treatment to women emanate from this single factor. The number of bride-burning cases has risen from 427 in 1983 to 6917 in 1998, a horrifying fact.

Notwithstanding the aforesaid development activities undertaken by the government, there still exists a wide gap between policies, plans, programmes and related mechanisms on the one hand and the grim situational reality of the status of women in India, on the other. This has been analysed and explained extensively in the Report of Committee on the Status of Women in India, Towards Equality, 1974 and highlighted in the National Perspective Plan for Women, 1988-2000, the Shramashakti Report, 1988 and the "Platform for Action, Five Years After-An Assessment".

Therefore, constitutional provisions are not enough to ensure the rights of women. Further steps are to be taken to bring them at par with menfolk. This can be possible with their empowerment. Therefore, besides a holistic approach to women's welfare and development special emphasis should be given to their needs and interests at all stages of life. The reduction of infant mortality as well as maternal mortality, the indicators of human development, should be given priority. They should have access to comprehensive, affordable and equality healthcare. Measures should be adopted to take into account the reproductive rights of women to enable them to exercise informed choices, their vulnerability to sexual and health problems together with endemic infections and communicable diseases such as Malaria, T.B. and water born diseases, hypertension and cardio-pulmonary diseases. Implementation of registration of births and deaths should be strictly ensured and registration of marriages should be made compulsory. The critical need of men and women is to have access to safe, effective and affordable methods of family planning of their choice. The issues of early marriage and spacing of children should be properly addressed. These steps will certainly go a long way in making women empowered.

Women Empowerment : A Question of Dependence

When we discuss about empowerment, a question comes to one's mind : whether women refuse to get empowered. For example, a recent study conducted in Lucknow has confirmed that Mahila Pradhans (Women Sarapanchas/Women Block Chairpersons) are still ruled by male relatives. A number of experts on Panchayatiraj, who attended a one-day seminar at Bakshi-Ka-Tabal (Lucknow), said the dependence of Mahila Gram Pradhans on their menfolk eventually forced the government to issue an order forbidding husbands and brothers of women gram pradhans from attending meetings.

In four of a the five assembly segments of Amethi, the condition of Gram Sabhas represented by women is precarious, as per the survey conducted by the Sabbhagi Sikshan Kendra. At least 143 Gram Sabhas here are represented by women (on the basis of 1995 polls). But most of them attended "sabha" meetings merely as escorts of their husbands, brothers or other male relatives, who actually function in authority. But it is different in case of urban legislators, as the present study revels who do not depend "much" on others and this attitude of independence can be attributed to their exposure to education, development, media, etc.

Women Empowerment : Strategies

The following strategies may be adopted to bring about a just socio-economic change to empowering women :

- To provide a conductive climate for women to exercise their rights, both within and outside home, as equal partners along with men, through early adoption of 'National Policy for Empowerment of Women' which also takes note of the commitments of the Ninth Five Year Plan in respect of empowerment of women.
- To legislate reservation of not less than 1/3 seats for women in the Lok Sabha and the State Assemblies and thus to ensure their adequate representation in decision making.
- To adopt an integrated approach towards empowering women through effective convergence of existing services, resources, infrastructure and manpower in both women specific and women-related sectors;
- To adopt a special strategy of women's component plan to ensure that not less than 30% of funds/benefits flow to women from other development sectors.
- To organize women into self help groups and thus make the beginning of a major process of empowering women;
- To accord high priority to reproductive, child health services and thus ensure easy access to maternal and child health services.
- To universalize the on-going supplementary feeding programme-Special Nutrition Programme (SNP) and Mid-Day meals (MDM).

- To ensure easy and equal access to education for women and girls through the commitments of the Special Action Plan of 1998.
- To initiate steps to eliminate gender bias in all educational programmes.
- To institute plans for free education for girls up to college level, including professional courses.
- To equip women with necessary skills in the modern upcoming trades which could keep them gainfully engaged besides making them economically independent and self-reliant; and
- To increase access to credit through setting up of a 'Development Bank of Women Entrepreneurs' in small and tiny sectors.

Women Empowerment : Role and Responsibility of Women Office-Bearers

As stated earlier, a new chapter was opened in the history of Indian democracy in 1992 when the 74th Amendment Act, as said earlier, was enacted to give sufficient representation to women in the urban local bodies. Aiming at the decentralization of planning and administration, the Act envisages that women representatives can effectively monitor and administer the schemes like health, education, family planning, etc. As mayors, chairpersons and councilors they will contribute significantly in respect of :

- Planning for economic and social development;
- Water supply for industrial and commercial purposes;
- Public health, sanitation, conservancy and solid waste management;
- Urban forestry, protection of environment and promotion of ecological aspects;
- Safeguarding the interests of the weaker sections of the society, including the handicapped;
- Slum improvement and up-gradation;

- Urban poverty alleviation programmes;
- Provisions of urban amenities and facilities such as parks, gardens and playgrounds;
- Promotion of cultural, educational and aesthetic aspects;
- Public amenities including street lighting, parking lots, bus stops and public conveniences.

As office-bearers, women can effectively manage the affairs of urban local bodies, promote the cause of responsive and responsible local-self government, and safeguard the interests of the urban poor, weaker sections, women and children as envisaged in the 74th Amendment Act. They can ameliorate their living conditions by providing the required assistance. They

- Should not only address the key civic issues, but also act as the voices of the poor and disadvantaged sections;
- Take necessary steps to motivate the latter to join the mainstreams of the development process;
- Play a vital role in sensitizing the municipal bodies to the problems of the masses;
- Ensure transparency in municipal administration and accountability to the electorate;
- Be instrumental in reorienting municipal budgets to support civic activities such as immunization of children, pre-school and primary education, primary and preventive health care, education of the girl child, economic empowerment of women, gender audit etc.;
- Try to mobilize and garner mass support to get rid of social evils from the society;
- And take steps to eliminate evil practices like dowry, torture and harassment of women, child abuse, smuggling of drugs, prostitution, etc.

Their area of concern should, thus, include all the facts of civil life including problems of security, health hazards, food, fuel, shelter, employment and civil amenities.

With a view to empower women urban local governments should take necessary steps. If necessary, special funds should be created to meet the demands. The earmarked expenditure be spent on the developmental activities of women and it should, by no means, be diverted. The funds provided by the Ministry of Women and Child Development may be made available to the aforesaid bodies for implementation of action programmes.

Ward Committees may be constituted by the urban local bodies and the former may act as 'Gram Sabhas'. These committees would be having direct contact with the voters. The women mayors, chairpersons and councilors should actively associate themselves with these committees.

It may be mentioned that the provision of district and metropolitan planning committees is mandatory. However, this provision is yet to be implemented in most of the states. These committees are meant to provide a critical decision making role to the elected municipal representatives in matters relating to regional and urban planning. The Government of India should ask the state governments to take immediate steps to implement this provision i.e. constitution of the district and metropolitan planning committees.

It is a foregone conclusion that if the urban governments do not have adequate resources at their disposal, implementation of welfare measures for women would be difficult. The Government of India should take up the matter immediately with the state governments and ask them to grant financial autonomy to the urban local governments. The latter's financial autonomy will certainly enable them not only in discharging their constitutional obligations effectively, but also helping them to protect the interests of the women by adopting welfare measures. The National Policy–2001 should be strictly implemented.[18]

Objectives

A great deal is said about elites among the present studies of behavioural research. Every modern society, however democratic its constitution is, in fact, ruled by elites. No modern society can claim to have a single comprehensive elite, because every modern society is having rather a complex system of specialized elites linked to the social order and to each other in a variety of ways. For virtually every activity and every corresponding sphere of social life there is an elite. There are elites of soliders, artists, business magnets, politicians, screen stars, scientists and even gamblers. All are elites in their respective sphere, with different responsibilities, sources of power and pattern of selection and reward. This plurality of elites reflects and promotes the pluralist characteristic of modern society in general. But elites are so numerous and varied that they seldom possess enough common features and affinities to avoid marked differences and tensions. However, some have more social weightage than others because not only they possess different skills and talents but because their activities have greater social impact than others. It is these elites, particularly the ruling ones, the top influential, who arouse particular interest, because they are the prime-movers and models for the entire society.

Politics is no more the sole concern of men. No more it is their sole profession. Over the years, they have been forced to share power, though reluctantly, with the other half of the human race. With the induction of more and more women into the arena of politics, because of reservation and exposure, their strength as elites and decision-makers has gone up at all levels including-urban local bodies. So it is but natural on the part of a student of political science to evince a keen interest in them : their functioning as effective legislators in urban councils, as able decision-makers, their political orientations, their attitudes towards problems, their socio-economic perceptions, their style and manner of functioning, their ability in delivering the goods, their capacity in promoting their cause and safeguarding their interests, their efficiency in bringing about socio-economic changes, their role in influencing the urban environment and giving direction to social change, their sense of identification with the urban systems, their participatory role, their change in status, image and position because of their newly acquired power, their socio-economic background which motivated them to join politics, etc.–all these naturally becomes the objectives of such a study.

The present work, therefore, has made a sincere attempt to identify the urban women elites of Berhampur Municipality in Ganjam District of Orissa as this will throw much light on their insight, perceptions and orientations. In present study, the term "women elites" refers to "women councilors, otherwise known as the political elites or the governing elites, of the Berhampur Municipality. These terms are also used interchangeably".

Purpose of the Study

It is in the context of the government's desire to empower women socially, economically and politically by adopting various developmental measures in all spheres, its sincerity and earnestness in framing the National Policy–2001 and its anxiety to enact the Protection from the Domestic Violence Bill–2001, an attempt has been made to study the empowerment of women councilors of Berhampur Municipality, who were in office during 1997-2001 A.D.

Methodology

The data for this present study are collected with the help of a questionnaire/schedule administered to all the ten women councilors who were in power from 1997-2001. The Council was dissolved on the ground of corruption by the Govt. of Orissa on 17th Nov. 2001, just three months before the completion of its full term of five years i.e. 1997-2002. Personal interviews were also held with all of them in order to elicit information on some of the matters not covered by the questionnaire. Besides, books, journals and articles are made use of for data collection.

Hypotheses

The present study seeks to test the following hypotheses:

(i) The women governing elites of Berhampur Municipality belong mostly to the middle income group.

(ii) Caste factor plays an important role in determining their status.

(iii) They fall mostly within the age group of 35-50 years. In other words they are middle aged.

(iv) They are literate and all of them are politically conscious.

(v) Their spouses are mostly engaged in business and agriculture.

(vi) They are independent in taking their decisions.

(vii) They can play an effective role in the affairs of the urban government.

(viii) They feel themselves empowered.

(ix) Their level of political efficacy and participation is high.

(x) They are politically matured and conscious.

Elites : A Conceptual Frame Work

In the realm of the social sciences, the term "elite" is placed in a specific context. One is treated as a member of the elite strata in that particular branch or field in which one is better placed vis-à-vis the rest of the society of one's companions. The specification is relative : one might be considered as a part of the elite strata in a particular sphere-academic, professional, vocational and the like; yet in another walk of life one might not be so placed and as such rated among the masses.

The world "elite" was used in the 17th century to describe commodities of particular excellence and the usage was later extended to refer to superior social groups such as crack military units or the higher ranks of the nobility. In the English language, the earliest known use of elites, according to the Oxford Dictionary, is in 1823. By this time it was already applied to social groups. But the term was not widely used in social sciences in the 19th century in Europe or until the 1930s in Britain and America, when it was diffused through the sociological theories of elite, notably in the writings of Vilfred Pareto.[19]

Pareto defines elites as people in a society who possess in marked degree qualities of intelligence, character, skill and capacity of whatever kind. According to him, the outstanding idea in the term elite is "superiority". He thinks that elites are those people who if awarded marks, will have the highest indices in their branches of activity. He further classifies elites as "governing elites"-those who participate more or less directly in political decisions and "non-governing elites"-those at the top of the non-political structures. It could, therefore, be maintained that the term "political elite" refers to persons in politics "who occupy posts of political command and who influence major political policies". Mosca explains in a similar vein that the elite consists of an organized minority, which rules over the unorganized majority. Parry describes elites as small minorities who appear to play an exceptionally influential part in political and social affairs[20]. C. Wright Mills maintains that elite is composed of men who have the most of what there is to have-money, power and prestige, who are able to realize their will, even if others resist it, whose positions enable them to transcend the ordinary environments of ordinary people and who are in positions to make decisions having major consequences. Aron[21] holds a pluralistic view of elites. He however, makes a distinction between elites and classes and examines the relationship between the intellectual elite and power structure. In the words of Laswell the political elite is distinct from other types of elites, comprises the power-holders of a body politic"[22]. Mannheim attributes actual policy-making and implementing roles to the elite[23]. In Marxian thinking, particularly the elitist thinking is contrary to Marxist position. Elitists believe that the power structure of any society is determined by the character and the abilities of its political leadership. It is political skill-or lack of it-which determines who will rise and how power may change hands. According to Marx, by contrast, the political leader from whatsoever class he may himself be drawn is but the "representative" of the dominant economic class.

Thus the term elite denotes such a class of people who have the highest indices in their branch of activity and those who are set apart from the rest of the society or group for their pre-eminence. This kind of pre-eminence may be in various fields. But Bottomore states that the term elite, now, is used generally for functional groups which have status in society. Take for example, the case of a highest paid cook in a posh hotel who has pre-eminence in the skill of cooking but he has no status in the society. Hence he cannot be brought under the category of elite. Therefore, the term elite refers to mainly functional and occupational groups which have a status in society. Individuals who reach the apex in various fields like politics, administration, education, jurisprudence, medicine, engineering, religion etc, are termed as the elites of the society.

Mosca divided elite into governing elite and non-governing elite. To Laswell, there are as many elites as there are values[24]. Besides the elite of power, there are elites of wealth, respect and knowledge. These value spheres are classified under eight categories : power enlightenment, wealth, well-being, skill, affection, respect and rectitude.

Elites may be classified under four functional problems which every society must resolve, namely goal attainment, adaptation, integration and pattern maintenance and tension management. Accordingly, four types of elites can be included (i) the current political elite (elite of goal attainment); (ii) the economic, military, diplomatic and scientific elites (elite of adaptation); (iii) elite exercising moral authority, priests, philosophers, educators (elite integration) and (iv) elite that keeps society knit together emotionally and psychologically consisting of artists, writers, filmstars and top figures in sports and games (elite of pattern maintenance and tension management).

It becomes clear from the above that elites generally belong to the following categories : political elite, administrative elite, intellectual elite, business elite, elite of special skill (like artists, film starts, religious heads) and military elite.

Factors which Help the Individual to Emerge as an Elite

According to Ralph Miliband, "Educational qualifications are obviously not enough to reach the top layers of management and may still, quite often, be unnecessary. But the trend is towards the professionalization of business, at least in the sense that getting a start in this particular race requires the kind of formal educational qualifications and this is even more true for other elite positions"[25].

Miliband further writes that the American political decision-makers are mostly sons of professional-men, proprietors and officials and farmers. This means that most of the political elites are recruited from wealthy families. Even in Germany recruitment to elite class is on the basis of wealth.

Similarly, Mosca writes that wealth is one of the important factors which helped an individual to emerge as an elite and that in some societies priestly class emerges as elite while in some other countries the positions of elites are occupied by heredity, castes. Mosca stressed that wealth rather than military valour tended to be the characteristic feature of the dominant class. The people who rule the society are certainly richer and they need not be brave and courageous.

Pareto's circulation of elite theory explains the way in which the non-elites are recruited to the elite positions. He contends that merit and reorganization constitute the factors responsible for the recruitment of elite. He does not rule out the possibility of elite being recruited from the lower classes.

Thus, from the above facts it can be said that the following factors help the individuals to emerge as elites : (i) hereditary i.e. birth in aristocratic families; (ii) wealth, (iii) religious dominance (being the head of the religious institutions), (iv) education and (v) individual ability.

Elite in India

In traditional Indian society the elite group was a closed network, the elite status was considerably rooted in the caste-system. It is evident from the Indian history that there were two types of elites–the priests and the kings-both of whom derived their positions by virtue of the caste into which they were born. Gradually, due to influence of western education a new middle-class composed of Brahmins, Kshatriyas, Vaisyas and Muslims emerged and it was from this middle class that most of the elites including political, bureaucratic, military and business have emerged.

The political elite in pre-independence days was composed of the landed gentry, lawyers, commercial classes, journalists, doctors and teachers[26]. As the political movement grew in strength the landed gentry was increasingly isolated and the political elite role passed on to the educated middle-class and professional groups[27]. After independence the political power passed into the hands of the people who were earlier engaged in the struggle for liberation and who then tended to widen their leadership from the political to the social and economic fields and thus direct all the social developments of the country. Studies now reveal that money plays an important role in determining elite positions. Protective discrimination has also helped women in India to emerge as political elites.

Setting

Berhampur City is situated in the southern part of Orissa. It is only eight miles away from the Bay of Bengal and twelve miles from the Andhra Pradesh. It constitutes the nucleus of six districts: Ganjam, Gajapati, Koraput, Nawrangpur, Rayagada and Phulbani. Free from communal riots, a meeting place of aboriginal and civilized people and the fusion spot of the Aryan and Dravidian cultures, Berhampur, right from early times, has been able to create a niche for herself in the glorious pages of history. With the waters of Bay of Bengal laping its eastern shore, the city is very famous for its silk sarees. A great centre of learning and commerce it was previously a part of the Mahuri Kingdom. With a population of around 4 lac, it has twenty seven wards and each one of them sends a representative to the municipal council. Of 27 urban councilors, 9 are women. Their strength in the Council has gone up because of reservation of seats. It is quite significant to note that a few years back there was not even a single woman councilor in Berhampur Municipality[28] which was established in 1864 by the Britisher. It was in the year 1964 it was reconstituted, comprising thirty-five villages. The total area under the municipality is 29.27 sq. km.

Socio-Economic Profile of Women Councilors

An individual's orientations, perceptions, attitudes, values, socialization, participation, efficacy, status and position all these, to a great extent, are shaped and influenced by the socio-economic environment in which he is born and brought up. The environment includes family, [29] education, caste, age, wealth, exposure, parents'/spouses' background, etc.

Family lays down the foundations of one's political belief,[30] besides constituting his primary and earliest reference group. Like family, education also plays an important role in shaping the human mind. It increases his awareness and helps him in imbibing certain qualities like sincerity, discipline, regularity, etc. It makes him aware of the complexity of the political system, including the understanding of the importance of the informal facets of the political process.[31]

Age also plays an important role as a determinant in throwing up municipal leadership and also in terms of their obligations vis-à-vis municipal affairs. Even after more than fifty years of independence, caste still plays an important role in the elections.

The following table presents the socio-economic profile of women councilors who were in office from 1997 to 2001:

It is quite interesting to observe that all the municipal councilors, except one, are in the age group of 35-50 yrs. It is because of this age factor they are active, dynamic, enterprising, hard-working and serious. They are not lazy and lethargic. In personal interviews all of them categorically told that they personally approached the officers of the Municipality to get their works done. It is further interesting to note that they personally supervised the developmental works like construction, roads, drains, buildings etc; went to the site from where the debris was to be removed; inspected the area where poles were to be removed; inspected the area where poles were to be erected.

Of course, age is not the sole factor for their involvement in the developmental activities. It is supplemented by their education. They are educated, some of them are highly educated. It is quite heartening to note that of the 9 councilors, 3 are graduates and 2 are post-graduates, of 2 one had done post-graduate in Economics and Public Administration. Others have read upto 9th standard. Their exposure to education has made them conscious of environment in which they are living. If age has made them active, education has made them matured, enlightened, wise, increased their understanding, widened their horizon of knowledge, helped them to think in proper perspective.

All the councilors, expect one, are married. One of them is a widow. Her husband was in the Police Department and he died at the age of fifty because of illness. Manjula Devi, because of her family problems, is yet to get married. Since her father is no more, she is looking after the family which consists of her mother, a widow, three brothers and two sisters.

Another interesting phenomenon is that all the councilors are actively engaged in social service activities. They have chosen it as a means to reach the people and win their hearts. Even though they are no more in power following the premature dissolution of the Municipal Council, they have been regularly meeting their people, going to them, trying to solve their problems. This selfless service, involvement and dedication has made them very popular in their respective constituencies.

It is pertinent to note that a few of them including Amita Sahu, J. Jayalakshmi are closely associated with a number of socio-economic and cultural associations, institutions and organizations. This has certainly given them a clear insight into the problems they face. Amita Sahu in personal interview said that she preferred to attend all the functions when invited. Because it helped her in building up her career. She also did not mind to spend some money in these functions, if she was asked to pay, she was of the opinion that this donation was an investment but not an expenditure. The same is the case also with other councilors. It may, therefore, not be unpalatable to say that in all their actions they are not philanthropic. They are also self seekers, like others, trying their best to achieve their goal at any cost and by any means.

Almost all the women councilors, barring a few, are house-wives and do not have any income of their own. Their financial needs and demands are mostly managed by their spouses or

Table 1 : Profile

Sl. No.	Name of the Councilor	Age	Qualification	Marital Status	Profession	Personal Income	Family Income (P.M) Spouse's/ Father's	Property Worth (P.M)
1.	Mrs. Amita Sahu	41	B.A. LL.B.	M	Politics & Social Service	–	Rs. 15,000/-	Rs. 10 lac.
2.	Mrs. Aímmayi Readdy	40	9th class	M	-do-	–	Rs. 10,000/-	Rs. 10 lac.
3.	Mrs. Jyoti Subudhi	50	7th class	M	-do-	–	Rs. 12,000/-	Rs. 10 lac.
4.	Ms. Manjula Devi	27	M.A.	UM	Politics & Business	Rs. 10,000/-	Rs. 10,000/-	Rs. 10 lac.
5.	Mrs. J. Jayalakshmi	45	M.A. (Eco. & P.A)	M	Politics & Business	Rs. 25,000/-	Rs. 40,000/-	Rs. 50 lac.
6.	Mrs. Annapurna Behera	53	4th class	M (W)	Sfocial Service	–	Rs. 10,000/-	Rs. 10 lac.
7.	Mrs. Bishnu Sahu	37.	7th class	M	"	–	Rs. 14,000/-	Rs. 8 lac.
8.	Mrs. T. Surya Prabha	30	B.A.	M	"	–	Rs. 10,000/-	Rs. 5 lac.
9.	Mrs. Tatini Sahu	43	B.A.	M	"	–	Rs. 20,000/-	Rs. 25 lac.

parents. However, two of them are financially independent; J. Jayalakshmi is running her own pharmaceutical industry with a monthly income of Rs. 25,000/- per month. With her own bunglow, four-wheelers, she is highly affluent, while Manjula Devi is looking after her own business. She is a contractor in her own right and earning around Rs. 10,000/- per month. Her elder brother looks after his own business.

It won't be wrong to say that women, irrespective of their socio-economic status, depend, to an extent, upon their parents, relatives or spouses. In other words, the latter exert some influence on them. It is, therefore, essential to know their socio-economic and political background. Of the eight, five of them are in service while the rest three are looking after their business. While one has done his M.A. in Labour Relations, two of them are graduates, while the rest have education upto 9th standard. All of them are very sound financially as their monthly income ranges from Rs. 10,000/- to Rs. 40,000/-. They have also permanent assets like house, land, etc. worth 5 to 50 lac rupees.

Political Orientation of Women Councilors

(i)Political Socialisation

It is interesting to note that all the women councilors, who were in office during 1997—2002, are novices as they are only five-year old in the arena of politics. It was for the first time they became councilors in 1997 and none of them had either contested or held any political office earlier. It is pertinent to know about their induction into such a new field which gave them a thrilling sensation, a kind of satisfaction, a feeling of happiness. In respect of their induction into politics, they were either influenced by their spouses or by their family members, relatives, party leaders, media, members of the locality, etc. It is significant to observe that in certain cases councilors were requested by the people to contest the election and all their (councilor's) election expenses were borne by the latter. It shows a kind of perfect understanding between the people and their representatives, between the "governors" and the "governed". The councilors were motivated by different socializing agents whose direct or indirect influence varied in degree but not in kind.

A few councilors had, however, a strong base in politics and they have imbibed or inherited their political orientations because or their parents' and relatives', motivations as well as their involvement with certain political and non-political organizations.

It is significant to note that though the women councilors entered into politics directly in 1997 by contesting and wining the election, they had developed their political orientation with the help of the aforesaid agents through discussion, deliberation and interaction. Their orientations have also been shaped by the mass media. Though most of them are not well educated, they are well informed because of their exposure to the media. They cannot read newspapers but sit before the TV for news at least for more than one hour a day. Those who are educated subscribe newspapers, both Language and English. Interestingly, none of them has a radio set either for entertainment of information or education purpose.

All the councilors are politically affiliated-3 belong to the Congress, 2 to the BJP and the rest 4 are independent. But all these independent candidates were pro-Congress in their activities and dealings because they extended full support and cooperation to the Chairman and Vice-Chairman who were from the Congress, for their personal benefit.

When they were asked why did they support the Chairman, who belonged to the Congress, they said that 'compulsion and expectation' forced them to extend their cooperation to the latter. Had they remained neutral, they might have incurred his displeasure. He in turn, out of political vendetta might not have sanctioned funds for any developmental works in their constituencies.

It is significant to note one incident, which is a slur on democracy. It relates to the election of Tatini Sahu to the office of Vice-Chairman. Amita Sahu and J. Jayalakshmi, the Congress councilors, were assured by the local leaders of their elevation as Chairman and Vice-Chairman respectively. But it was later decided that Amita Sahu and Bhimudu, who belonged to O.B.C., will be elected as Vice-Chairman and Chairman respectively. But when the actual game started, a few powerful elements of the Congress forcibly entered into the office violating all norms and ethics and threatened the councilors of dire consequences unless they obliged them by electing Tatini Sahu as the Vice-Chairman. They shouted, "heads would roll" if their demands were not met. This 'fear and force' factor went against the interest of Amita Sahu. She had to bow down and yield to their demands. This is certainly a sordid affair, a dark chapter in the history of Berhampur Municipality, an onslaught on one's freedom to choose without fear or favour, bias or prejudice.

It is further interesting to point out that for the office of the Vice-Chairman there were two candidates in the fray: Tatini Sahu (Congress) and Manjula Devi from the B.J.P. Despite the whip issued by the Congress, the latter, to her utter dismay and surprise, secured eight votes in her favour. It shows that some councilors (both men and women) belonging to the Congress defied the party whip and cast their votes in favour of Manjula Devi. It further shows their resentment against the choice of Tatini Sahu, an inefficient, ineffective candidate.

Some councilor also told that Tatini Sahu spent nearly four lac rupees to purchase the votes. With money she could snatch away the second highest post in the Council, though she did not deserve it at all. It is the personal opinion of her colleagues.

As most of the councilors are less educated they have not gone through the manifestoes of their political parties. Some of them are even not aware of it. And those who are educated, have also not read them because of their lack of interest. But it is to be noted that some of them like Amita Sahu, "whose body", in her own words, belongs to Congress but mind and soul to the BJP, and Manjula Kumari Devi, a BJP Member, regularly read the BJP literature like Rashtradipa, Organizer, Panchajanya, etc. Because of their exposure to such literature they are more matured than their colleagues.

(ii) Political Awareness

The political awareness of the councilors is quite high. They are well aware of the problems like corruption, Ayodhya tangle, burning of train a Godhra, crime against women, dowry, bride-burning, etc. Most of them were of opinion that crime against women could be checked if they are given proper education. According to J. Jayalakshmi it is the rural women who suffer more than their urban counterparts. Law alone cannot bring justice to them. It is the political will and change in the mindset of the male members that will bring a change in the living conditions of women. This, in turn, will empower them.

All of them, as expected, supported, wholeheartedly 33% of reservation of seats for them in the urban councils as it has given them a chance to serve the people and solve their problems by bringing a change. This reservation, to them, should be a permanent phenomenon. It is significant to note that the Congress councilors are terribly annoyed with the functioning of their local leaders and of the opinion that they should be immediately sacked from the party and replaced by those who are competent, honest and hardworking. But BJP councilors are very happy with their leaders and have a very good report with them even after the dissolution of the Council. They do not feel that women are neglected in the society, though they are aware of their problems. They believe that things will improve in future and they will have a better world to live in.

(iii) Political Participation

Not only the councilors are well aware of the social problems and issues, their level of participations is also quite high. All of them after having become majors, have exercised their franchise and never they have missed even a single election without going to the polling booths. Most of them have attended almost all the Council meetings and successfully put forth their view without fear and prejudice. None of them makes any financial contributions to any political party. Those who have become life members of political parties they had made some payments at the time of applying for life membership.

None of them gave any information about the money they spent in their election. Some of them said that it was their strong supporters who managed and worked the show. It is significant to observe that J. Jayalakshmi, the wife of Dr. Surya Rao, resigned from her office as she could not tolerate the way the Council functioned. She was very unhappy and dissatisfied with the behaviour of male councilors. She told in a personal interview to the researcher that level of participation in the Council was very low and it was often marred by pandemonium and indiscipline.

(iv) Political Efficacy

Councilors' political efficacy is too high. They are confident of their position and capacity in delivering their goods. Given a chance, most of them are prepared to contest in the elections to the Assembly and the Parliament. The office, their 'new assignment' gave them a new status, a new image, a new position, a new hope, and this, in turn, shaped their personality and perceptions and helped them to discover a 'new person' in them.

Conclusion

The women councilors, who are also known as "governing elites", "political elites", decision-makers, of Berhampur Municipality are well exposed as their orientations towards politics, as studied above under four different dimensions like political socialization, political awareness, political participation and political efficacy, are of high order and quite satisfactory.

It is significant to note that the last few years have witnessed in India extensive and intensive developments in the sphere of women and the law. The rapid pace of developments can be attributed to a number of factors. The doctrine of equality of the sexes, which is now accepted as an established one, is one factor. Increase in literacy and education amongst the females is another contributory factor. The Judicial approach on various issues concerning women has, by and large, been progressive and liberal. World-wide movement for women's freedom has not left India untouched even though the form which the movement has assumed in India may not be identical with the form assumed by it elsewhere[32].

Swami Vivekananda, an Indian saint, has very rightly said :

> There is no chance for the welfare of the world unless the condition of women is improved. It is not possible for a bird to fly on one wing.

But, unfortunately, since the ages, the bird has been forced to fly on one wing as the other one is not only battered but also amputed. Quite a large chunk of Indian women is paying dearly the price of some legacies of history, culture and social traits. This process has caused substantial harm to the body politic. Hence the crying need of the hour is to bring to an end the sufferings of the Indian women. The issue of their empowerment has, therefore, been given top priority by the Government of India. Time has come to create an awareness in them about their rights and opportunities, legal means and enforcement, economic empowerment paving the way for economic independence, etc. This will go a long way in making them confident of their status and position in the society.

Any discussion on the rights of women cannot be completed without referring to the Essay on the Subjection of Women by John Stuart Mill. He observed in 1869 in the course of that Essay[33] thus:

> "That the principle which regulates the existing social relations between the two sexes–the legal subordination of one sex to the other –is wrong in itself, and now one of the chief hindrances to human improvement; and that it ought to be replaced by a principle of perfect equality, admitting no power or privilege on the one side, nor disability on the other."

J.S. Mill gave tremendous importance to women's development, their participation in the decision-making, their role in bringing socio-economic development, etc. Hence, it has been very rightly said that a woman's place in society marks the level of civilization[34]. The reason for such a wide gap between the ideal and the practical is not only due to historical reasons but mainly because of attitude of inferiority and bondage towards women who are thus deprived of basic freedom and thereby explored to easy exploitation[35].

In India, women are equal to men. This is enshrined in its Constitution. But, in practice, the principle of equality remains inoperative for the majority of women who are handicapped by the illiteracy, lack of training and access to productive assets. The idea of equality of opportunity nestled in the egalitarian framework of our Constitution has remained as an abstract principle in a society characterized by social and economic inequalities. This plight of women can be overcome only with their empowerment.

It is, therefore, to be kept in mind that movement towards gender equality is not a technocratic goal, it is a political process. It requires a new way of thinking in which, women and men give way to a new philosophy that regards all people, irrespective of gender, as essential agents of change[36].

March 8th, 1917. A red-letter day, a historic day, a day of much importance and great significance. It has gone down in the annals of history for having laid the foundation of a new age for women by giving them a new lease of life, a new hope, a new future, a new meaning to their goal particularly in the sphere of politics. In the history of mankind a new era was ushered in: an era which witnessed women fighting for a cause, for their rights against exploitation, for their survival, for their empowerment and for their around development. It is significant to note that the International Women's Movement had come a long way since the early years of 20th century when on that historic Sunday in February the Russian women chose last Sunday of Feb. in 1917 to strike for "bread and peace" with two million Russian soldiers dead in the war. The rest was history. Four days later the Czar was forced to abdicate the throne and the provisional governments led by the Communists granted women the right to vote. Thus emerged a new era in the history of mankind. The historic Sunday fell on Feb. 23 as per Julian Calendar then in use in Russia but on 8 March, on the Gregorian Calendar in use elsewhere.

Though the movements for women's rights differed in their ideological moorings from the communist-led struggles that were organizing working class women, it was in a similar background that International Women's Day came about. The women working in garment factories in New York marched on 8th March for better work conditions. The day was declared as International Women's Day in 1910 by Clara Zetkin, the German Communist leader. The "Second Wave" feminism of the 1960s too was an intense upheaval all over the world, this time against the external manifestations of patriarchy and the internal ones within political groups and the family.

History often repeats itself. In Aug. 1970, thousands of American women joined the national Organization of Women (NOW) in America and women putting aside their domestic duties came out in the streets in a national strike. The movement for the Equal Rights Amendments Act was a prolonged one, showing that women's liberation was much more than burning bras.

It is, therefore, not out of context to note that on 8th March the focus is on women. Right from government organizations, NGOs, media to the multi-billion dollar industries worldwide that sell their products–right from a pin to personal computers and pickles and pampads to powerful machines–celebrate the International Women's day in their own way. Organisations are coming with a Women's Special. On one hand she is treated as a commodity and money-minting machine which is not in good taste in the days of liberalization and globalisation, while, on the other, she is worshiped as Shakti. It is because of this, many a woman falls into the trap of living upto the stereotypical image that society has created and nurtured for her since ages. It is this dilemma that the modern women who is intelligent and educated enough to choose her own course vis-à-vis the changing perceptions in the contemporary society, is trying to resolve and evolve a role for herself as she decides the best.

It is because of this change in the attitude of women the International Women's Day is celebrated. The day has, indeed, been the story of ordinary women as makers of history. It is rooted and reflected in centuries–old struggle of women to actively participate in the decision making on an equal footing with men.

The women's movement had been marked with several high victories over the decades and the United Nations, too, started commemorating the day from Mar, 8, 1976, and four UN conferences had been held from Cairo on Population and Development to Beijing on "Platform for Action: from economic empowerment to intellectual emancipation". It is significant to observe that the movement had, over the years, managed to trickle down to the grassroot level. An average woman, whether literate or illiterate, living in urban or rural areas, has learned to assert herself with a new found confidence that came with her ability to supplement the family income.

Needless to say there are few women in every society who have proved themselves on par with men and created a niche for themselves in their chosen fields–not only in the traditional teacher and doctor roles but as tough and efficient administrators in the higher echelons of public service and of course in politics. But, for the majority of middle class women the empowerment in true sense remains a dream, an eluding goal, an illusion.

They may be qualified, well-educated and employed but when it comes to decision-making at home or outside, they have no role or see no role for themselves having abdicated that responsibility to either the man of the house or to the elders in the joint family as tradition would not expect them to be otherwise. It is unfortunate that women themselves do not see any 'injustice' in this arrangement, having lived with that mind set for centuries together.

We may have one Medha Patekar leading the Narmada Bachao Andolan with courage and conviction and without caring for the dire consequences, Arundhati Roy, a Broker Prize winner-turned-activist, whose literary works including The God of Small Things created sensations in the literary world, or that representative from Revolutionary Association of Afghanistan Women, Sehar Seba, who came all the way to Visakhapatnam in Andhra Pradesh (India) to participate in the All-India Democratic Women's Association Conference just to tell the world the inhuman torture and untold sufferings and agonies to which they were subjected by Talibans. But these brave women's campaigns which have certainly a positive impact on millions of middle class women and inspire them to achieve intellectual emancipation too alongwith economic independence.

No doubt the Women's Representation Bill is yet to become a reality, but their initiation into political and democratic process had commenced with 33 per cent representation in local bodies, as well as government jobs and educational institutions.

Those responsible for crime against women, be it in the family or outside, should not be allowed to go scot-free, does not matter whether they are finally persecuted or not. The role of media in giving a wide coverage to violence against women has sent a powerful message to the perpetrators of crime.

Another encouraging feature is recognition of women as the major actors in brining peace and change, progress and property and in helping the governments worldwide in resolving the conflicts.

The day is not far-off when their contribution to social, economic and political spheres of society would be acknowledged and appreciated openly. That would be the day of true happiness for them[37].

The measures adopted by the Government of India, as discussed above, to empower women are certainly encouraging and remarkable. Recently, the Union Finance Minister, Yasawant Sinha, assigned the two departments the task of encouraging women scientists in his budget speech which he delivered in the Lok Sabha in Feb. 2002. Bachi Singh, the Minister of State for Science and Technology, has said the strategies are being worked out to attract women into careers in science and engineering. This is certainly a positive step in direction of women empowerment.

The Prime Minister, A.B. Vajpayee's greetings to women of the country on the occasion of the International Women's Day also reflect the Government's desire to improve the status of women. He said:

> The Women of today are equal and rightful partners in the country's march towards progress. The women of the new millennium are taking giant strides in different walks of life, lending a multifarious hue to their persona.

It is significant to note while the cosmetic companies like Ponds launched advertising campaigns for International Women's Day on March 8th senior officers in the government organizations were ordering meek women employees to organize functions to mark the day of women's empowerment. These two forms of celebration have generated extreme reactions among activists and those who have been connected with the women's movement. While some see celebrations by cosmetics as a victory, arguing that the movement is growing and turning into a festival a sorts, others are disappointed. This group of people is not only irked by the shallow ritualism of commemorating particular days, but also the slow erosion of the thrust of women's liberation as the axis of the movement[38].

Those who are unhappy with the co-option of the Women's Day by forces of consumerism maintain that institutionalization of a vibrant anti-establishment movement is an antithesis of the radical values embodied in early feminism[39].

In India, the Mathura Rape case in 1980 sparked off the autonomous Women's Movement and Women's Organizations emerged in several towns, dealing with violence against women in its various manifestations. Militant Campaigns against rape and dowry deaths, with actions like blackening the face of wife-murderers and their social boycott led to important changes in the rape laws and those pertaining in family violence, marriage and divorce. This has certainly empower Indian women.

However, vibrant as this movement was, the slow and insidious process of co-option began to dull the edge of militancy. The increasing trend of making careers in the movement, of taking up jobs and research projects became easy options.

This has lead to a proliferation of crisis centers for women in distress. But what may have began as pooling of individual resources to provide shelters and legal aid gradually turned into professional non-governmental organizations (NGOs) where paid staff render professional services.

A debate has been continuing within the movement: whether women's consciousness will be reached by making them politically aware, so that they can participate in broader movements for social change or they should be doing "case work" i.e. mitigating the problems of individual women in a practical way.

In India, voluntary organizations have mushroomed in towns and villages–organizing workshops and seminars on women's issues, giving legal aid, health training, providing for self-help savings and other schemes, doing developmental activities, creating an image of tremendous growth and proliferation of the women's movement.

In such a scenario, it is time to evaluate the work of voluntary organizations in making women conscious of their rights and enabling them to handle their own problems.

With politics of piurality being the order of the day, certain questions can be posed. For instance, would the profession of modeling or participation in beauty contests be an expression of independence and entry into feminist space or falling a victim to a consumerist culture that turns women into sex objects? Would 33 per cent reservations for women in elected bodies, in the police force, judiciary and bureaucracy be expression of their improvement or merely their assimilation into the exploitative state machinery.

Years of torture, humiliation, suffering, neglect and discrimination against women cannot be brought to an end in a day with a magic wand. Bur sincere efforts, strong will and careful planning by the government will definitely safeguard the interest of women. Steps should be taken to increase their level of education which will ultimately help them to shape their own future, build up their own career, take their own decisions, and lead an independent life which will give them strength and security, peach and prosperity. Education will certainly increase their awareness, empower them to participate in decision-making process at home and outside and make them economically strong and independent. Empowerment of women also requires the participation and co-operation of men in all fields. India has adopted several measures to empower them. We have to march ahead along with other developed countries of the world. Women empowerment can be possible only when we change our mindsets that allow women a second class status in the society.

Today women happen to be the most vulnerable and neglected lot in the development strategy and it would be imperative to give special attention to this group. For the purpose of analyzing and evolving meaningful strategy of development, they must be treated as a separate social category.[40] Steps should be taken to undo the wrongs done to them so that we can have an integrated, well-developed and balanced society. This can be possible only with their empowerment.

Developmental programmes undertaken by the Government and different policies adopted by it, particularly the National Policy–2001 and the Protection from the Domestic Violence Bill-2001, have gone a long way in empowering women: a dream which has come true. Still, we have to walk many a miles.

REFERENCES

Manu is said to be the descendant of self-existent Brahman who is the creator or progenitor of the whole world. To some, he belonged to 1200 B.C. while others opine that he lived in 12th or 13th century A.D. For details see K.S. Padhy, Indian Political Tradition (Berhampur: Tara Tarini Pustakalaya, 1997), pp. 1-52.

Source: Atharva Veda. It has discussed the role of women in socio-economic life in the society.

In "Ram-Gita", Lord Ram tells his younger brother Laxman about the role of a woman in the society.

K.S. Lal, History of the Khilijis (New Delhi: Asia Publishing House, 1967).

Agha Mehdi Hussain, Tughlaq Dynasty (New Delhi: S. Chand & Co., 1978).

R.C. mazumdar, H.C. Ray Choudhury & K.K. Dutta, An Advanced History of India (London: Macmillan, 1967).

The Constitution of India has guaranteed certain rights to women, so that their interest can be safeguarded. They are as follows:

Art. 14 : The State shall not deny to any person equality before law or equal protection of law within the territory of India.

Art 15(1) : The State shall not discriminate against any citizen on grounds oniy of religion, race, caste, sex, place of birth or any of them.

Art. 15(2) : No citizen shall, on grounds only of religion, race, caste, sex, place of birth or any of them, be subject to any disability, liability, restriction or condition with regard to:

(a) Access to shops, public restaurants, hotels and places of public entertainment; or

(b) The use of wells, bathing ghats, roads and places of public resort maintained wholly or partly out of State funds or dedicated to the use of the General Public.

Art. 15(3) : Nothing in this Article shall prevent the State from making any special provision for women and children.

Art. 16(1) : There shall be equality of opportunity for all citizens in matters relating to employment or appointment to any office under state.

Art. 16(2) : No citizen shall, on grounds only of religion, race, caste, sex, descent, place of birth, residence or any of them, be ineligible for, or discriminated against in respect of, any employment or office under the state.

Art. 39 : The state shall, in particular, direct its policy towards securing :

(a) That the citizens, men and women equally, have the right to an adequate means of livelihood.

(b) That there is equal pay for equal work for both men and women.

(c) That the health and strength of workers, men and women, and the tender age children are not abused and that citizens are not forced by economic necessity to enter avocations unsuited to their age or strength.

Art. 42 : The state to make provision for recurring just and humane condition of work and for maternity relief.

Art. 46 : The State to promote with special care the educational and economic interests of the weaker sections of the people and to protect them from social injustice and all forms of exploitation.

Art. 47 : The State to raise the level of nutrition and the standard of living of its people and the improvement of public health.

Art. 51(A) : It shall be the duty of every citizen of India to promote harmony and the spirit of common brotherhood amongst all the people of India transcending religious, linguistic and regional or sectional diversities to renounce practices derogatory to the dignity of women.

Art. 243 (D) (3) : Not less than one-third (including the number or seats reserved for women belonging to the Scheduled Castes and the Scheduled Tribes) of the total number of seats to be filled by direct election in every Panchayat to be reserved for women and such seats to be allotted by rotation to different constituencies in a Panchayat.

Art. 243 (D) (4) : Not less than one-third of the total number of offices of Chairpersons in the Panchayats at each level to be reserved for women.

Art. 243 (T) (3) : Not less than one-third (including the number of seats reserved for women belonging to the Scheduled Castes and the Scheduled Tribes) of the total number of seats to be filled by direct election in every municipality to be reserved for women and such seats to be allotted by rotation to different constituencies in a Municipality.

Art. 243 (T) (4) : Reservation of offices of Chairpersons in municipalities for the Scheduled Castes, the Scheduled Tribes and women in such manner as the legislature of a State may by law provide.

Notwithstanding the aforesaid constitutional provisions guaranteeing several rights to women, it is very unfortunate they are yet to receive their dues. Inequality between men and women continues to exist in respect of their access to health and nutrition education and socio-economic and political participation. Hence their empowerment.

Ashok Kumar, Some Theoretical Aspects of People's Participation in Wamen's Welfare Activities, in Mukta Mittal (ed.), Women Power in India (New Delhi : Anmol Publication Pvt. Ltd., 1995), p. 114.

Decision-making includes: (a) activities such as generation of ideas, formulation of plans; (b) activities such as prioritizing and formulation of plans; (c) operational aspect such as procedures and delivery of benefits.

Implementation includes resource mobilization or contribution, administration and co-ordination and benefit sharing.

S.N. Mishra, Development through participation, course material, India Institute of Public Administration, New Delhi, p. 48.

G.N. Reddy, The Rural Poor (Allahabad : Chugh Publication, 1991), p 49.

E.D. Setty, People's Participation in Rural Development : A Critical Analysis, The Indian Journal of Social Work, Vol. XI, VI, No. 1, April 1985, pp. 73-83.

Robert E. Dowse and John A. Hughes (London : John Wiley & Sons, 1972), p. 289.

The RMK was created in 1993 to meet the micro credit needs of poor and asset-less women in the informal sector. From its inception a total credit of Rs. 77.36 crore was sanctioned to benefit 350,000 women. It has expanded its institutional base at grass root level through self-help groups for expanding its credit services.

The WCP introduced as a major strategy for the first time during the 9th Plan (1997-2002) was reviewed in Aug. 2002. It took note of funds having been made available by a number of Ministries and Departments such as Health and Family Welfare, H.R.D., Labour, Agriculture, Rural Development, Social Justice & Empowerment, Tribal Affairs etc. to benefit Women.

Protection from the Domestic Violence Bill, 2001.

Like the National Policy 2001, the Protection from the Domestic Violence Bill 2001 is another bold and progressive step by the Governmental of India in the direction of women empowerment. On the eve of the International Women's Day the Government wanted to introduce and pass the Protection from Domestic Violence Bill, 2001 in the current session of Parliament (Feb. –Mar-2002). It was formulated in response to a campaign by women's groups across the country demanding a specific law that deals with violence against women committed in their homes. Although there is a provision under the Criminal Law, Sec. 498 A, women do not have access to any civil remedies.

The Women's groups that have strongly criticized the Bill are: Jagori, Nirantar, Action India, Ankur, Lawyers Collective, All-India

Democratic Women's Association, Saheli, Akshara (Mumbai), Women's Centre (Mumbai), PLD, Anweshi (Calicut), Young Women's Christian Association (India0, National Federation of Indian Women, Ekta (Madurai0 Amnesty, Asli (Lucknow), Manara (Bangalore) and Shakti Shalini.

Led by the Supreme Court Advocate, Indira Jaising, and the Lawyers' Collective, and in consultation with different women's groups who had been dealing with cases of domestic violence for over two decades, a model draft was prepared in 1999 and presented to the Vajpayee Government.

There were three important factors that this draft had to address to prevent violence within the home. It had to recognize that the place of residence, called the "shared household" is the site of abuse and unequal power relations. As neither society nor family provide a safety net and shelter for women in such situations, the women should have the right to reside in the shared household. This concept of a shared household would then include daughters, widows, mothers and women in bigamous marriages and in common law relationships. The Court should have the power to pass "protection orders", restrain the abuser from entering the shared household, order repossession and grant emergency monetary relief. So, any law that addresses domestic violence must prevent it, protect the right of woman to live in the shared household and make provision for her maintenance.

This draft cannot be construed as a marriage law. It does not seek to define rights within the marriage or rights at the break-up of the matrimonial tie. Its mandate is to provide the woman with a safe space, free from violence, to make her decisions. Domestic violence is one of the tools used to force a woman out of the home, to snatch away her rights to property and sometimes her own children. None of our matrimonial laws provides for the sharing of matrimonial assets, maintenance proceedings are long drawn out and execution of maintenance orders is even harder. Women are forced to leave the home with empty laws or suffer the abuse in silence. It is this situation that the law must address.

The Government of India has recognized and accepted that violence exists within the family. On 11 Dec. 2001, the Ministry of Human Resource Development printed and circulated "The Protection from Domestic Violence Bill 133 of 2001". It was a welcome step but it falls short of providing effective and meaningful steps to deal with domestic violence.

The Domestic Violence Bill, 2001, approved by the Cabinet, is strongly as expected, opposed by the Women's groups because it is a far cry from what these groups had proposed. The principal and most glaring omission in the Bill lies in the very definition of domestic violence. While the draft of the Lawyers' Collective (Delhi) stuck to the internationally accepted definitions of domestic violence as seen in The Convention on Elimination of All Forms of Discrimination Against Women (CEDAW), the Government's Bill has a vague and loose one. This definition has also excluded sexual, economic and child abuse. It does not list specific acts of violence and leaves the interpretation of the cause of action to the discretion of the judge and so it becomes subject to the judicial officer's perception of violence.

The Bill speaks of "habitual assault" and vague concepts such as actions that make "the life of the aggrieved miserable". As a result, it does not take into account one time physical assault and allows for a great deal of subjective interpretations as to what "constitutes" domestic violence.

Sub-Section 2 of Clause 4, which defines domestic violence, cancels out any efficiency that even this inadequate definition might have had. This Section says that if the respondent follows a course of conduct which is "reasonable for his own protection or for the protection of his or another's property", then the Section that defines domestic violence as any conduct that "otherwise injures or harms the aggrieved person" will not apply. In other words, if an abusive husband can prove that he beat his wife to protect his property, he will not fall under the ambit of the law.

The Government's Bill has also ignored the needs of women and children, the victims of domestic violence, for shelter. As said earlier, the Lawyers' Collective draft had gone into this aspect in detail and suggested "protective orders" which could ensure that the victim could remain in her marital or natal home. The Bill is completely silent on the need for both shelter and financial support.

The Bill also restricts the application of the law to women who are within a "valid marriage". This, the women's groups argue, leaves out almost half the women who are the victims of domestic violence. Such women are often second wives, with no legal standing, or have cohabited without legal documents to prove their marital status or have been duped into so-called legal marriages which do not hold up in a court of law. This also excludes women who are victims of cruelty in their natal homes, before marriage. And it also excludes widows.

The Government Bill, as said earlier, ignores the concept of shared household. No existing law gives the women an absolute right of residence in the home and if this aspect remains untouched it fails to address the root cause of their vulnerability.

Another omission is the failure to provide for restraining orders. Violation of an order of protection entails a term of imprisonment for one year or a fine of Rs. 20,000/-. In such a situation the woman would have to go back to the court to enforce this order, whereas, a composite order with a suspended warrant would make it more effective for implementation.

While important aspects to prevent violence have been overlooked, the Bill empowers the Magistrate, as said earlier, to order for mandatory counseling for the victim jointly with abuser and for an "amicable settlement". No one could object to this but given the track record of the existing mandate of the family counseling centers, family courts and Lok Adalats, where reconciliation is treated as synonymous with "preservation of the family unit at all costs" and "adjustment" on the part of the woman even if it means that she has to live with violence, this will work against her. Mandatory counseling is necessary for the abuser. It is to be noted that this provision is dysfunctional. The information from the counseling session cannot be used in the case and is akin to "writing on water". The Bill makes provision for protecting officers and for help from NGOs, referred to as Service Providers. The Bill gives impunity to Protection Officers for acts done in good faith. This impunity should be extended to the Service Providers also.

It is pertinent to note The Domestic Violence Bill is meant to be a short-term measure for women in violent and abusive situation. It does not contemplate transfer of rights in property. Long term rights will have to be worked out under the existing laws. This Bill is to be in addition to and not in derogation of other family laws.

If the Protection from Domestic Violence Bill is to make any difference in the lives of women it must take effective steps to prevent violence within the home because domestic violence is a violation of women's human rights. When rights are violated in the public sphere the state takes active remedial steps but when the violations are within the private sphere the state turns a blind eye. The definition of violence and shared household must be clearly spelled out. The relief granted must prevent further violence. The Courts must be easily accessible with simple procedures. The Bill lacks these necessary provisions and needs reconsideration and substantial review if it is to address domestic violence in a meaningful way. In its present form it offers abused women the choice between a home with violence or homelessness. Representatives of women's groups have, therefore, rejected the Bill in its totality and urged the Government to modify it so that it covers "non-negotiable provisions" which include changing the definition of what constitutes domestic violence so that it conforms with the UN definition, ensuring that the law includes all categories of women, not just those legally married, and providing abused women the right to shelter, including in their marital home.

National Policy-2001.

The Government of India has taken a bold and progressive step by adopting the National Policy 2001 to empower women.

A. Goals and Objectives

The Policy seeks to advance the cause of women by bringing them all kinds of development-social, economic and political–and making them empowered. Steps will be taken to disseminate if so that maximum women will be encouraged to participate in the decision making. The objectives of this policy are to:

(i) Create proper environment by adopting positive economic and social policies for full development of women. This will certainly help them in realizing their potential;

(ii) Allow them to enjoy their rights and exercise their power on equal basis with men in all spheres-political, economic, social cultural and civil.

(iii) Give them an opportunity to have equal access to health care, equality in education at all levels, career and vocational guidance, employment, equal remuneration, occupational health and safety, social security and public office, etc;

(iv) Strengthen the legal system to remove all kinds of discrimination against women;

(v) Change the social attitudes and community practices by allowing both men and women to play an active participatory role in the system;

(vi) Mainstream a gender perspective in the development process;

(vii) Eliminate all kinds of discrimination and violence against women and the girl child and

(viii) Build and strengthen partnerships with civil society, particularly women's organization.

B. Decision Making

To achieve the goal of empowerment of women, measures will be adopted to ensure equality between women and men and allow the former to actively participate in decision making in every sphere and at all levels : the legislative, executive, judicial, corporate and statutory bodies, as also the Advisory Commissions, Committees, Boards, Trusts, etc. Affirmative actions such as reservations/quotas, including in higher legislative bodies, will be taken wherever necessary on a time-bound basis.

C. Violence

Women are subject to (both in home and outside) all kinds of violence, mental and physical-like sexual harassment, rape, dowry torture, molestation, kidnapping, eve-teasing, discrimination, overwork, etc. The irony is that nowhere, even in their mothers' wombs, they are safe. The Policy seeks to adopt measures to prevent all these evils which have become a painful part of their life.

D. Education

Women and girls will have an equal access to education, special measures will be adopted to eliminate discrimination against them, universalize education, create a gender sensitive educational system, reduce dropouts, eradicate illiteracy, increase enrolment and retention rates of girls and improve the quality of education to facilitate the life long learning and development of vocational/ technical skills by them. The existing gender gap between women and men in respect of secondary and higher education will be bridged Gender sensitive curricula will be developed at different levels of educational system in order to address sex stereotyping as one of the causes of gender discrimination.

E. Legal-Judicial Systems

Legal-Judicial systems will be made more responsible and gender sensitive to women's needs, especially in case of domestic violence and personal assault. They must get justice without delay and this will be possible with enactment of new laws and by reviewing the existing ones.

F. Mainstreaming a Gender Perspective in the Development Process

Policies will be made, programmes undertaken and systems established to ensure that women's perspectives are given due weightage in all developmental processes. In case there are gaps between policies and programmes, attempts will be made to bridge them. Coordinating and monitoring mechanisms will also be devised to assess from time to time to what extent progress has been made in respect of such mainstreaming mechanisms.

G. Economy

While disguising and implementing macro-economic and social policies women's perspectives will be included by ensuring their participation in such processes. Their significant contributions to socio-economic development as workers and producers are to be recognized in the formal and informal sectors. Appropriate policies will be made to take care of their employment and working conditions.

H. Agriculture

Since women are playing a critical role in agriculture and allied sectors as producers, sincere and concerted efforts will be made to ensure that benefits of training, extension and various pogrammes reach them in proportion to their numbers. Training should be imparted to them in soil conservation, social forestry, dairy development and other occupations allied to agriculture like horticulture, livestock including small animal husbandry, poultry, fisheries etc. This training will also be expanded to benefit them (women workers) in the agriculture sector.

I. Industry

Women's contributions to industry are certainly significant as they have joined electronics, information technology, food processing, agro-industry and textiles. To encourage their participation in industries there should be sufficient enactment of law. Enough security should be provided to them so that they can, if they wish, work in night shifts. This will be accompanied with support services for security, transportation etc.

J. Support Services

Without support services women will find it difficult to work in industries or elsewhere. Not only an environment will be created to provide them security but also support services like child care facilities, including crèches at work places for the aged and the disabled. These services will be improved and expanded to create favourable environment for their effective participation in the political system.

K. Health and Nutrition

Measures will be adopted to improve the health condition of women. They should have an easy, comprehensive and affordable access to heath care. Proper steps will also be taken to meet their nutritional needs at all stages of the life cycle: infancy and childhood, adolescence and reproductive.

L. Drinking Water and Sanitation

Special attention will be given to women particularly those living in urban slums and rural areas by providing and improving drinking water and toilet facilities, removing the debris, etc.

M. Housing and Shelter

Adequate provisions will be made to provide sufficient accommodation to women particularly those who are working, students, apprentices and trainees. They face insurmountable difficulties when posted outside. While framing housing policies and plans, their perspectives will be taken into consideration.

N. Environment

Policies and programs for conservation and restoration of the environment will reflect the perspectives of women. Considering the impact of environment on their working conditions and livelihood, their participation will be ensured in protecting the environment from being polluted and degraded. Since the vast majority of rural women still depend on the locally available non-commercial sources of energy such as animal during, crop waste and fuel wood, steps will be taken to ensure the efficient use of these energy resources in a environmental friendly manner. They will be encouraged to make use of solar energy, bio-gas, smokeless chulahs and other rural application so as to have a visible impact of these measures in influencing ecosystems and changing the life styles of rural women.

O. Science and Technology

Women will be motivated to be more and more scientific in their approach and attitude. Their scientific orientations will be developed through appropriate policies in this regard. Girls will be asked to opt for science subjects in schools and colleges. Women will be involved in all developmental projects with scientific and technical inputs. They will be provided training in areas where they have special skills like communication and information technology.

J.B. Bottomore, Elite and Society (Middle Sex: Penguin. 1966).

Vilfred Pareto, "The Circulation of Elites" in Parsons, Naegela and Pitts (ed.) Theories of Society (New Work: Free Press, 1961), p. 552.

Gaetano Mosca, The Ruling Class (New York: McGraw Hill, 1939), pp. 50-53.

Parry Geriant, Political Elites (London: George Allen of Unwin Ltd., 1969), p. 13.

Aron Raymond, Social Structure and the Ruling Class, British Journal of Sociology, Part-I, 1950.

H.D. Laswell, et al, The Comparative Study of Elites (Stanford: Hoover Institute Series, 1952), Vol. I.

Karl Mannheim, Ideology and Utopia (London: Kegan Paul, 1936).

Harold D. Lasswell. Daniel Larners, The Study of Political World Revolutionary Elite. (Cambridge, Massachuaoetts: The MIT Press, 1966), p. 8.

Ralph Miliband, The State in Capitalist Society (London: Weidenfeld and Nicolson, 1970), p. 40.

K.S. Padhy & S. Choudhury, "Social Status of the Decision-Makers of the Berhampur Municipal Councillors", the Research Journal, Behrhampur University, Vo. IV, No. 4, Dec. 1984, pp. 53-65.

James C. Davis, "The Family's Role in Political Socialization", Annals, 361, Sept. 1965, p. 11.

Robert E. Lane, "Fathers and Sons: The Foundation of Political Belief", American Sociological Review, 24, 1959, pp. 502-11.

K.S. Padhy & D. Sabat, "Political Socialization of the Rural Elites: A Case Study of an Orissian panchayat" in K.S. Padhy (ed.), Political Sociology: A Perspective Analysis (New Delhi: Discovery Publishing House, 1989), p. 71.

E.S. Venkataramiah, "Women and the Law" in B.K. Pal (ed.), Problems and Concerns of Indian Women (New Delhi: ABC Publishing House, 1987), p. 12.

On Liberty, Representative Government, The Subjection of Women– Three Essays by J.S. Mill (UK: Oxford University Press, 1960), p. 427.

Sunanda Bhandare, "Crime Against Women" in B.K. Pal (ed.), Problems and Concerns of Indian Women (New Delhi: ABC Publishing House, 1987), p. 65.

Ibid., pp. 65-66.

Sumitra Mahajan, "Empowerment of Women: Philosophy, Goals and Achievements", Yojana, Vol. 45, New Delhi, August 2001, p. 5.

M.M. Maitreyi, "Women's Emancipation : More hype than action", The Hindu, 8 March 2002.

Shoma Sen, "Politics of Plurality", The Hindu, 10 March 2002.

Born in a poor family in the 18th Cei tury and the author of the path breaking document, "A Vindication of the Rights of Women", Mary Wollenstonecraft a feminist struggled for her education and career as a writer and strove for a relationship with men based on intellectual mutual compatibility. The 19th Century feminists, fighting for the rights to vote, resorted to militant tactics like chaining themselves to the gates of public offices. Around the same time, Marxist thinkers like Friedrich Engles identified the bourgeois family as one of the chief oppressors of women, something that the radical feminists would reiterate more than 100 years later. In India, in the same century, Jyotiba Phuley, a social reformer from Maharastra, strove to educate the lower castes and women. He taught his wife, Savitri, to read and write and she became the first woman teacher in state. Bur Savitri had to face the humiliationof being pelted with stones and cow-dung as she set her daunting task.

Mukta Mittal, "Role of Electronic Media in Women's Development" in Mukta Mittal (ed.) Women Power in India (New Delhi: Anmol Publication Pvt. Ltd., 1995), p. 141.

EMPOWERMENT OF WOMEN : NATIONAL POLICY–2001

The Principle of gender equality is enshrined in the Indian Constitution in its Preamble, Fundamental Rights, Fundamental Duties and Directive Principles. The Constitution not only grants equality to women, but also empowers the State to adopt measures of positive discrimination in fabour of women.

Within the framework of a democratic polity, our laws, development policies, Plans and programmes have aimed at women's advancement in different spheres. *From the Fifth Five Year Plan (1974-79) onwards, there has been a marked shift in the approach to women's issues from welfare to development. In recent years, the empowerment of women has been recognized as the central issue in determining the status of women. The National Commission for Women was set up by an Act of Parliament in 1990 to safeguard the rights and legal entitlements of women.* The 73rd and 74th Amendments (1993) to the Constitution of India have provided for reservation of seats in the local bodies of panchayats and Municipalities for women, laying a strong foundation for their participation in decision making at the *local levels.*

India has also ratified various international conventions and human rights instruments committing to secure equal rights of women. Key among them is the ratification of the Convention on Elimination of All Forms of Discrimination Against Women (CEDAW) in 1993.

Report of Department of Women & Child Development, Ministry of Human Resource Development

The Mexico Plan of Action (1975), the Nairobi Forward Looking Strategies (1985), the Beijing Declaration as well as the Platform for Action (1995) and the Outcome Document adopted by the UNGA Session on Gender Equality and Development & Peace for the 21st century, titled "Further actions and initiatives to implement the Beijing Declaration and the Platform for Action" have been unreservedly endorsed by India for appropriate follow up.

The policy also takes note of the commitments of the Ninth Five Year Plan and the other sectorial policies relating to empowerment of Women.

The women's movement and a wide spread network of non-government organizations which have strong grassroots presence and deep insight into women's concerns have contributed in inspiring initiatives for the empowerment of women.

However, there still exists a wide gap between the goals enunciated in the Constitution, legislation, policies, plans, programmes and related mechanisms on the one hand and the situational reality of the status of women in India, on the other. This has been analyzed extensively in the Report of Committee on the Status of Women in India, Towards Equality, 1974 and highlighted in the National Perspective Plan for Women, 1988-2000, the Shramshakti Report, 1988 and the "Platform for Action, Five years After-An assessment".

Gender disparity manifests itself in various forms, the most obvious being the trend of continuously declining female ratio in the population in the last few decades. Social stereotyping and violence at the domestic and societal levels are some of the other manifestations. Discrimination against girl children, adolescent girls and women persists in parts of the country.

The underlying causes of gender inequality are related to social and economic structure, which is based on informal and formal norms, and practices.

Consequently, the access of women particularly those belonging to weaker sections including Scheduled Castes/

Scheduled Tribes/Other Backward Classes and minorities, majority of whom are in the rural areas and in the informal, unorganized sector—to education, health and productive resources, among others, is inadequate. Therefore, they remain largely marginalized, poor and socially excluded.

Goal and Objectives

The goal of this policy is to bring about the advancement, development and empowerment of women. The policy will be widely disseminated so as to encourage active participation of all stakeholders for achieving its goals. Specifically, the objectives of this policy include :

(i) Creating an environment through positive economic and social policies for full development of women to enable them to realize their full potential;

(ii) The de-jure and de-fac to enjoyment of all human rights and fundamental freedom by women on equal basis with men in all spheres—political, economic, social, cultural and civil;

(iii) Equal access to participation and decision making of women in social, political and economic life of the nation;

(iv) Equal access to women to health care, quality education at all levels, career and vocational guidance, employment, equal remuneration, occupational health and safety, social security and public office etc.;

(v) Strengthening legal systems aimed at elimination of all forms of discrimination against women;

(vi) Changing societal attitudes and community practices by active participation and involvement of both men and women;

(vii) Mainstreaming a gender perspective in the development process;

(viii) Elimination of discrimination and all forms of violence against women and the girl child; and

(ix) Building and strengthening partnerships with civil society, particularly women's organizations.

Policy Prescriptions

Judicial Legal Systems

Legal-judicial systems will be made more responsive and gender sensitive to women's needs, especially in case of domestic violence and personal assault. New laws will be enacted and existing laws reviewed to ensure that justice is quick and the punishment meted out to the culprits is commensurate with the severity of the offence.

At the initiative of and with the full participation of all stakeholders including community and religious leaders, the policy would aim to encourage changes in personal laws such as those related to marriage, divorce, maintenance and guardianship so as to eliminate discrimination against women.

The evolution of property rights in a patriarchal system has contributed to the subordinate status of women. The policy would aim to encourage changes in laws relating to ownership of property and inheritance by evolving consensus in order to make them gender just.

Decision Making

Women's equality in power sharing and active participation in decision making, including decision making in political process at all levels will be ensured for the achievement of the goals of empowerment. All measures will be taken to guarantee women equal access to and full participation in decision making bodies at every level, including the legislative, executive, judicial, corporate, statutory bodies, as also the advisory Commissions, Committees, Boards, Trust etc. Affirmative actions such as reservations/quotas, including in higher legislative bodies, will be considered whenever necessary on a time bound basis. Women-friendly personnel policies will also be drawn up to encourage women to participate effectively in the development process.

Mainstreaming a Gender Perspective in the Development Process

Policies, programmes and systems will be established to ensure mainstreaming of women's perspective in all developmental processes, as catalysts, participants and recipients. Wherever there are gaps in policies and programmes, women specific interventions would be undertaken to bridge these. Coordinating and monitoring mechanisms will also be devised to assess from time to time the progress of such mainstreaming mechanisms. Women's issues and concerns as a result will specially be addressed and reflected in all concerned laws, sectorial policies, plans and programmes of action.

Economic Empowerment of Women

Poverty Eradication

Since women comprise the majority of the population below the poverty line and are very often in situations of extreme poverty, given the harsh realities of intra-household and social discrimination, macro economic policies and poverty eradication programmes will specifically address the needs and problems of such women. There will be improved implementation of programmes which are already women oriented with special targets for women. Steps will be taken for mobilization of poor women and convergence of services, by offering them a range of economic and social options, along with necessary support measures to enhance their capabilities.

Micro Credit

In order to enhance women's access to credit for consumption and production, the establishment of new, and strengthening of existing micro credit mechanisms and micro-finance institution will be undertaken so that the outreach of credit is enhanced. Other supportive measures would be taken to ensure adequate flow of credit through extant financial institutions and banks, so that all women below poverty line have easy access to credit.

Women and Economy

Women's perspectives will be included in designing and implementing macro-economic and social policies by institutionalizing their participation in such processes. Their contribution to socio-economic development as producers and workers will be recognized in the formal and informal sectors (including home based workers) and appropriate policies relating to employment and to her working conditions will be drawn up. Such measures could include:

(a) Reinterpretation and redefinition of conventional concepts of work wherever necessary e.g. in the Census records, to reflect women's contribution as producers and workers.

(b) Preparation of satellite and national accounts.

(c) Development of appropriate methodologies for undertaking (a) and (b) above.

Globalization

Globalization has presented new challenges for the realization of the goal of women's equality, the gender impact of which has not been systematically evaluated fully. However, from the micro-level studies that were commissioned by the Department of Women & Child Development, it is evident that there is a need for re-framing policies for access to employment and quality of employment. Benefits of the growing global economy have been unevenly distributed leading to wider economic disparities, the feminization of poverty, increased gender inequality through often deteriorating working conditions and unsafe working environment especially in the informal economy and rural areas. Strategies will be designed to enhance the capacity of women and empower them to meet the negative social and economic impacts, which may flow from the globalization process.

Women and Agriculture

In view of the critical role of women in the agriculture and allied sectors, as producers, concentrated efforts will be made to ensure that benefits of training, extension and various programmes will reach them in proportion to their numbers. The programmes for training women in soil conservation, social forestry, dairy development and other occupations allied to agriculture like horticulture, livestock including small animal husbandry, poultry, fisheries etc. will be expanded to benefit women workers in the agriculture sector.

Women and Industry

The important role played by women in electronics, information technology and food processing and agro industry and textiles has been crucial to the development of these sectors. They would be given comprehensive support in terms of labour legislation, social security and other support services to participate in various industrial sectors.

Women at present can not work in night shift in factories even if they wish to. Suitable measures will be taken to enable women to work in night shift in factories. This will be accompanied with support services for security, transportation etc.

Support Services

The provision of support services for women, like child care facilities, including creches at work palaces and educational institutions, homes for the aged and the disabled will be expanded and improved to create an enabling environment and to ensure their full cooperation in social, political and economic life. Women-friendly personnel policies will also be drawn up to encourage women to participate effectively in the developmental process.

Social Empowerment of Women

Education

Equal access to education for women and girls will be ensured. Special measures will be taken to eliminate discrimination, universalize education, eradicate illiteracy, create a gender-sensitive educational system, increase enrolment and retention rates of girls and improve the quality of education to facilitate the life-long learning as well as development of vocational/technical skills by women. Reducing the gender gap in secondary and higher education would be a focus area. Sectorial time targets in existing policies will be achieved, with a special focus on girls and women, particularly those belonging to weaker sections including the Scheduled Castes/Scheduled Tribes/Other Backward Classes/ Minorities. Gender sensitive curricula would be developed at all levels of educational system in order to address sex stereotyping as one of the causes of gender discrimination.

Health

A holistic approach to women's health which includes both nutrition and health services will be adopted and special attention will be given to the needs of women and the girl at all stages of the life cycle. The reduction of infant mortality and maternal mortality, which are sensitive indicators of human development, is a priority concern. This policy reiterates the national demographic goals for Infant Mortality Rate (IMR), Maternal Mortality Rate (MMR) that are set out in the National Population Policy 2000. Women should have access to comprehensive, affordable and quality health care. Measures will be adopted that take into account the reproductive rights of women to enable them to exercise informed choices, their vulnerability to sexual and health problems together with endemic, infectious and communicable diseases such malaria, TB, and Water brone disease well as hypertension and cardio-pulmonary diseases. The social, developmental health consequences of HIV/AIDS and other sexually transmitted diseases will be tackled from a gender perspective.

To effectively meet problems of infant the maternal mortality, and early marriage, the availability of good and accurate data at micro level on deaths, birth and marriages is required. Strict implementation of registration of births and deaths would be ensured and registration of marriages would be made compulsory.

In accordance with the commitment of the National Population Policy (2000) to population stabilization, this policy recognizes the critical need of men and women to have access to safe, effective and affordable methods of family planning of their choice and the need to suitably address the issues of early marriages and spacing of children. Interventions such as spread of education, compulsory registration of marriage and special programmes like Balika Samridhi Yojana should impact on delaying the age of marriage so that by 2010 child marriages are eliminated.

Women's traditional knowledge about healtn care and nutrition will be recognized through proper documentation and its use will be encouraged. The use of Indian and alternative systems of medicine will be enhanced within the framework of overall health infrastructure available for women.

Nutrition

In view of the high risk of malnutrition and disease that women face at all the three critical stage viz., infancy and childhood, adolescent and reproductive phase, focused attention would be paid to meeting the nutritional needs of women at all stages of the life cycle. This is also important in view of the critical link between the health of adolescent girls, pregnant and lactating women with the health of infant and young children. Special efforts will be made to tackle the problem of macro and micro nutrient deficiencies especially amongst pregnant and lactating women as it leads to various diseases and disabilities.

Intra-household discrimination in nutritional matters vis-à-vis girls and women will be sought to be ended through appropriate strategies. Widespread use of nutrition education would be made to address the issues of intra-household imbalances in nutrition and the special needs of pregnant and lactating women. Women's participation will also be ensured in the planning, superintendence and delivery of the system.

Drinking Water and Sanitation

Special attention will be given to the needs of women in the provision of safe drinking water, sewage disposal, toilet facilities and sanitation within accessible reach of households, especially in rural areas and urban slums. Women's participation will be ensured in the planning, delivery and maintenance of such services.

Housing and Shelter

Women's perspectives will be included in housing policies, planning of housing colonies and provision of shelter both in rural and urban areas. Special attention will be given for providing adequate and safe housing and accommodation for women including single women, heads of households, working women, students, apprentices and trainees.

Environment

Women will be involved and their perspectives reflected in the policies and programmes for environment, conservation and restoration. Considering the impact of environmental factors on their livelihoods, women's participation will be ensured in the conservation of the environment and control of environmental degradation. The vast majority of rural women still depend on the locally available non-commercial sources of energy such as animal dung, crop waste and fuel wood. In order to ensure the efficient use of these energy resources in an environmental friendly manner, the policy will aim at promoting the programmes of non-conventional energy resources. Women will be involved in spreading the use of solar energy, biogas, smokeless chulahs and other rural application so as to have a visible impact of these measures in influencing eco systems and in changing the life styles of rural women.

Science and Technology

Programmes will be strengthened to bring about a greater involvement of women in science and technology. These will include measures to motivate girls to take up science and technology for higher education and also ensure that development projects with scientific and technical inputs involve women fully. Efforts to develop a scientific temper and awareness will also be stepped up. Special measures would be taken for their training in areas where they have special skills like communication and information technology. Efforts to develop appropriate technologies suited to women's needs as well as to reduce their drudgery will be given a special focus too.

Women in Difficult Circumstances

In recognition of the diversity of women's situations and in acknowledgement of the needs of specially disadvantaged groups, measures and programmes will be undertaken to provide them with special assistance. These groups include women in extreme poverty, destitute women, women in conflict situations, women affected by natural calamities, women in less developed regions, the disabled widows, elderly women, single women in difficult circumstances, women heading households, those displaced from employment, migrants, women who are victims of marital violence, deserted women and prostitutes etc.

Violence Against Women

All forms of violence against women, physical and mental, whether at domestic or societal levels, including those arising from customs, traditions or accepted practices shall be dealt with effectively with a view to eliminating its incidence. Institutions and mechanisms/schemes for assistance will be created and strengthened for prevention of such violence, including sexual harassment at work place and customs like dowry; for the rehabilitation of the victims of violence and for taking effective action against the perpetrators of such violence. A special emphasis will also be laid on programmes and measures to deal with trafficking in women and girls.

Rights of the Girl Child

All forms of discrimination against the girl child and violation of her rights shall be eliminated by undertaking strong measures both preventive and punitive within and outside the family. These would relate specifically to strict enforcement of laws against prenatal sex selection and the practices of female foeticide, female infanticide, child marriage, child abuse and child prostitution, child abuse and child prostitution etc.

Removal of discrimination in the treatment of the girl child within the family and outside and projection of a positive image of the girl child will be actively fostered. There will be special emphasis on the needs of the girl child and earmarking of substantial investments in the areas relating to food and nutrition, health and education, and in vocational education. In implementing programmes for eliminating child labour, there will be a special focus on girl children.

Mass Media

Media will be used to portray images consistent with human dignity of girls and women. The policy will specifically strive to remove demeaning, degrading and negative conventional stereotypical images of women and violence against women. Private sector partners and media networks will be involved at all levels to ensure equal access for women particularly in the area of information and communication technologies. The media would be encouraged to develop codes of conduct, professional guidelines and other self regulatory mechanisms to remove gender stereotypes and promote balanced portrayals of women and men.

Operational Strategies

Action Plans

All Central and State Ministries will draw up time bound Action Plans for translating the policy into a set of concrete actions, through a participatory process of consultation and Centre/State Departments of Women and Child Development and National/State Commissions for Women. The plans will specifically including the following:

(i) Measurable goals to be achieved by 2010.

(ii) Identification and commitment of resources.

(iii) Responsibilities for implementation of action points.

(iv) Structures and mechanisms to ensure efficient monitoring, review and gender impact assessment of action points and policies.

(v) Introduction of a gender perspective in the budgeting process.

In order to support better planning and programme formulation and adequate allocation of resources, Gender Development Indices (GDI) will be developed by networking with specialized agencies. These could be analyzed and studied in depth. Gender auditing and development of evaluation mechanisms will also be undertaken along side.

Collection of gender disaggregated data by all primary data collecting agencies of the Central and State Governments as well as research and academic institutions in the public and private sectors will be undertaken. Data and information gaps in vital areas reflecting the status of women will be sought to be filled in by these immediately. All ministries/corporations/banks and financial institutions etc. will be advised to collect, collate, disseminate and maintain/publish data related to programmes and benefits on a gender disaggregated basis. This will help in meaningful planning and evaluation of policies.

Institutional Mechanisms

Institutional mechanisms, to promote the advancement of women, which exist at the Central and State levels, will be strengthened. These will be through interventions as may be appropriate and will relate to, among others, provision of adequate resources, training and advocacy skills to effectively influence macro-policies, legislation, programmes etc. to achieve the empowerment of women.

National and State Councils will be formed to oversee the operationalisation of the policy on a regular basis. The National Council will be headed by the Prime Minister and the State Councils by the Chief Ministers and will be broad in composition having representatives from the concerned Departments/Ministers, National and State Commissions for Women, Social Welfare Boards, representatives of non-government organizations, women's organizations, corporate sector, Trade Unions, financing institutions, academics, experts and social activists etc. These bodies will review the progress made in implementing the policy twice a year. The National

Development Council will also be informed of the progress of the programme undertaken under the policy from time to time for advice and comments.

National and State Resource Centres on women will be established with mandates for collection and dissemination of information, undertaking research work, conducting surveys, *implementing training and awareness generation programmes etc.* These centers will link up with women's studies centers and other research and academic institutions through suitable information networking systems.

While institutions at the district level will be strengthened, at the grassroots, women will be helped by government through its programmes to organize and strengthen into self-help groups (SHGs) at the Anganwadi/village/town level. The women's groups will be helped to institutionalize themselves into registered societies and to federate at the Panchayat/Municipal level. These societies will bring about synergistic implementation of all the social and economic development programmes by drawing resources made available through government and non-government channels, including banks and financial institutions and by establishing a close interface with the Panchayats/municipalities.

Resource Management

Availability of adequate financial, human and market resources to implement the policy will be managed by concerned departments, financial credit institutions and bank, private sector, civil society and other connected institutions. This process will include:

(a) Assessment of benefits flowing to women and resource allocation to the pogrammes relating to them through an exercise of gender budgeting. Appropriate changes in policies will be made to optimize benefits to women under these schemes;

(b) Adequate resource allocation to develop and promote the policy outlined earlier based on (a) above by concerned departments.

(c) Developing synergy between personnel of Health. Rural Development. Education and Women & Child Development Department at field level and other village level functionaries.

(d) Meeting credit needs by banks and financial credit institutions through suitable policy initiatives and development of new institutions in coordination with the Department of Women & Child Development.

The strategy of Women's Component Plan adopted in the Ninth Plan of ensuring that not less than 30% of benefits/funds flow to women from all Ministries and Departments will be implemented effectively so that the needs and interest of women and girls are addressed by all concerned sectors. The Department of Women and Child Development being the nodal Ministry will monitor and review the progress of the implementation of the Component Plan from time to time, in terms of both quality and quantity in collaboration with the Planning Commission.

Efforts will be made to channelize private sector investments too, to support programmes and projects for advancement of women.

Legislation

The existing legislative structure will be reviewed and additional legislative measures taken by identified departments to implement the policy. This will also involve a review of all existing laws including personal, customary and tribal laws, subordinate legislation, related rules as well as executive and eliminate all gender discriminatory references. The process will be planned over a time period 200-2003. The specific measures required would be evolved through a consultation process involving civil society, National Commission for Women and Department of Women and Child Development. In appropriate cases the consultation process would be widened to include other stakeholders too.

Effective implementation of legislation would be promoted by involving civil society and community. Appropriate changes in legislation will be undertaken, if necessary.

In addition, following other specific measures will be taken to implement the legislation effectively:

(a) Strict enforcement of all relevant legal provisions and speedy redressal of grievances will be ensured, with a special focus on violence and gender related atrocities;

(b) Measures to prevent and punish harassment at the place of work, protection for women workers in the organized/unorganized sector and strict enforcement of relevant laws such as Equal Remuneration Act and Minimum Wages Act will be undertaken;

(c) Crimes against women, their incidence, prevention, detection and prosecution will be regularly reviewed at all Crime Review for a and conferences at the Central, State and District levels. Recognised, local, voluntary organizations will be authorized to lodge complaints and facilitate registration, investigations and legal proceedings related to violence and atrocities against girls and women;

(d) Women's cells in police stations, women police stations, family courts, mahila courts, counseling centers, legal aid Centers and Nyaya Panchayats will be strengthened and expanded to eliminate violence and atrocities against women;

(e) Widespread dissemination of information on all aspects of legal rights, human rights and other entitlements of women, through specially designed legal literacy programmes and rights information programmes will be done.

Gender Sensitization

Training of personnel of executive, legislative and judicial wings of the state, with a special focus on policy and programme framers, implementation and development agencies, law enforcement machinery and the judiciary, as well as non-governmental organizations will be undertaken. Other measures will include:

(a) Promoting societal awareness to gender issues and women's human rights;

(b) Review of curriculum and educational materials to include gender education and human rights issues;

(c) Removal of all references derogatory to the dignity of women from all public documents and legal instruments;

(d) Use of different forms of mass media to communicate social messages relating to women's equality and empowerment.

Panchayati Raj Institutions

The 73rd and 74th Amendments (1993) to the India Constitution have served as a breakthrough towards ensuring equal access and increased participation in political power structure for women. The PRIs will play a central role in the process of enhancing women's participation in public life. The PRIs and the local self governments will be actively involved in the implementation and execution of the National Policy for Women at the grassroots level.

Partnership With the Voluntary

Sector Organizations

The involvement of voluntary organizations, associations, federations, trade unions, non-governmental organization, women's organizations, as well as institutions dealing with education, training and research will be ensured in formulation, implementation, monitoring and review of all policies and programmes affecting women. Towards this end, they will be provided with appropriate support related to resources and capacity building and facilitated to participate actively in the process of the empowerment of women.

International Cooperation

The policy will aim at implementation of international obligations/commitments in all sectors on empowerment of women such as the Convention on All Forms of Discrimination Against Women (CEDAW), Convention on the Rights of the Child (CRC), International Conference on Population and Development (IPCD+5) and other such instruments. International, regional and sub-regional cooperation towards the empowerment of women will continue to be encouraged through sharing of experiences, exchange of ideas and technology, networking with institutions and organizations and through bilateral and multi-lateral partnerships.

MAHARASHTRA GOVERNMENTS POLICY FOR WOMEN (1994)

Background

Women's development in India is rooted in the constitution where equality of the sexes before the Law is one of the most fundamental rights. However, the Constitution also legitimizes positive discrimination in favour of women and children by the State.

While accepting that women were a distinct category for whom special and separate programmes were to be formulated, it was expected that voluntary agencies would in some way deliver the benefits of social welfare measure to this group. Even the education and health agencies were expected to achieve a wide coverage of women without any separate machinery to focus on the special needs and problems of the group. The approach towards women was coloured by the "welfare" orientation where women were seen as an object of State munificence rather than as participants in the development process.

It was only in the Seventies that the shift in approach from "welfare" to "development" slowly emerged. The break-through came with the Sixth Plan (1975-80), chapter on women where for the first time there was an emphasis on the potential of women to become agents of development. The document also emphasized the need to boost their self-image and self-confidence.

Although the concept has been accepted, not much work has been done to attune Government thinking and Government machinery to the different but equally valid and relevant needs of women. The concepts of the "Man" and the "Public" domain the "women" and the "private" domain still continue to dominate Government thinking and therefore training programmes and plan schemes still do not clearly tackle the issues of infrastructure, support services and specific training which are so essential for women's development.

Alongwith the concept of development came one of participation. The Constitutional Amendment to give statutory status to the Panchayat Raj institutions was a major step in devolving powers to local bodies and thereby to women. Maharashtra was one of the first States to implement the amendment. It went one step further by creating Statutory Committees in each Zilla Parishad for the development of women and children. Women are to constitute 70 per cent of the strength of the committees which are to be chaired by a woman. Funds both from government and from the Zilla Parishad are earmarked for the use of its Committee.

After the National Commission for women was set up. Maharashtra was the first State to follow with a State Legislation setting up a State Commission for women in January 1993. To focus on the specific needs of this very vulnerable sector of society, the Government also created a separate department for women and child development in June 1993.

This policy is an attempt to identify the immediate steps that the State can take to improve the position of women. This policy marks the beginning of a process. These decisions will be reviewed every three years to ensure that policy keeps pace with evolving social needs in a fast changing world.

Education

There is compelling evidence to demonstrate that completed primary education and increased female literacy have a positive effect in raising the age of marriage and reducing infant mortality rate, reducing crude birth rate and total fertility rate, on poverty alleviation and overall social economic development. However in spite of the overwhelming evidence that female literacy has a positive effect on social development, the female literacy rate in India is unfortunately low.

In order to accelerate the pace of female literacy, Government of Maharashtra has recently formulated an action plan. High priority will be given to implement schemes formulated an the action plan for achievement of universal primary education for girls. Village Education Committees and Women's groups will be persuaded to actively involve themselves in promoting primary education and literacy as a means to increase awareness, develop confidence and improve their living conditions.

The removal of women's illiteracy and obstacles inhibiting their access to and retention in elementary education will receive over-riding priority though provision of special support services, setting up of targets, and effective monitoring.

For effective preschool education, anganwadis will be attached to the primary schools and will be encouraged to start day-care centres so that older girls can leave their younger siblings in the centre to pursue their studies in the school. Mahila Mandals will be encouraged to take the responsibility of running such day-care centers.

In order to tackle the problems of female literacy and the unfortunately high female drop-out rate, the following steps will be initiated:

— Financial provision for formal or non-formal education for all girls upto elementary stage will be made top-priority.

— Lowering the direct and indirect cost to the parents. One of the hindrances in girls' education is that the direct costs for textbooks etc. and hidden costs for uniforms and opportunity costs in terms of girls' household tasks and responsibilities are perceived as being greater than the benefits of education. Therefore, an economic approach to increase demand for girls education is to reduce direct or hidden opportunity cost. To start with, this will be achieved by providing incentives, provision of free uniforms, writing materials, provision of textbooks, provision of day-care centers to free girls to pursue their study providing of attendance allowance to girls below the poverty line. In the long run, when the families realize the importance of girls' education, the incentives can be slowly withdrawn.

— Increasing the number of female teachers so that 50 per cent of teachers are women.

— To increase community participation through Village Education Committees (VEC) and Mahila Mandalas.

— To start need based functional/vocational courses for girls with the held of NGOs and Directorate of Vocational Education.

— A scheme of incentive will be introduced for Mahila mandals and Village Education Committees and Gram Panchayats which increase retention among girl students.

— Reduction in female drop-out rates will be included as a factor while evolving a formula for devolution of finances to Gram Panchayat.

— To increase the awareness of women that literacy is a vehicle to improve their living conditions and to empower them both individually and collectively to change their living conditions, small modules on empowerment through literacy will be prepared and introduced, and circulated amongst Mahila Mandals, Village Education, Committees, NGOs and other groups to enable them to participate in the overall literacy promotion activity.

— The Mahila Kendra will be promoted as a space for women to acquire functional literacy and for post-literacy activities.

Technical Education

The importance of inculcating technical skill specially in non-conventional areas to women is becoming increasingly evident. The State has a large network of Engineering Colleges, Polytechnics, Industrial Training Institutes (ITIs) and basic training centres which will be used for this purpose. Today the percentage of girls in polytechnics in Maharashtra ranges from 6 per cent to 17 per cent. The percentage of women faculty and women entering industry is even less. The main factor responsible for this situation are : (a) lack of residential facilities in the Polytechnics, (b) lack of parental knowledge and encouragement, (c) lack of industry institute coordination, and (d) high costs of education.

Government will, in a phased manner, increase residential facilities for girls at all technical education institutions.

A vocational guidance centre for girls will be set up in each secondary school to educate the parents of the girls entering secondary school about the advantages and options open to their girls in technical courses.

The vocational training directorate will be asked to identify new schemes for vocational training in non-conventional areas for girls specifically in the certificate courses where more girls can obtain admission.

The Maharashtra Centre for Entrepreneurship Development (MCED) will be given grant in aid to start a special training course on business management for women entrepreneurs in the small scale sector.

Industries will be encouraged to set up a fund for providing scholarships for girls who go through the technical education and entrepreneurship courses and also for sponsoring women faculty in various technical education institutions.